Regime Support Beyond the Balanc

This book challenges the conventional wisdom that policy performance is the most important determinant of regime support. It does so by focusing on two countries where performance and support do not match. Chile is the economic envy of every country in Latin America, yet support has been surprisingly anemic. By contrast, Venezuela managed to maintain extremely high levels of support during the reign of Hugo Chávez despite severe failures of governance. Resolution of these paradoxes requires turning away from policy decisions and focusing instead on how those decisions are made. Taking inspiration from democratic theory and social psychology, this book argues that extensive opportunities for direct participation in the political process engenders in citizens strong feelings of efficacy – a sense of control over the course of politics. Rhodes-Purdy uses a mixed-methods approach to test this theory, including qualitative case studies, analysis of survey data, and experimental methods.

MATTHEW RHODES-PURDY is a postdoctoral research associate in the Department of Political Science at Washington University in St. Louis. He received his PhD in Government from the University of Texas at Austin. He is an alumnus of the Fulbright Student Program in Chile. His research interests include legitimacy and regime support, populism, and participatory governance. His work has appeared in *Comparative Politics, Political Research Quarterly, Latin American Research Review*, and *Political Studies*.

Regime Support Beyond the Balance Sheet

Participation and Policy Performance in Latin America

MATTHEW RHODES-PURDY
Washington University in St. Louis

CAMBRIDGE
UNIVERSITY PRESS

CAMBRIDGE
UNIVERSITY PRESS

University Printing House, Cambridge CB2 8BS, United Kingdom

One Liberty Plaza, 20th Floor, New York, NY 10006, USA

477 Williamstown Road, Port Melbourne, VIC 3207, Australia

314-321, 3rd Floor, Plot 3, Splendor Forum, Jasola District Centre, New Delhi - 110025, India

79 Anson Road, #06-04/06, Singapore 079906

Cambridge University Press is part of the University of Cambridge.

It furthers the University's mission by disseminating knowledge in the pursuit of education, learning and research at the highest international levels of excellence.

www.cambridge.org
Information on this title: www.cambridge.org/9781108413305
DOI: 10.1017/9781108332958

© Matthew Rhodes-Purdy 2017

First published 2017
First paperback edition 2020

A catalogue record for this publication is available from the British Library

Library of Congress Cataloging in Publication data
Names: Rhodes-Purdy, Matthew, author.
Title: Regime support beyond the balance sheet : participation and policy performance in Latin America / Matthew Rhodes-Purdy.
Description: 1 Edition. | New York : Cambridge University Press, 2017.
Identifiers: LCCN 2017018754| ISBN 9781108420259 (hardback) | ISBN 9781108413305 (printback)
Subjects: LCSH: Latin America–Politics and government. | Political participation–Latin America. | Populism–Latin America.
Classification: LCC JL966 .R46 2017 | DDC 320.98–dc23
LC record available at https://lccn.loc.gov/2017018754

ISBN 978-1-108-42025-9 Hardback
ISBN 978-1-108-41330-5 Paperback

To Lindsey and Hank. For seeing me through it.

Contents

Figures

Tables

Acknowledgments

Many people have provided valuable commentary and assistance on this project. First, I would like to thank my supervisor, Kurt Weyland. His ability to seek out a weak argument or a flaw in logic verges on superhuman; the argument presented here would be much poorer without his contributions. The members of the committee for the dissertation on which this book is based also provided valuable feedback and support: Wendy Hunter (who deserves particular credit for suggesting using Venezuela as a second case), Zachary Elkins, Raul Madrid, and Pamela Paxton. In addition to serving on my committee, Dr. Paxton's course on structural equation modeling introduced me to a statistical technique that has become one of my most important methodological tools, and her advice on the models and techniques used in this book was invaluable.

Special thanks are due to Fernando Rosenblatt, who shared his time, his knowledge of political science and Chile, and even his office, during a critical phase during this project's development. Patricio Navia of the Universidad de Deigo Portales is also due a major thank you. His critiques of my approach, especially the fact that dissatisfaction with democracy in Chile is clustered among the middle sectors, ultimately led me to develop one of the central arguments of this book, specifically the moderated relationship between efficacy and support.

I would also like to thank Alexandra Panzarelli and Quinlan Bowman. Venezuela is an extremely difficult country in which to conduct fieldwork (indeed even day-to-day living is quite a challenge), and their assistance in navigating that difficult terrain was critical. Daniel Budny's assistance in dealing with the peculiarities of being a foreigner living in Caracas was essential; without his help and advice,

I would likely have been both homeless and penniless during my fieldwork in Venezuela.

The research described here has benefited immensely from a few important funding sources. The Macdonald Fellowship program at the University of Texas at Austin provided financial support for my fieldwork in Venezuela. The Fulbright Student Program supported my fieldwork in Chile; an exploratory trip to Chile several years prior was funded by the Tinker Foundation. A generous grant from the College of Liberal Arts, University of Texas at Austin, supported the drafting of the dissertation that would eventually give rise to this book.

In addition to financial support, specific pieces and arguments contained within this book have benefited from previous publication. Some of the material on Venezuela (mostly in Chapter 5 but also scattered throughout) was previously published in *Political Research Quarterly* (Rhodes-Purdy, 2015). An article summarizing the argument of the book previously appeared in *Comparative Politics* (Rhodes-Purdy, 2017). Material from both of these articles is reprinted with permission of the journal in which they were originally published. Throughout this project I have relied on the comments of anonymous external reviewers from a number of journals. I would particularly like to thank the two anonymous reviewers of Cambridge University Press, whose commentaries were some of the most thorough, thoughtful, and constructive I have ever received. I would also like to thank all the staff at the press for their tireless efforts to bring this book to fruition.

Finally, and most importantly, I would like to thank my family. First my parents, Mark and Betty. Both schoolteachers, my love of and dedication to education and scholarship has been their greatest gift to me. As anyone who has completed a doctoral program can attest, this love of learning does not mean the process is not frequently trying, even grueling. In that spirit, my greatest thanks go to my wife Lindsey, and my son Hank. When the grind of academia gets to be too much, they always know how to make things better.

I Introduction

The impetus for this project came in the spring of 2006, while taking refuge from a cloud of tear gas in a metro station in Santiago, Chile. The street above had been clear for some time, but the noxious remnants of the state's response to a student protest march, one of many that spring, were still very much in evidence. The wave of protests had taken nearly everyone by surprise. Aptly summarizing the conventional wisdom that still held on the eve of the protests, political scientist Kenneth M. Roberts stated that "the mass social mobilizations of the 1960s, early 1970s and mid-1980s have been conspicuous by their absence ... there is little indication that they are looming on the horizon for years to come" (1998, p. 157). Despite lingering worries about inequality and atavistic institutions that had survived the transition away from military rule, most observers viewed Chile as one of Latin America's great success stories, both economically and politically. The eruption of a major wave of contentious politics (which turned out to be merely the first of many such waves to come) demonstrated that a significant portion of the Chilean population did not share this view. How could deep-seated discontent continue to fester, and eventually explode into the streets, within an economic and political system that was (and is) the envy of the region?

Years later, while conducting fieldwork in Caracas, another brush with violence provoked a bizarrely inverted sense of déjà vu. Sitting in my apartment in the affluent neighborhood of *Los Palos Grandes* late at night, the sudden sound of gunfire (and later grenade explosions) from the street below erupted as police battled a group of hoodlums who had been interrupted during an attempted kidnapping in another district. The event was shocking (and of course terrifying), though not the least bit surprising. These kind of violent incidents (this one left several of the kidnappers dead and their victim bleeding but alive on the stoop across the corner from my building) had become nearly a matter of course. The gunfight recalled my experience in Chile years before, not because they were comparable in terms of danger or chaos, but because they both occurred alongside a clear and inexplicable divergence of public attitudes and "objective" reality. For despite the endemic violence, chronic inflation, shortages of basic goods, and the deterioration of society in to warring camps, I knew from my examination of public opinion surveys (as well as my day-to-day discussions with ordinary residents of Caracas) that many Venezuelans were deeply enamored with their leader, Hugo Chávez. They admired his penchant for unadorned rhetoric (including the use of profanities that would have been unthinkable coming from more traditional *politicos*), his passion for the poor and the dispossessed, and even his willingness to resort to violence, as he did in an attempted coup in 1992, which brought him to prominence. It became clear to me that Chile and Venezuela had become mirror images of one another. Or if you prefer, one was the other's evil twin; I leave it to the reader to decide which is which, although my personal view is that each country has had successes in some areas and failures in others, none of which should be ignored. Both countries, despite vast differences of culture, history, and economy, had inexplicable levels of public support for their regimes, given their respective policy performance. Chile's governments continually did as much right as could be expected, yet Chileans remained surprisingly cool to the political system that had generated such gains. Meanwhile, the grind of death and deprivation crushed Venezuelans day in and day out, yet many maintained faith in Chávez and his political project.

These circumstances appear to be contradictory due to the implicit assumption that all regimes need do in order to ensure the support of their citizens is tend to their material needs, or at least provide an environment in which citizens can easily provide for themselves. It is a common assumption, both in popular discourse and in academic literature on regime support and legitimacy.

Studies of these topics have, in recent years, privileged the quality of governance as the source of legitimacy almost to the exclusion of any other potential sources (Crozier, Huntington, & Watanuki, 1975; Hardin, 2000; Mainwaring, Scully, & Vargas Cullell, 2010; Miller & Listhaug, 1999; Newton & Norris, 2000; Rogowski, 1974). While studies may include any number of ancillary variables, be they institutional, behavioral, cultural, and so forth, such factors usually exert their influence based upon the utilitarian logic of rational self-interest, and are viewed as interesting because they enable or hamper a regime's provision of economic goods to its citizens.

The idea that a political system that routinely fails to provide desired goods and services, whether through incompetence or malice, would gradually lose its legitimacy is intuitively appealing and perfectly reasonable. It is also completely inadequate. Figure 1.1 presents average levels of regime support (as measured by two commonly used indicators, satisfaction with democracy and perceived level of democracy), and the relatively objective performance index used by Mainwaring et al. (2010).

Both graphs show that, while there is clearly a relationship between support and performance, there is a great deal of unexplained variation, as can be seen by a number of cases lying far above or below the regression line. For both indicators, Chile is the most extreme outlier (except Honduras for perceived level of democracy), but it is not the only one. While regime support in Chile has remained anemic (Angell, 2010; Madrid, Hunter, & Weyland, 2010; Mainwaring et al., 2010) despite inarguably strong economic performance (Angell, 2010; Posner, 1999, 2004), Venezuela presents an opposite, mirror-image of the Chilean case. Under the Chávez government, and the regime he helped to bring about, the quality of governance has been abysmal by nearly any standard (Corrales, 2010; Mainwaring et al., 2010, p. 39). Although some of the social programs instituted by Chávez and his government undoubtedly improved the lives of poor Venezuelans, these gains are dwarfed by the rising wave of violence, inflation, and stagnation that engulfed the country as Chávez's reign continued.

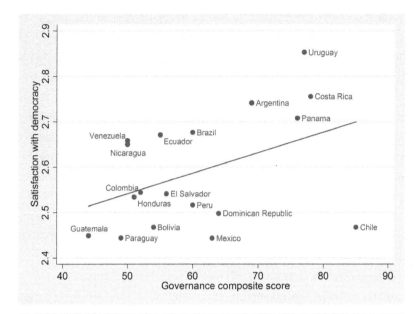

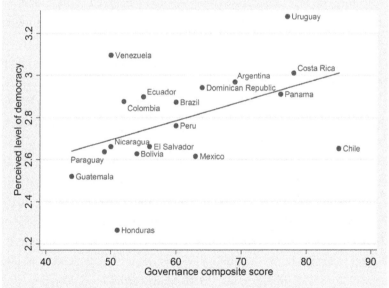

FIGURE I.I: Satisfaction with democracy and perceived level of democracy by performance

Data on the y-axis are from the 2012 wave of the Latin American Public Opinion Project's (LAPOP) Americas Barometer survey. See Mainwaring et al. (2010) for data years, but which correspond roughly to 2009–2010.

Some of the blame for these issues can be laid at the feet of others, including prior administrations and the chaos of international oil prices, but a considerable amount (especially for inflation) belongs to the policy choices of Chávez's government. And yet the Bolivarian state was viewed by its citizens as more legitimate than the majority of its regional neighbors during much of Chávez's reign (The Latin American Public Opinion Project, 2012; Canache, 2007; *Latinobarómetro*, 2007). Just as Chile is an extreme "underperformer" in the graphs in Figure 1.1, Venezuela is an extreme overachiever; it is the largest outlier above the line for satisfaction with democracy, and the second largest of perceived level of democracy (after Uruguay).

Ironically, the Venezuelan and Chilean paradoxes are exactly the sort of puzzle that the concept of regime support was intended to resolve. Easton (1975) saw support as a potential explanation for why equivalent economic or social troubles produced only mild disruptions in some polities but full-blown political crises in others. To resolve this, Easton differentiates between "specific" and "diffuse" support. Specific support refers to attitudes regarding what Easton calls "outputs": the actual decisions, policies, and actions. Diffuse support, which Easton argues pertains to the political regime, "refers to evaluations of what an object is or represents ... not of what it does. It consists of a reservoir of favorable attitudes or good will that helps members to accept or tolerate outputs to which they are opposed" (1975, p. 444). Various analysts sought to explain this sort of enduring support (Easton argued that experience and especially socialization were key antecedents), but the drift toward performance-centric theoretical frameworks, encouraged by the ascendency of rational choice in political science, abrogated this line of analysis. Utilitarian conceptions of support cannot resolve this sort of paradox; if regime support is assumed to be largely or entirely a product of economic success, then Chile and Venezuela are inexplicable.

1.1 THE ARGUMENT: BRINGING PROCEDURES BACK IN

The purpose of this research is to account for the paradoxes described earlier by restoring Easton's insight that inputs matter to its proper place in regime support theory. That said, Easton's explanations relying on direct experience of interactions with the political system (which for most citizens are infrequent) and socialization are unconvincing. As both Chile and Venezuela show, support can both erode and build too quickly for socialization to be the primary force at work. And the support literature's utilitarian drift has resulted in a dearth of alternatives to Easton.

Another source can fill this gap: democratic theory. Both classical and participatory democratic theorists (e.g. Barber, 1984; Pateman, 1970; Rousseau, 2002) have long argued that the process of self-governance has intrinsic value to individuals, regardless what policies such processes eventually produce. Psychological theories of organizational and procedural justice have also recognized the power of intrinsic procedural characteristics in shaping organizational attitudes, developing a bidimensional framework of organizational support that takes both procedures and outcomes into account (Folger & Cropanzano, 2001; Lind, 2001; Lind & Tyler, 1988; McFarlin & Sweeney, 1992; Thibaut & Walker, 1975; van den Bos, Lind, & Wilke, 2001). Although political theory and social psychology have very different epistemological foundations, on the topic of support they converge on a common proposition: that *how* decisions are made is as important as the decisions themselves, and that whether or not those bound by decisions have a say in them is among the most important procedural variables for explaining individual attitudes toward decision-making processes. In the context of democratic governance, the extent to which citizens as a group have a say in the policy process is called citizen autonomy. My most important and central argument throughout this book is that citizen autonomy is a critical (and neglected) source of systemic support. The term autonomy is used here as in democratic theory, meaning "self-governance," i.e. that decision-making authority is granted to those who are bound by those decisions, rather than separation or independence from another authority, as it is used in common parlance. Citizens are kinder in their evaluations of regime institutions if they feel they

have the ability to participate in the processes by which those institutions decide and implement policy.

The preceding discussion raises a question: how do political
systems create autonomy? And what types or varieties of political
systems are most able to *convince* citizens they have autonomy?
Before diving into this issue, some discussion of the scope of the
theory and evidence presented here is necessary. Although most of
the normative theory I employ concerns democracy, the social psychological work cited earlier and throughout this book indicate that
autonomy is a fairly universal human need, regardless of regime type.
This may provide some insight on why authoritarian regimes, which
often deny citizens *personal* autonomy, much less collective autonomy, have such difficulty maintaining legitimacy even when they are
not brutally repressive. It may also shed light on why authoritarian
regimes (Cuba comes to mind)[1] that give citizens some role in the
political process have less trouble in this regard, even if that role is
entirely subordinate. Indeed, one of the cases of interest here, Venezuela, experienced at least some authoritarian drift during the period
of analysis.

That said, this book focuses on cases that are at least nominally
democratic, and caution should be taken in extrapolating the findings
presented here to fully authoritarian contexts. Mechanisms for engen-
dering perceptions of citizen autonomy in authoritarian regimes may
well exist, but they are likely to be complex and difficult to identify,
and their effects will likely be extremely dependent upon the particular details of specific regimes. Authoritarianism is, given its emphasis
on leaders who dominate the societies they govern, essentially antagonistic to citizen autonomy, and exceptions to that rule are just that:
exceptions, idiosyncratic departures in unique cases. Further research
would be necessary to determine if the theories developed in this book
apply in authoritarian contexts.

---

[1] Thanks are due to the anonymous reviewers of the manuscript, who first broached
this issue. One of the reviewers also specifically mentioned Cuba.

Democracy, however, is another matter entirely. Although some democracies are (as this book argues) better than others at making their citizens feel politically capable, all democracies must grant at least some power to the citizenry as a whole. On this, there can be no exceptions: popular power, if only in limited form, is *the* defining characteristic of democracy; it is what makes democracy distinct from other forms of rule. Of course democratic regimes may grant radically different levels of power to citizens (reserving the remainder for elites), and that power may be granted using different mechanisms in different proportions. Describing how political institutions and practices either encourage or inhibit autonomy (and perceptions of it) is a necessary first step to developing testable hypotheses about which ways are best suited for encouraging autonomy. Doing so requires a conceptual framework, and democratic theory provides a solid foundation on which to build such a framework. I identify two broad categories of mechanisms – summarized here and described in detail in Chapter 3 – that democracies use to grant citizens the ability to influence the political process: representation and participation.

1.1.1 The Sources of Autonomy: Representation and Participation

Representation is the dominant mechanism of autonomy in modern democracy, and hues closely to Schumpeter's (2008) minimalist view of democracy as the granting of the power to govern to specific individuals or groups (usually political parties) based on elite competition for the votes of citizens. It assigns to citizens a largely passive role; citizens select elites, who then make decisions. Yet citizens do have some (albeit indirect) influence on the political process here because elites must consider their wishes and preferences if they are to successfully compete for votes. Two submechanisms must be present for this indirect empowerment to work: accountability and choice. Citizens must at a bare minimum be able to evict from office elites who provoke their displeasure. Yet accountability alone does not even imply the usual "free and fair election" standard that many scholars cite as the defining feature of democracy. It would be possible for elections to allow accountability without competition: retention elections where the vote is to retain or remove a single, unopposed incumbent, as are sometimes used for local judicial elections in the United States, would suffice. A second criterion must be added here: choice. To be truly granted effective voice in the political system, citizens must have multiple options from which to choose. This would imply specific systemic features such as free entry in the electoral arena and multiple parties with a realistic chance of winning. A broader view of representation would include in its ideal vision a vibrant multiparty system, where the number of parties is sufficiently large to give every ideological bloc or social group a patron party to advocate for its interests or ideology.

Although representation does provide a significant amount of autonomy, it is far from a perfect mechanism. Representation reflects a view of the democratic process that is analogous to the processes of interaction between firms and consumers in a free market. Consumers can influence the behavior of firms, either as individuals (through their purchasing choices) or collectively (e.g. through the organized use of voice [Hirschman, 1970] or boycotts). Firms must adapt to consumer tastes and preferences or risk being strangled to death by the invisible hand. Likewise, under representation, citizens influence elites primarily by "consuming" (i.e. voting for or otherwise supporting) this or that leader or faction, and those who fail to respond to citizen demands, like intransigent firms, will perish. Yet citizens and civil society remain fundamentally divided from the democratic state, just as consumers do not become part of a business by consuming its products.

Some democratic theorists view this fundamental division as woefully inadequate for fulfilling democracy's purpose. Such scholars have an entirely different view of why democracy is valuable. Advocates of classical or participatory democracy such as Jean-Jacques Rousseau, Carole Pateman, C. B. Macpherson, and Benjamin Barber all dispute that true citizen autonomy can ever be created when the state and society are so neatly cleaved. Generally these theorists also hold that "true" democracy, one in which the people play an active role, has some intrinsic value (e.g. moral, educational, or psychological development) that elite-directed forms of representative government can never satisfy. One of this book's most important arguments is that citizen autonomy, and its subjective perception by citizens, is a crucial benefit of giving citizens a relatively direct political role. Yet much of the literature on participatory theory is hypothetical, and due to its inherent suspicion of mediated forms of democracy, largely ignores representative institutions and structures as they currently exist. To overcome this, an alternative mechanism based on participatory theory must be derived and constructed, rather than lifted relatively unaltered, as representation was from liberal democratic theory.

To do so, I define participation as a mechanism for creating citizen autonomy; it is an alternative to representation, although I will argue that it can be used to evaluate many institutions and practices that are normally associated with representative democracy. Throughout this book, the term "participation" will, unless otherwise noted, refer to this mechanism, and not the actual behavior of any group or individual. Participation is defined as the extent to which citizens are given a direct role in the political process where possible, and where any indirectness or mediation necessitated by practical concerns (such as the scale of modern societies) is kept to a minimum. Like representation, participation can be decomposed into submechanisms. The first, which I call participatory opportunities, are the focus of much of this book, and are what empirical scholars have in mind when using the term "participatory democracy": institutions, programs, and fora where citizens make decisions without intermediaries. These sorts of opportunities are far more practical at the local level (within cities and neighborhoods), and thus participatory democrats often favor devolution of power to municipal-level institutions such as participatory budgeting programs, or the communal councils of Venezuela, which Chapter 5 discusses in considerable detail.

Chapter 6 also uses an experiment and a qualitative evaluation of a rare participatory program in Chile to test the importance of this aspect of participation on autonomy.

Participatory opportunities may be the most effective aspect of participation in generating autonomy, but they are also the most limited. By their nature, they are constrained in scope, usually operating at the neighborhood or municipal level. Perhaps there are ways in which national political issues can be settled by the citizenry as a whole. Such methods are not, with the partial exception of direct democracy institutions like referenda and initiatives and very recent experiments with e-governance, widely used, and thus cannot provide much comparative leverage. As a result, a new way of looking at existing democratic systems and practices is necessary, one that takes inspiration from participatory theory but that adapts its vision to the real world as it currently exists. In this vein, I identify two additional submechanisms of participation: the delegate model and ease of governance. The delegate model is inspired by Marxian delegative democracy (Macpherson, 1977, ch. 5),[2] which allows for mediated democracy, but where those who actually make decisions are tightly bound by the policy preferences and dictates of their constituents. In other words, elected leaders are to act more as delegates than as representatives. They are expected to do what those who elect them direct them to do, with rules and procedures designed to prevent delegates for substituting their own preferences or judgments for those to whom they are responsible. Obviously all modern, representative democracies depart from this standard, but some do so more than others. When analyzing existing systems, the delegate model of citizen-leader relationships can be used, for example, to suggest that parties should compete on the basis of policy preferences (i.e. programmatic parties), and should have deep roots in and connections

---

[2] This should not be confused with O'Donell's (1994, 1998) more recent concept of delegative democracy, which is little more than a form of extreme presidentialism, perhaps combined with illiberal tendencies, rather than a distinct model of democracy. It is in many ways the antithesis of citizen-directed rule as conceptualized by MacPherson and other democratic Marxists.

to civil society and social organizations. It further suggests that governing majorities should be allowed to implement their stated policies with relatively few constraints. Although ultimate power is held by professional politicians, a system that maximized these traits would give its citizens a relatively active role in the policy process. Parties would shape their platforms according to demands rising from civil society, voters would select from competing parties based on policy preferences, and those policy preferences would be enacted in relatively undiluted form. In short, such a system would minimize any distortions or garbling of the translation of public opinion into actual policy.

This raises another issue, one on which participatory theory has been largely silent. Even if representatives act in perfect accordance with the preferences of those who elect them to the best of their ability, participation is not guaranteed. This is because the substitution of elite judgement for that of the people is only one way in which people's role can be minimized. Political systems can and do place varying constraints on the ability of elites to turn policy preferences, whether those of the people or their own, into practice. Checks and balances, separation of powers, veto players, and supermajorities can all be used to thwart even the most faithful delegates from taking popular preferences and reifying them as laws and policies. Thus I include a second submechanism for participation as applied to mediated politics: ease of governance. Participation requires that majorities be allowed a relatively free hand to enact the platforms chosen by the people through elections, without excessive interference from those factions that failed to secure a majority.

Before concluding, one final note needs to be emphasized: the submechanisms of both representation and (with one exception, discussed presently) participation are mutually reinforcing. In other words, if accountability is present but choice is not, the quality of representation will not be moderate, but poor: both submechanisms are necessary. This is even more the case for the elements of participation pertaining to relationships between citizens and leaders. It matters little how faithful delegates are if they can be blocked at every turn and thus cannot accomplish the tasks assigned to them by the citizenry. And if delegates are faithless, implementing their own agenda with little regard for the desires of those in whose name they claim to act, it would not be terribly comforting to know that their chicanery can be accomplished with minimal effort. Participatory opportunities are a partial exception to this: because they do not rely on mediation, the operate parallel to the other submechanisms, and thus are not directly affected by them.

This lengthy dissection of two competing mechanisms was necessary for a number of reasons. First, I will argue that participation is a major factor in explaining citizen autonomy. By participation, I do not mean the actual political behavior or engagement of any individual or group. Nor do I refer simply to participatory fora, although such fora play a crucial role in Venezuela's support paradox, as I describe in Chapter 5. Rather participation, as reconceptualized here, is not an institutional subtype but a set of criteria for evaluating *all* institutions and practices occurring under a given regime. This will become vital during the discussion of Chile in Chapter 6, in which I argue that, contrary to the popular discourse of a "crisis of representation," by representative criteria Chile is a model democracy. Chile's legitimacy woes are instead attributable to failures of participation.

I.2   AUTONOMY IN CHILE AND VENEZUELA

Chile and Venezuela vary a great deal on the various mechanisms of autonomy discussed earlier, and in this case the difference is parallel to the opposing patterns of support in each case. Although both Chile and (until recently)[3] Venezuela are at least nominally democratic, the similarity in their political systems ends there. Each has embraced a

---

[3] Venezuela's status as a full democracy was debatable during the last few years of the Chávez administration. Under his successor, Nicolás Maduro, violent repression of street demonstrations and manipulation of supposedly autonomous institutions such as the courts and the electoral commission have decisively ended democracy in the country. This research deals only with the period during which Chávez was in power, although the concluding chapter does engage in some speculation regarding Maduro.

radically different view of what democracy is for, how it should operate, and how extensive a role the public should be granted in the process of making political decisions. Chile returned to democracy at the end of the 1980s. The country's relatively long history of stable democracy had come to an abrupt end during a period of intense polarization under the democratic socialist government of Salvador Allende. Under Allende and the *Unidad Popular* (UP, Popular Unity) coalition he led, society became deeply politicized, driven by rising expectations on the left and a perception of existential threat on the right. This bitter divide extended to virtually all social sectors; even the Christian Democratic center, which previously eschewed ideological fervor and had acted as a moderating force, polarized into warring camps (Scully, 1992). When this intense conflict rendered the country all but ungovernable, the military (with the implicit support of the right and center and moral support from the United States) elected to resolve the crisis with bombs and bullets in 1973. The trauma of this democratic failure, and the extent to which it shaped the political attitudes of ordinary citizens and political elites, cannot be overstated.

When democracy was restored seventeen years later, the Chilean political class had come to fear "populism" and the politicization of society that it could engender at least as much as the possibility of renewed military interference in politics. This fear of public involvement in politics was perhaps more acute among the parties of the right, but the partisan center and left were also deeply suspicious of mass democracy. The left bore the brunt of the military's campaign of repression, and a newfound respect for even pro forma, "bourgeois" democracy came to be a widely accepted norm in the post-Pinochet left. Whatever imperative to organize and mobilize the citizenry the left might have had was tempered by the lessons taken from the Allende era: that the benefits of an engaged and mobilized citizenry must be sacrificed, if necessary, to protect representative politics and civilian rule (Roberts, 1998). As a result, while the political class fought for and won significant concessions from the military during the transition process, many features of the regime that placed barriers between citizens and the state were allowed to remain. I discuss the specific aspects of the Chilean regime that inhibit popular participation in Chapter 6. To put it briefly, the Chilean electoral system interacts with extensive supermajority requirements for critical policy areas (e.g. education, labor, taxation) to incentivize political parties to abandon mobilization of society in favor of elite bargaining to achieve policy goals. The constitution essentially precludes the possibility of one party or coalition gaining sufficiently sizable majorities necessary to enact major reforms. As a result, parties must reach across the aisle and win the assent of their ideological rivals to accomplish any significant changes. Mobilization of the populace, in other words, has little strategic value to parties and could make elite bargaining more difficult if one of the parties (especially those on the right) found it threatening. Consequently, parties in Chile have largely abdicated one of their most important social functions: to organize and enable ordinary citizens to get involved in politics. Parties have little interest in cultivating a broad base of militants or establishing ties with social organizations (Rosenblatt, 2013). Given the dearth of alternative mechanisms for participation in Chile, the absence of parties at the grassroots has left a significant void. It is hardly surprising the Chileans feel a great deal of both apathy and helplessness vis-à-vis the state. Although successive governments have, largely through effective management of the economy, managed to avoid a full-blown legitimacy crisis, the benefits-for-passivity bargain that forms the heart of state–society relations in Chile seems to be breaking down (Luna, 2016).

If one wanted to see what such a breakdown could look like (at least if it were to go beyond a breakdown and become an utter calamity), one would only need look to Venezuela prior to the ascension of Hugo Chávez. Like Chile, Venezuela experienced a period of rule by the left (under Rómulo Betancourt) that was brought to an abrupt end by the military. When the military was pushed out of power in 1958, the Venezuelan political elite sought to avoid the mistakes of the past by prioritizing stability over inclusion, much the same as their Chilean counterparts would decades later. The *Punto Fijo* pact between Venezuela's three largest parties ensured the stability of competitive politics but also established oligopolistic partisan competition, with two parties (the center-left *Acción Democrática* [AD] and the center-right *Comité de Organización Política Electoral Independiente* [COPEI]) using oil rents and penetration of civil society to keep rival political movements out while alternating power between themselves (Coppedge, 1994). Although this system was successful in preserving civilian rule when most of the region was falling under the iron fist of the military, economic crises and corruption eventually undermined this system of "presidential partyarchy"; citizens ceased to accept their dominance and enforced passivity by party hacks once the good times stopped flowing.

As the economic crises in Venezuela during the 1980s eroded public support for the regime, gradually producing a full-blown legitimacy crisis in the 1990s, the political environment became increasingly propitious for political outsiders. Although a number of political leaders and movements, from Carlos Andrés Pérez (an AD stalwart who abandoned the party as *puntofijismo* came into disrepute) to the upstart leftist party *La Causa R*, no one capitalized on latent populist sentiments and attitudes more effectively than Hugo Chávez Frias. Chávez burst dramatically onto the political stage in Venezuela as the leader of a failed coup in 1992. Although he eventually forsook bullets for the ballot box, and recognized (if only ambivalently) the wisdom of forming alliances with civilian movements, his contempt for the oligarchic political class that had ruled for nearly fifty years never wavered. Once elected to the presidency in 1999, he immediately sought to enact a new constitution and a new political regime, one that would take an entirely different view of democracy and popular sovereignty. Gone were the days when parties dominated society; instead Chávez, partnering with a collection of newly awakened social organizations that had risen as the *Punto Fijo* parties' control faltered, sought to craft a political regime based upon the principle of "participatory, protagonist democracy." Giving a nod to his major inspiration, Simón Bolívar, he labeled his movement the "Bolivarian Revolution."

Despite these noble ambitions, Bolivarian Venezuela is not and never has been a neo-Athenian participatory democratic paradise. Chávez, like most populists, used rhetoric and the power granted to him as the occupant of a powerful executive office to polarize society, attack political rivals (including social organizations that advocated for subaltern groups, such as labor unions, which he saw as dominated by the oligarchy), and generally focused as much on empowering himself as his followers, especially after achieving full control over the government in 2006. Yet his detractors, who see him as little more than a strongman who used oil money to buy whatever support he could not get using his personal charisma to enthrall the masses, are just as wrong about the nature of the Bolivarian regime. Chávez (and the constitution he helped shape) did implement a broad variety of new participatory governance mechanisms at the local level, dealing with everything from land titles to water delivery to community development. As I will argue later, these programs gave many Venezuelans a newfound sense of empowerment and inclusion after decades of enforced passivity and neglect under *Punto Fijo*. These new participatory opportunities, ennobled further by Chávez's lofty rhetoric of a grand struggle between the people and the oligarchy, are the reason why the Bolivarian regime was able to maintain legitimacy despite its nearly total failure to govern the country. Without a concrete manifestation of "participatory, protagonist democracy," in the form of participatory opportunities at the local level, Chávez's claims would have eventually rung hollow, and his government (and quite likely the regime he helped to build) would have been crushed under the weight of his policy failures. And the programs themselves, which as I will demonstrate are participatory but are also quite limited in their scope, took on a much grander meaning because they were part of a broader democratizing revolution. In other words, populism and participatory opportunities each amplified the effect of the other on the public's imagination; working together in a mutually reinforcing fashion, they created a plausible narrative among huge swaths of the Venezuelan public that Chávez was indeed a new Bolívar, come to restore the people's sovereignty at long last.

Although citizen autonomy is a plausible explanation for the support paradox in Chile, it seems somewhat inadequate to account for the paradox in Venezuela without some elaboration. Governance problems are so acute in Venezuela that it is unlikely that any variable could overrule the impact of shortages, endemic violent crime, and runaway inflation. Psychological theory suggests that citizen autonomy can also account for the failure of these very real economic grievances to manifest in a mass withdrawal of support. Psychological research has repeatedly found that perceptions of control dramatically alter responses to external stimuli. Specifically, an individual who believes that he or she can substantially influence the course of a given process can be expected to respond to negative outcomes with more tolerance and less anxiety than an individual who feels at the mercy of forces beyond his or her control. In other words, feelings of autonomy increase support both directly and by ameliorating the deleterious effect of bad policy, fore-stalling erosions of legitimacy that might otherwise lead economic plights to devolve into full-blown regime crises. In the language of quantitative modeling, perceptions of autonomy moderate the relation-ship between performance and regime support.

Citizen autonomy is a promising solution to the paradox because it varies concomitantly with the stated priorities and philosophies of each regime. While Chile has focused on political stability and economic development since its return to democracy, often by intentionally insu-lating policymakers from popular pressure, Bolivarian Venezuela has emphasized the creation of channels for the direct participation of ordin-ary citizens in politics. A sense of empowerment and political inclusion is one of the *chavista* movement's most important promises to its militants, and the primary source of its claim to popular legitimacy. By incorporating the presence or absence of institutionally guaranteed par-ticipatory opportunities, it is possible to fully specify a theory of support that can explain cross-national variation, with clear connections between national-level and individual-level variables. I find that the provision of opportunities for direct participation in the policymaking process is an important source of widespread perceptions of citizen autonomy. Moreover this relationship apparently holds even for tightly circumscribed participatory opportunities occurring in a context of creeping authoritarianism and discredited representative mechanisms, as prevail in contemporary Venezuela. Figure 1.2 summarizes this theoretical framework.

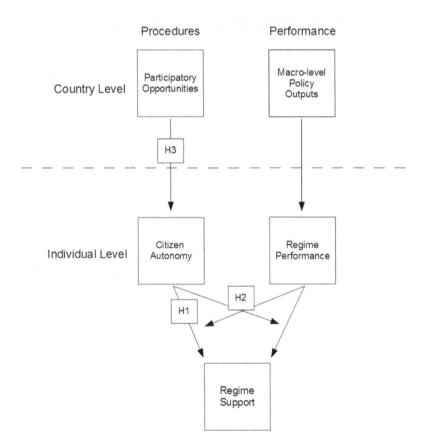

FIGURE 1.2: Theoretical framework

1.3 WHY AUTONOMY MATTERS: THE INTERACTIVE STRUCTURE OF REGIME SUPPORT

The cases studied in this research show the importance of adopting an interactive model of regime support that does not ignore questions of procedural justice. No theoretical framework without these modifications fits well in both Chile and Venezuela. The durability of legitimacy in Venezuela despite the erosion of representative democracy, especially when considered simultaneously with the impeccable democratic credentials and anemic support of Chile, requires a reevaluation of what makes democratic politics desirable. This research suggests that many individuals disagree with the primacy of liberal conceptions of democracy that reign in academia, which see elections and political competition as the *sine qua non* of democracy. Venezuela and Chile provide significant caveats to that belief. Chile shows that representative democracy cannot alone ensure legitimacy if it fails to enforce some measure of popular sovereignty by binding elites to the popular will. Bolivarian Venezuela shows that, in a political context where competitive multiparty politics have been discredited, large swathes of the citizenry will happily surrender their ability to hold elites accountable in exchange for direct participation in politics, even if that participation is tightly circumscribed to the level of the *barrio*.

The primary concern of this work, beyond explaining support patterns in the cases of interest, is to evaluate claims about why democracy matters. Normative democratic theories rest upon competing claims regarding human nature, and particularly on some conceived ideal typical relationship between the citizen and the state that is a product of that nature. Specifically, the existence of "the political man" is at issue here (Lipset, 1963): Are human beings inherently inclined toward politics, as classical democratic theory holds (Aristotle, 1959; Pateman, 1970; Rousseau, 2002), or do citizens yearn for their polities to simply protect their interests, provide their services, and leave them in peace (Downs, 1957; Hibbing & Theiss-Morse, 2001, 2002; Sartori, 1987)? One cannot directly evaluate these sorts of assumptions, but by drawing out their implications into clear hypotheses, empirical analysis can be brought to bear on these otherwise intractable debates.

The findings presented here are unambiguous: opportunities for direct engagement with the political system have strong positive impacts on those citizens who live under regimes that grant them. Nowhere in this work do I argue that utilitarian concerns are absent from the minds of most individuals, but the prominence of such questions in setting the tone of state–society relations is somewhat illusory. Quantitative scholars are often accused of ignoring context,[4] and such charges would be more than fair when applied to rational choice, economistic arguments for how states build support. While performance may act as a causal variable, the impact of participatory access is both causal and contextual. It shapes not only support itself, but how other factors contribute to the process. Citizens who, through direct access to the political system, come to feel a sense of control over their fates, act in much the way that classical democratic theory predicts. Here we find a mechanism, grounded in decades of psychological research, for the participatory democrat's claim that participation causes citizens to become more conscientious, more responsible, and less prone to panic or anger when confronted with economic or social problems. States can claim legitimacy entirely based upon competent governance, but such support appears quite tentative, revocable and (thanks to globalization) disturbingly dependent upon forces outside of the regime's control.

I.4   REBUTTING ELITISM: LEGITIMACY AND THE RESURGENCE OF POPULISM IN LATIN AMERICA

The findings have some clear practical implications, some hopeful, others more troubling. Discussion of these implications must be somewhat limited, as they require positing support not as a dependent

---

[4] In the interests of fairness, I should, as a quantitative scholar myself, concede that such accusations are frequently justified.

variable, as it is treated in all chapters here, but as an explanation of something else. Nevertheless, some effects of support, especially in light of the theoretical framework developed here and the case studies to which it is applied, are apparent enough to discuss at some length. Specifically, the findings I present here have some very clear implications regarding regime stability and breakdown, and the rise of populism.

Many of the more prominent works on regime support concern its impact on systemic stability and regime survival (e.g. Almond & Verba, 1963; Crozier et al., 1975; Easton, 1975; Pharr, Putnam, & Dalton, 2000). As the dire predictions of these authors failed to materialize, with imperfect democratic regimes in the industrial world limping along relatively untroubled by their citizens' waning confidence, many began to question the relevance of support altogether. Theories which gave an important causal role in regime transition to mass actors, such as those based upon class conflict (Acemoglu & Robinson, 2006; Bellin, 2000; Boix, 2006; Rueschemeyer, Stephens, & Stephens, 1992) or cultural values (Inglehart & Welzel, 2005) fell out of favor by the 2000s, especially in Latin American studies. Instead, attention turned to the importance of powerful political actors and elites (e.g. Higley & Burton, 2006; Mainwaring & Pérez-Liñán, 2013; McFaul, 2002; Schmitter & O'Donnell, 1986). Within this line of inquiry, the opinions and attitudes of the public are largely irrelevant to the question of regime stability; social and political elites determine the institutional structure of the state.

That said, the wave of populist leaders that came to power beginning with Chávez seems to have reawakened interest in how the political attitudes and values of citizens can influence democratic outcomes. For example, Booth and Seligson (2009), in their important work on support in Latin America, argue that citizens with "low legitimacy levels [could] facilitate the actions of antidemocratic elites" (p. 242). Yet even Booth and Seligson downplay the risks to democracy of low legitimacy by arguing that for democracy to fail, a critical mass of citizens must have negative attitudes regarding performance, regime institutions, and democratic norms (pp. 246–247). Booth and Seligson find this situation unlikely, because although existing regime practices has lost support, support for democratic norms remains relatively strong.

While the corrosive effect of weak support on regime stability may well have been overblown, it would be a mistake to overcorrect and dismiss it entirely. Even if one accepts that elite agency is the most direct factor that determines whether regimes stand or fall, their strategic maneuvering does not occur in a vacuum. The foundational text of the elite transition paradigm in Latin American studies, Schmitter and O'Donnell's *Transitions from Authoritarian Rule* (1986), is instructive here. While its theoretical narrative is entirely focused upon a tiny fraction of the population, not just elites but regime insiders, one need not look too deeply to see a role for mass actors in the story. All theories that involve a considerable role for the agency of actors must still acknowledge the contextually determined incentives and constraints under which these actors operate. Even elite theorists who are dismissive of the public as an actor in its own right acknowledge that "public opinion is one of the most valuable resources which actors can employ" (Mainwaring & Pérez-Liñán, 2013, p. 12). When crises occur, bringing elites who wish to save a regime and those who wish to bring about its end into direct conflict, the presence or absence of regime support can provide one side or the other a powerful weapon. The fall of representative democracy in Venezuela is a fairly unambiguous example of this. Although a series of economic crises weakened the elitist *puntofijismo* regime, the repeated flouting of popular preferences, exacerbated by long-simmering resentments over the regime's elitist and hierarchical style of rule, put the final nail in the regime's coffin. Hugo Chávez was undoubtedly a canny politician, but his fabled charisma owed much to the illegitimacy of his opponents. It has been noted that charisma is, in part, simply the ability to make oneself a *tabula rasa* on to which individuals can project their hopes and expectations (e.g. Panizza, 2005), and in part on circumstantial conditions such as a hostile environment combined with feelings of helplessness (Madsen & Snow, 1991). Chávez would not have been able to so thoroughly unmake the *ancién regime*, nor to construct one so completely matching his own vision, without such a deep well of anger and resentment from which to draw.

Even if one concedes that most regime transitions are determined at the elite level, Venezuela is a glaring exception to this. The attitudes of the populace, especially widespread antipathy toward *puntofijismo*, cannot be ignored in this instance; the role of public opinion in general and regime support in particular is so clear that no theory that ignores them need be taken seriously. In other words, regimes may differ considerably in their vulnerability to their populaces' displeasure, and those who use public opinion to fell one regime may well find themselves uniquely dependent upon cultivating the same force to protect their own. While it may be that democracies and certain types of authoritarian regimes are not responsive to citizen discontent, populist regimes are acutely dependent upon the enthusiastic support of ordinary citizens for survival. Populist regimes tend to be, by their very nature, giants with feet of clay. Without wading into the morass that is the conceptual debate over defining populism, one relatively uncontroversial characteristic of such movements is a strong anti-systemic bent. Populists tend to embrace the notion of creative destruction, seeking to uproot institutions sooner and build replacements later (if at all).

Given this tendency, as well as the affinity of such regimes for self-inflicted economic wounds, shaky foundations are the norm, which leaves populists few institutional or organizational resources that they can use to anchor themselves. Strong popular support therefore tends to be of critical importance for such movements to survive. Even those movements that do eventually build institutions and organizations, as the Bolivarian movement has, tend to do so around the task of mobilizing support in times of crises or vulnerability. Legitimacy may be neither necessary nor sufficient for regime survival in many contexts, but when a populist loses it, his or her days are numbered. This drive is reflected in support statistics; nearly all top-ranking states in terms of support are led by populists (The Latin American Public Opinion Project, 2012).

The theoretical framework I develop and its direct application to a populist context in Venezuela both provide clear insight into one way in which populists maintain legitimacy. Populists tend to be poor economic performers, and they often ignore or actively subvert representative and liberal institutions. In this analysis, I show how non-representative mechanisms for political incorporation, especially direct and participatory programs, provide an alternative procedural way for populists to meet their commitments to their bases and thus ensure their survival. Left populism seems to be making a comeback in Latin America after going out of fashion for some time. Populism of both left and right varieties has also seen something of a renaissance in the United States and Europe as well. In light of this proliferation, theories that can explain how these regimes build support and thus ensure their survival are of clear relevance.

1.5   SIMMERING DISCONTENT: REGIME SUPPORT AND CONTENTIOUS POLITICS

Even in liberal democracies like Chile, where low support appears not to be a terminal malady, one need only count the demonstrations to see its relevance. Stability is not a binary variable; it presents in shades of degree, and when taken as such the importance of legitimacy is much more readily apparent. An enormous body of scholarship exists demonstrating the link between dissatisfaction with democracy as practiced and contentious and even anti-systemic political behavior (Booth & Seligson, 2009; Carlin, 2011; Crow, 2010; Klosko, Muller, & Opp, 1987; Lichbach, 1995; Madsen, 1987; McAdam & Tarrow, 2010; Muller & Opp, 1986; Opp, Burow-Auffarth, & Heinrichs, 1981; Rhodes-Purdy, 2012; Tarrow, 2000). Since the original march of *los pingüinos* in 2006, waves of protests have crested in Chile, one after another, with almost no respite. While none of these movements has ever come close to threatening the survival of democracy, the disruptions of day-to-day life, injuries, arrests, property damage, and other negative externalities of contention have become cause for concern.

Successive governments in Chile have long employed a "kitchen sink" approach to this issue, attempting to placate disaffected citizens (and especially students) with both public goods and institutional reform. My findings have clear implications for this strategy: specifically, they indicate that greater emphasis should be placed on political reform. Not only are procedural justice concerns the root cause of disaffection, but my findings suggest that economic grievances could also be ameliorated through institutional reform alone. Even if no reforms to taxation, education funding, or the pension system (to name only a few highly contentious issues that have risen in recent years) were undertaken, increased systemic responsiveness and opportunities for participation would weaken the negative impact of these issues on legitimacy. Currently the country is beginning a slow (but for Chile surprisingly participatory) process of rewriting the constitution. Discarding the current constitution, with its dictatorial roots, is a long overdue step, but it remains to be seen whether the Chilean elite will overcome its fear of unleashing the populace on the political system.

1.6 RESEARCH DESIGN, METHODS, AND CASE SELECTION

The two primary theoretical contributions of this study are the emphasis on direct participation and the interactive relationship between performance, process, and regime support. I test hypotheses based on these insights using a multimethod research design, employing statistical analysis, an experiment, and a comparison of the two cases of interest. Results of large-N statistical analyses are presented in Chapter 4. These analyses test both the direct impact of citizen autonomy on support and its moderating effect on the support–performance relationship. I also test whether perceptions of autonomy are, on average, higher in those countries with extensive opportunities for direct participation.

The limited number of second-level units of analysis and the possibility of conjunctural causal pathways limits the power of statistical examination of my argument at the regime level. Therefore in Chapters 5 and 6, I present case studies of Venezuela and Chile respectively to further support this portion of the argument. The case study portions of this book do not directly follow either a most similar or most different systems design; Chile and Venezuela share a common political and cultural history as former Spanish colonies, but differ radically in any number of additional characteristics. Their joint inclusion serves two primary purposes. First, even imperfect case comparisons that could not reliably "prove" true hypotheses can help rule out false ones (Cohen & Nagel, 1934, ch. 9; Rihoux & Ragin, 2009, ch. 1). Arguments based on policy issues of great concern to the popular sectors (e.g. poverty reduction) and substantive representation are both ruled out by comparing these two cases in Chapters 2 and 3, respectively. Second, each case can independently provide a "road test" of the theory developed and tested in earlier Sections 1.1-1.5. One of the most valid critiques of quantitative analysis is that it often operates at a fairly high level of abstraction, and thus the relationships between variables that it establishes may be "valid" but are so far removed from the real world as to be of limited value when understanding outcomes in real-world cases. To guard against this, I apply the theoretical insights developed in Chapter 3 and tested in Chapter 4 to the cases of interest, starting with Venezuela in Chapter 5 and moving on to Chile in Chapter 6.

Before proceeding further, a brief note about the scope of this book is necessary. The support paradoxes in question cannot be neatly excised from the historical contexts that gave rise to them. In a sense, these paradoxes were years, or even decades, in the making. This book, while not neglecting these historical processes, focuses on the same time period for both countries: roughly 2006 to 2012. Part of the reason for this focus can be attributed to the old adage about drunkards searching for keys under streetlights. LAPOP has without question the most valid and reliable measures of the concepts of interest to be found in any survey of the region, but 2006 is the earliest wave in which all countries were included, and many important indicators are unavailable even in included countries prior to this time. By happy accident, this time period happens to when each country's paradox was the most pronounced, as explained in the detailed treatment of each case in Chapters 5 and 6.[5]

The study of Venezuela examines the complex role of participatory programs in a populist, semi-authoritarian regime; I find that these programs were absolutely crucial for the regime's legitimacy during the reign of Chávez, especially given the countervailing pressures and constraints under which the Bolivarian regime operates. I use a statistical analysis specifically tailored to the Venezuelan context, supplemented with interview data, to show that engagement with participatory programs has the predicted impact on perceptions of citizen autonomy to support this argument. The fact that such direct participation exists alongside debased liberal and representative institutions at the national level, and in fact exists in part to excuse these violations of democratic norms, sheds considerable light on what citizens actually expect from and value in politics.

Chile presents a more difficult analytical puzzle. It is "the dog that did not bark," where high quality governance has not had its widely assumed legitimating effect. Beyond that, it is difficult to attribute low support in Chile specifically to the absence of participatory opportunities; any number of absent factors could potentially be at work. To overcome this, I use three primary approaches, the first theoretical, the last two empirical. Theoretically, the modification of "participation" as a mechanism that can be applied even to mediated forms of democracy, which I specified earlier in this chapter, allows

---

[5] Chile is a partial exception to this, as support has continued to decline, although weakening economic performance and a series of corruption scandals make that decline significantly less inexplicable than during the period under investigation here. Venezuela's support has also declined markedly, but the death of Chávez (among other factors, some of which are discussed in the Chapter 7: Conclusion) makes this less interesting.

for a rigorous evaluation of Chile's democratic institutions. Applying this framework, I find that participation is not merely *absent* in Chile, but that its institutions are actively antagonistic to participation. Theory can only take one so far, and thus I employ two empirical tactics to test the hypotheses of interest: a statistical deconstruction of party-system antipathy, which runs very deep in Chile, and experimental research, buttressed by qualitative analysis of a real-world example of the experimental treatment. Using public opinion data from the Center for Public Studies (CEP), I find that regime support in Chile is inextricably linked to confidence (or lack of same) in the country's political parties and party system. I further find that discontent with parties is driven by a lack of faith in their willingness and ability to enable citizen participation in politics, rather than their representative role. Finally, I use an experiment to demonstrate that participatory opportunities improve evaluations of the sponsoring entity, especially among those who are dissatisfied with policy choices. Although these results do conform to the predictions of my theory, a small experiment conducted among a student population has limited external validity. Fortunately, a participatory program in Providencia municipality allows for a real-world test of dynamics suggested by experimental and statistical analysis. I find that tense relationships between the municipality and civil society organizations became much more amicable due to the program, which follows what theory would predict quite closely.

1.7 GOING FORWARD: STRUCTURE OF THE ARGUMENT

The development of the theoretical framework utilized here will proceed over the next two chapters. In Chapter 2, I turn first to conceptual issues regarding the exact definition of regime support; this is not a trivial matter, as many terms (often with conflicting definitions from author to author) have been employed which might be reasonably considered instances or specific subtypes of "support" and it is absolutely crucial to be very specific about the dependent

variable before proceeding further. Additionally, I find that disagree-
ments over conceptualization closely mirror the debate over causal
factors, with two groups becoming clear with some sorting of the
literature: those works emphasizing outcomes and those emphasizing
intrinsic characteristics of regime processes. I then review the body of
theory that highlights outcomes; I find that such variables are important but incapable of shedding light on the question of interest here.
Indeed, the research puzzle I seek to solve has its basis in this inad-
equacy. Then in Chapter 3, I turn to procedural theories of support,
finally arriving at citizen autonomy (and its regime-level antecedent,
participatory opportunities) as the most likely source of the discrepancies in Chile and Venezuela. The remaining chapters involve empirical testing of the hypotheses developed in these two chapters.

2 Conceptualizations and Existing Explanations of Regime Support

2.1 ASSENT OR APPROVAL: CONCEPTUALIZING REGIME SUPPORT

Debates concerning explanations for regime support are not over a simple choice of including or excluding this or that variable, but rather arise from fundamental differences in conceptualization. In other words, what shapes support tends to depend on how one defines it. The literature on the subject is a confusing mélange of definitions, with little consistency from one work to another, even among works that use the same term. Yet it is possible to organize conceptualizations of support into two broad categories. The resultant conceptual schema is important to note because it largely mirrors (indeed it is in part responsible for) the divide between procedural and performance variables, which will be reflected in the analytical framework I develop in this chapter and in Chapter 3.

Before proceeding with examination of what the term "regime support" means, it is important to note what it does not mean. There is a common misconception – particularly when the accurate but unhelpful term "support for democracy" is used in lieu of the more precise "regime support" – that the term refers to evaluations of democracy as an ideal, rather than as practiced. This is a common instance of a wider problem that frequently crops up in the support literature: that of separating the various objects to which support attitudes may pertain. Easton (1975) was the first author who attempted to systematically organize empirical objects into a schema of support. He arranged political community, political regime, and political leaders along a continuum, running from "diffuse" to "specific" based upon the relative abstractness of the object.

Klingemann (1999) elaborated on this schema, adding political ideals and specific policies, and empirically verified the distinct existence of each object using Confirmatory Factor Analysis (CFA). A thorough parsing of the various levels that may or may not be included in such a schema is beyond the scope of this work. Yet two points on this topic must be noted. First, while some (perhaps most) authors would disagree (e.g. Inglehart, 2003; Linde & Ekman, 2003; Sarsfield & Echegaray, 2005), I reserve the term "support" to refer to an attitude directed at objects at least as concrete as the political regime. To further ensure conceptual clarity, I avoid using the term "support for democracy" altogether, in favor of the term "regime support." The word "support" has strong empirical connotations; it implies the existence of a very real object being held up or buttressed by the subject. One can speak of commitment to or pride in political community, or of belief in or preference for democratic ideals, but to use the term "support" for these sentiments is inappropriate because the intension of the term (which includes concreteness) not only does not fit with the characteristics of these objects but in fact does fit with closely related but empirically and theoretically distinct objects (see Sartori, 1984). This is a recipe for confusion; especially should one wish to conduct an analysis involving multiple objects, which brings us to the second point.

Given the omission of the word "democracy" from the term's label, a brief reminder about the scope of this project is in order here. I restrict the domain of my analyses to regimes that are at least nominally democratic. However, this restriction is due to an abundance of caution, rather than a positive conviction that the relationships I describe (particularly the relationships between autonomy, performance, and regime support) would not operate in authoritarian contexts. It is likely that these relationships *do* hold even in non-democracies, but because my primary cases and the rest of the countries in Latin America that provide public opinion evidence, are at least minimally democratic, I cannot say that they hold for sure without further research. Venezuela, of course, is a partial exception;

by the end of the Chávez era the regime's authoritarian leanings had become very pronounced. Yet, because I grapple with this case in considerable detail, I am able to explain and analyze how its unique characteristics, including its democratic failures, conform to the theories here. So while I am confident that the framework used here would apply broadly to all democracies, and that it also pertains to one case that is semi-authoritarian, that is as far as I can responsibly go.

The preceding discussion is relevant primarily because different conceptualizations of regime support, among other characteristics, tend to emphasize their affinity for different immediately proximate objects on the scale of abstractness used by Easton, Klingemann, and others. While there is sufficient empirical evidence to be confident that objects are evaluated separately by citizens (Booth & Seligson, 2009; Klingemann, 1999), attitudes toward different objects may well impact one another. Additionally, evaluations of different objects may share a common attitudinal "mode," or type of support. For example, political leaders and the policies that they enact may be evaluated separately, but both evaluations will be made largely on instrumental grounds, i.e. the extent to which each satisfies individual needs and preferences. Conversely, political ideals (like democracy) are evaluated largely on moral, normative grounds (Klingemann, 1999, p. 54).

Unlike the separation of objects, a challenge which is largely at the periphery of analysis and consists mostly of getting such difficulties "out of the way" of the main argument with sound measurement strategies, the issue of attitudinal mode gets to the heart of conceptualizing support. The political regime stands at the midpoint of Easton's continuum, demarcating (and blurring) the border between abstract and concrete objects. The rules and institutions that collectively comprise the democratic state are in part a reflection of various philosophical and moral notions about the proper distribution of political power. Regimes determine which leaders are granted access to power and how such leaders are retained or removed, which can have a significant impact on the extent to which various social groups

Table 2.1: *Characteristics of approval and attachment*

	Approval	Assent
Related terms and concepts	Confidence, rational legitimacy	Legitimacy, loyalty, allegiance
Citizen orientation	Private	Public
Basis of evaluation	Instrumental/ utilitarian	Moral/psychological
Nature of low support	Dissatisfaction	Alienation
Important related object of support	Political leaders, specific policies	Regime principles, democratic ideals
Class of causal variables	Outputs	Throughputs/Inputs

benefit or suffer from state policy. It therefore is reasonable to assume that both instrumental and moral evaluations are relevant for determining regime support.

Which of these modes has the greater causal force (and under which sets of circumstances) is at the root of the most profound debates over the sources of support, and this divide can be used to roughly bifurcate conceptual work on the subject. These two groups can be considered constitutive dimensions of support, meaning that these two concepts (which are probably not observable or measureable separately from support) jointly form the umbrella concept. A list of characteristics belonging to each dimension, which I label "assent" and "approval," is presented in Table 2.1.

Assent and approval are not perfect terms, but they have the advantage of being infrequently used in the existing literature, therefore avoiding the confusion that some more commonly employed words might engender. I turn first to those conceptions of regime support that might be included under the assent dimension.

2.1.1 Assent

The oldest works on those attitudes that can be included under the umbrella of regime support tended to assume a relationship between citizen (or subject) and state that was much deeper and more enduring than the quid-pro-quo utilitarianism of later works. Among the earliest of these were Weber's classic works on legitimacy (Weber, 1978). Although he defined the state based upon on violence and coercion, he also emphasized the importance of the widespread acceptance of the state's monopoly on force. Early analyses from the nascent subfield of public opinion hewed closely to this understanding of how citizens evaluated their regimes when developing the concept of political allegiance (and its negation, alienation) (Almond & Verba, 1963; Gamson, 1968; Lane, 1962, ch. 10). These works differed a great deal in details, but they agreed that one's acceptance or rejection of the state was based primarily on moral, psychological, or emotional considerations.

A few key implications can be gleaned from the preceding discussion. The term assent, which implies both acceptance of the regime and an emotional basis of that acceptance (having its origins in the Latin verb meaning "to feel"), captures the core of this dimension of support. It is emotional, psychological, and moral, rather than instrumental or utilitarian. Indeed, this dimension assigns little importance to what is actually done under the aegis of a given regime, exclusively focusing upon the inherent qualities of the procedures and institutions of the state. Regimes are evaluated based upon their adherence to abstract principles or political ideals, as implied by Weber's concept of legal authority. The exact standard by which these inherent characteristics are assumed to be judged is a source of considerable debate; there is no consensus on this subject, which is likely one of the reasons why this area of the literature, though originating well before the more outcome-oriented works which I discuss presently, is so underdeveloped. Easton and Dennis held that support and other regime attitudes were likely the result of early childhood socialization (Easton & Dennis, 1967, 1969); the normative value of a regime was inculcated during childhood, along with other moral precepts. This is somewhat similar to Weber's concept of traditional authority, where a regime was valued because it had existed since time out of mind. In other words, the original psychological works on support treated it more like a fixed personality trait, or at least a deeply held value, than an attitude, which might vary over time as circumstances changed.

Other works on the subject departed from Dennis and Easton's focus on socialization, instead assuming that some independent set of standards were being applied when citizens evaluated their regimes (Almond & Verba, 1963; Gamson, 1968; Lane, 1962). The importance of belief in political ideals (the next most abstract object after the regime) is clear here. Discovering the source of support requires a clear notion of the standards of evaluation. The literature on conceptions of democracy attempts to identify such standards by specifying characteristics of democracy that citizens might value (D. Collier & Levitsky, 1997; Crow, 2007, 2010; Diamond, 1996). Such analyses have been consistently hampered by the extreme difficulty of classifying survey respondents as this or that type of democrat. This often requires making herculean assumptions about the political knowledge of citizens. For example, this literature makes an unstated assumption that citizens are aware of alternative conceptions and consciously compare existing regime practices to those ideals. This is not overly taxing for comparative studies of support at a given point in time, but it raises serious issues when trying to explain change over time within a given polity. Explaining change over time would require one to show that a regime either completely adopted a new form of democracy, or that a large number of citizens drastically changed their beliefs about what democracy means.[1] Either would require far more demanding and less plausible assumptions than will be made in support of my argument.

---

[1] Canache (2007) attempts to avoid this trap in Venezuela, arguing that support for Chávez and his government was driven by a change in perceptions, induced by the Bolivarian movement, in conceptions of democracy, from representative to participatory. This argument, if true, would be not be inconsistent with the approach I develop here. At most it would imply an alternative mechanism than the psychological/emotional one on which I rely, and even then the two could be complimentary rather than competing.

Behavioralist and political psychological works would contest this assumption, arguing that unconscious emotional and psychological needs are often in play, which may only be vaguely understood by citizens. For example, an alienated individual may well be responding to a lack of institutional allowance for her active participation (Almond & Verba, 1963; Gamson, 1968; Lane, 1962), but having never been exposed to alternative democratic forms that allow citizens a more active role, she cannot be reasonably expected to cite participatory opportunities as a critical (and absent) aspect of democracy. Additionally, asking respondents to identify specific characteristics of democratic subtypes leads to biased findings in favor of outcome-oriented definitions. Respondents who believe in political equality and popular control over economic policies may cite high prices as a sign of democratic failure, not because they define democracy in terms of prices or inflation, but because high prices are the manifestation of the gulf between democracy as practiced and their belief in democracy as direct sovereignty over policy choices (Schaffer, 2010).

Given this confusion and lack of clarity, it is perhaps unsurprising that scholars have turned away from the morass altogether in search of less contentious sets of standards. While normative debates raged on, a more utilitarian approach to regime support, which makes very clear and uncontroversial assumptions about individual preferences, has gained prominence.

2.1.2 Approval

The ascendency of rational choice in political science impacted conceptions of support, just as it did throughout the discipline. With it came new ideas about how citizens evaluated their political systems, which were far removed from Weberian notions of a normative basis for legitimacy. Rogowski (1974) coined the term "rational legitimacy" to describe this new notion, arguing that citizens were much more influenced by materialistic and utilitarian concerns than previous authors had recognized. This implied that support was likely far less resilient than early authors had assumed, because it responds to a rapidly changing political environment. Within a rationalist framework, regime evaluations are almost fickle.

To the extent that rational support can be durable, it does so through the related concept of confidence. Confidence is also sometimes called trust, but this is inappropriate as the kind of recurring face-to-face interactions that are needed to develop real trust cannot occur between citizens and political leaders, much less faceless institutions (Hardin, 2000). Confidence then is generally assumed to be a kind of aggregate assessment; that is, a belief in the ability of the political regime to produce leaders who are competent and who will act in the best interest of citizens (Craig, Niemi, & Silver, 1990; Hardin, 2000, 2002; Lipset & Schneider, 1983). While patterns of good or poor performance may be recognized and thus fortify support at the regime level, the underlying logic is still that of instrumental rationality.

2.1.3   What Matters More? Assessing the Dimensionality of Support

The current state of the literature is a seemingly irreconcilable conflict between the two constituent dimensions of support. A great deal of work has been done within each conception (although virtually all recent work favors approval), but very little has been done to bridge the gap between the two. This raises the obvious question: which dimension should be given primacy? The clear answer, conceptually speaking, is neither, at least not on an *a priori* basis. Although theoretically interesting, it would be extremely difficult to measure these two dimensions separately from the more general variable that they constitute. It is relatively simple to measure the minimalist concept of support, but getting at the gradations of meaning inherent in assent and approval would risk repeating the errors of the conceptions of democracy literature; namely, it would attempt to measure fine distinctions based on highly abstract theoretical concerns with quantitative survey analysis, which is ill-suited for the purpose. Furthermore, whatever may or may not be possible in theory, currently available

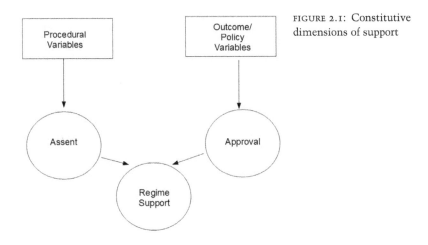

FIGURE 2.1: Constitutive dimensions of support

cross-national surveys only allow one to measure the minimalist support concept, not its constitutive dimensions.

It is possible to evaluate the relative importance of each dimension even if they cannot be independently measured. The discussion of each dimension clearly implied causes of regime support that can be theoretically assigned to one dimension or the other. If assent was more important, one would expect procedural variables to have the greatest impact. On the other hand, advocates of approval would predict that variables concerned with the quality of policy produced by a given regime would be the most important. In other words, by evaluating different theoretical narratives empirically we can gain insight not only into the causes of support but also into its inherent nature. Figure 2.1 shows this schema.

The most important point of this conceptual discussion for the task at hand is that it provides a clear schema for organizing the literature on support. It can be difficult in practice to declare this or that work as a "performance" argument; this will become readily apparent when discussing institutional approaches to support, which would appear to be procedural but which are, in fact, based on performance. What matters is not whether or not procedural or output variables are included, but rather which is the proximate cause of support, and what is the underlying logic of the argument. As I will show, institutionally grounded arguments can still favor the approval dimension if they focus not on intrinsic characteristics but on the policy impacts of institutional variants.

With this in mind, a second important implication of the preceding discussion needs to be underlined: the paradoxes that form the basis of this work are paradoxes if and only if one assumes that the approval dimension is dominant. If assent is the more powerful determinant of support, and if approval shapes support only weakly or not at all, then the incongruence between performance and support ceases to be a paradox.

2.2 PERFORMANCE ÜBER ALLES: RATIONAL LEGITIMACY AND UTILITARIAN SUPPORT

Performance is, broadly speaking, the quality of governance and policy produced under a given regime. It is theoretically distinct from the performance of political actors, but difficult to untangle in practice, since "the regime" does not do anything independently of those to whom it grants positions of power. A regime is an aggregate: if incompetent leaders repeatedly gain power under the rules of a given regime, individuals will turn against those rules. This is an especially difficult distinction to make in the case of Venezuela, which until recently had only one ruler under the existing regime: Hugo Chávez. In that case, I argue that regime performance and the performance of political leaders were one and the same until Chávez's death. In most cases these are separate objects and are treated as such.

2.2.1 The Theoretical Basis of Performance Arguments

Sorting works on support into those based on performance and those based on procedure seems straightforward, but can in practice be rather complicated. For example, many analyses include institutional variables (such as parliamentary vs. presidential, electoral systems, etc.), and thus appear to be arguments based upon process. Upon closer inspection, the impact of these institutions is not directly on support but on patterns of winners and losers; whether one benefits or not is, in these cases, the driving force behind support. Democratic theory can provide clarity here. Pateman (1970) divides democratic theory into two families: classical and contemporary. The primary assumption that divides these two schools of thought rests in their beliefs about the utility of democratic participation: classical theory held that such participation had intrinsic value to those who participated, whereas contemporary theory viewed democracy as a means to an end, to be praised only for the outcomes it produced, such as stability, the protection of civil liberties, and so forth. This closely aligns with David Held's (2007) and C.B. Macpherson's (1977) theoretical schemas, wherein democratic variants were divided into protective (which I rechristen as "instrumental") and developmental families. The latter group was so named because of the positive impact democratic politics were thought to have on the psychological and moral development of participants.

Performance arguments can therefore be identified not by those variables that they include but by their embrace of instrumental conceptions of democracy. Such conceptions originate in liberal theory, which holds that democracy is desirable only because it effectively promotes and protects individual rights and facilitates the pursuit of private interests (Hobbes, 1985; Locke, 2003; Madison, 1952). A strong suspicion of politics (especially mass politics) underlies this body of theory. The communitarian and public-oriented assumptions of "classical" democratic theory were explicitly rejected by proponents of liberalism in favor of "delimit[ing] the sphere of politics carefully [and] unleash[ing] individual energies in civil society" (Held, 2007, p. 48). This is not to say that liberals were not concerned with the impact of political institutions; to the contrary, the structure of democratic regimes was a matter of great import. Yet liberalism values institutions for different reasons than classical democratic theory. To liberals, institutions of democracy are preferable only because they constrain the excesses of both elites and masses better than any other conceivable political arrangement (Madison, 1952).

While the need to protect individual rights necessitates some form of democracy within a liberal framework, the fear of excessive government interference in the private pursuit of citizens is not allayed simply because a government is democratic. Indeed, a central contradiction of liberalism arises from the necessity of some form of popular sovereignty and the fear that the sovereign people will attempt to deprive some individuals of those rights which democracy is meant to defend (Adams, 2000; de Tocqueville, 1990). As a result of this inner conflict proponents of such philosophies strongly support the right of the people to choose their leaders, but they tend to be far less sanguine about granting an expansive political role to the masses, with their short-term demands and lack of policy expertise. Excessive involvement of the ordinary citizens in politics is viewed as unnecessary at best and potentially even threatening to systemic stability (Crozier et al., 1975; Huntington, 1965; Schumpeter, 2008).

Later theorists took the normative assumptions of instrumentalism and adapted them into empirical assumptions; these works became the direct (if not always explicit) inspiration for performance-based theories of regime support. Specifically, they took the proposition that excessive mass participation in politics was normatively undesirable and went a step further, arguing that it was also empirically impossible due to the apathy of average citizens (Michels, 2001; Mosca, 1939; Sartori, 1984). These authors assumed that most people were not and would never be concerned with politics, and would therefore rationally and voluntarily limit their political participation to that which is necessary for the pursuit of their private interests (Crow, 2007, 2010; Downs, 1957; Hibbing & Theiss-Morse, 2001, 2002). Within this paradigm, participation is viewed as a cost or an expense, something rational individuals are expected to avoid if possible.

In short, individuals should prefer those regimes that maximize the quality of governance while minimizing the need for active input.

The insights of the instrumentalist school have clear implications for the study of regime support, because it deduces strong hypotheses about regime preferences based on those philosophical and normative assumptions its progenitors developed about human nature. Specifically, it argues for a rational, self-interested view of democratic citizens, who care little about how decisions are made unless those procedures have some predictable consequences for which policies are eventually chosen. Any and all concern for institutions is filtered through policy outputs.

2.2.2   Empirical Predictions of Performance-Centric Theories

Two important implications of output-centric theories arise from the preceding discussion. These implications can be distilled into a simple flow chart; this chart is presented in Figure 2.2.

First, they posit a fairly direct, sequential relationship between evaluations of policy, political leaders, and regime institutions in turn. That is, evaluations of policy output are the basis by which political leaders are judged, and the prevalence of high-performing political actors over time is the primary source of regime support (Finkel, Muller, & Seligson, 1989; Muller, 1970; Muller & Williams, 1980; Newton & Norris, 2000). Performance arguments, taking inspiration from instrumental views of democracy, assume the causal primacy of the approval dimension, focusing on objects on the concrete side of the support continuum.

Second, to the extent that throughput-oriented variables are included in such models, they matter only because they impact policy outputs. One of the most influential works on support, Crozier, Huntington, and Watanuki's (1975) study of democratic malaise in the Trilateral nations, focused on changing state-society relations and their impact on declining support. Their analyses were inspired by Huntington's work on institutionalization, in which he argued that political breakdown was often due to excessive participation that existing institutions could not manage or control (Huntington, 1965). Taking this proposition as the key assumption of their

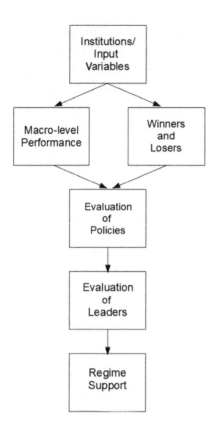

FIGURE 2.2: Relationship chart for performance-oriented explanations of support

theoretical framework, the authors argued that this inability of state institutions to cope with increasing demands from society was leading to poor quality governance, and thus low support.

Not all analyses that include institutional reactions to popular participation shared this pessimistic view. Robert Putnam's work on social capital (Putnam, 1993, 1995) provided a rationale for a relationship between participation, institutional reactions to participation, and support that was directly opposed to that argued by Huntington and his coauthors. Specifically, a highly participatory citizenry, according to Putnam, actually facilitated quality governance through effective and disciplined demand-making (Putnam, 1993). Putnam later linked this argument directly to regime support, arguing that declining legitimacy was the result of depleted social capital, which inhibited the kind of civic engagement necessary for good governance (Hardin, 2000; Newton & Norris, 2000; Pharr et al., 2000).

A final group of institutional theories of support ignores the macroeconomic effects of specific institutions, instead focusing on how specific institutional variants structure patterns of support within polities. These works assume that "winners," i.e. those individuals or social groups that benefit from government policy, can be institutionally determined. Furthermore, institutions can either exacerbate or lessen the pain that those who are not unambiguous beneficiaries of government policies suffer (Anderson & Guillory, 1997; Carlin & Singer, 2011; Norris, 1999a). For example, following Lijphart's (1984) work on consensual and majoritarian democratic subtypes, Anderson and Guillory (1997) argue that citizens who are part of the political majority are more satisfied, but minority status has a much more severe negative impact on support in majoritarian democracies than in those closer to the consensual end of Lijphart's continuum; this argument has been referred to as "the losers' hypothesis." Norris (1999a), operating on essentially the same logic, conducted a similar analysis but also included party and electoral systems and state structure (federal vs. unitary), with a directly opposing finding to Anderson and Guillory that majoritarian institutions actually encouraged slightly higher levels of support.

Although these works make radically different arguments about which variables matter, sometimes finding effects of the same variable in completely different directions, they all have one thing in common. Despite their inclusion of institutional variables, none of these works can be categorized as "procedural"; they are simply elaborate performance arguments. Here the importance of the earlier conceptual discussion becomes clear. The type of variables included is only part of the picture: the underlying theoretical logic and causal mechanisms are equally crucial for understanding theories of support. In this case, talk of winners and losers and of crises of governability clearly link these works to the approval dimension. These analysts make competing claims about how institutions shape performance; all agree that performance is the direct predictor of regime support.

2.2.3 The Inadequacy of Performance Arguments

I do not deny that performance issues can negatively impact regime support. Regimes that continually fail to meet the needs and expectations of their citizenry cannot expect to indefinitely maintain their loyalty. Long-term deprivation under democratic regimes may even turn people off to democracy as an ideal (Sarsfield & Echegaray, 2005). That said, this exclusive focus on outputs provides an incomplete picture. Theoretically, utilitarian arguments cannot shed light on the puzzle that Easton sought to solve via the concept of diffuse support: namely, they cannot explain why similar declines in the quality of governance produce political crises in some contexts yet only minor disturbances in others.

This is a fatal flaw for a study such as this, which focuses on cases where support and performance are severely mismatched. A brief presentation of descriptive statistics from the 2012 LAPOP survey is sufficient to demonstrate just how large the gap between support and performance is in these two countries. Table 2.2 shows each country's rank on the latent index of support used in this book (see the statistical model in Chapter 4 for details), as well as two single-indicator measures of support: satisfaction with democracy and perceived level of democracy.

Regardless of which indicator is used, Venezuela consistently outranks Chile (and most of Latin America) in terms of regime support. Chile is in the lower half of Latin American countries on all indicators, and nearly last on one. The ranking for perceived level of democracy is particularly shocking, given that it is completely at odds with "objective" measures of democracy provided by international databases; Venezuela was (in 2012) the second most democratic state in the region according to its own citizens, but is among the least democratic according to outside observers. All of these support

Table 2.2: *Regime support ranks by country*

Indicator	Chile	Venezuela
Regime support	10	5
Perceived level of democracy	13	2
Satisfaction with democracy	15	7
Average	13	5

Table 2.3: *Performance rankings by country*

Indicator	Chile	Venezuela
Freedom house score	3	18
Polity IV scores, 2012	1	18
Rule of Law	1	18
Control of corruption	2	16
GDP growth	1	17
Inflation	2	17
Formal sector jobs	1	11
Poverty reduction	1	6
Homicides	1	17
Combined governance score	1	14

All data except Polity IV scores taken from Mainwaring et al. (2010). Polity IV scores taken from the Polity online database. Many students of democracy object to Freedom House scores as a measure of the concept, due to their bias in favor of democracies that are highly liberal (i.e. which embrace laissez-faire capitalism). Polity IV scores are included to correct for this.

rankings have nearly the opposite values that the performance rankings of each case would predict. These are presented in Table 2.3.

The difference between "objective" performance and subjective support is twelve ranks for Chile and nine ranks for Venezuela. The discrepancy is large enough to rule out any ambiguity: if regime performance does in fact cause support, then virtually all of the common macrolevel factors which are used to evaluate governance are useless.

2.2.4   Pocketbook Issues and Alternative Performance Arguments

The preceding discussion, and the support/performance paradox which it established, is based upon one major assumption that bears examining: that citizens evaluate regime performance on the basis of the health of the national economy. While sociotropic factors like those described earlier almost certainly have an important impact on performance evaluations (Dettrey, 2013; Kinder & Kiewiet, 1981), they are not the only factor. In fact the rationalist perspective that privileges governance as the primary explanation for support also emphasizes the importance of "pocketbook" economic concerns (Downs, 1957; Lewis-Beck, 1985). Even in poorly governed countries, some groups may be spared the pain of their regime's failures. These fortunate groups may make aggregate levels of support higher than they would otherwise be in societies with the same average performance levels.

Lending support to the possibility that intra-national variation in benefits derived from macrolevel regime performance may be driving the support paradoxes of interest here is the fact that support in Chile is patterned around social class. However, it is not the poor in Chile who are the least supportive, as their circumstances have improved a great deal since the return to democracy (Mainwaring et al., 2010). The middle class in Chile is where dissatisfaction is most intense, and unsurprisingly they benefit the least from government policy. They carry significant tax burdens but receive few benefits from the government, although they certainly benefit from Chile's strong economy. Quantitative analysis bears out the prediction that Chile's middle classes are significantly more dissatisfied with the regime than poorer and richer *chilenos*. The results of a regression analysis, with support as the dependent variable and socioeconomic status as the predictor with a nonlinear relationship to support, are presented in Figure 2.3.

As the graphs in Figure 2.3 show, the very poor in Chile are relatively content with the way democracy functions. The impact of

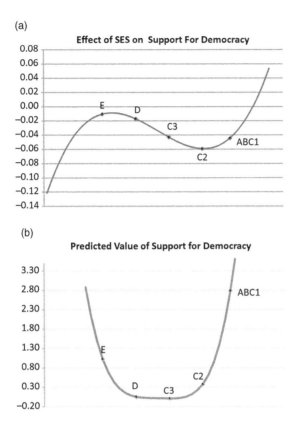

FIGURE 2.3: Support by socioeconomic status in Chile

Source: The Center for Public Studies (CEP) of Chile. Support is measured using a latent variable that predicts a series of institutional confidence questions in the same manner as later models using CEP data; see Chapter 6 for more detail. The underlying model is Support $= \gamma_0 + \gamma_1 SES + \gamma_1 SES^2 + \gamma_1 SES^4$. This model was chosen based on comparison of the Bayesian AIC statistics of all models containing all configurations of quadratic models up to the fourth root.

socioeconomic status on support declines as one moves toward higher social strata, reaching a nadir among the middle sectors. It then rises dramatically among the wealthiest citizens. This issue will be discussed in more detail in Chapter 6, but it needs to be addressed here briefly. Chilean social policy combines a relatively laissez-faire state with generous social spending on behalf of the most impoverished. This has been an effective tactic for reducing poverty and its consequences through a combination of declining unemployment and amelioration of misery through social spending. An unfortunate side effect of this strategy has been to put the middle class in a political economic vice. Taxes for the wealthy are kept relatively low in the name of encouraging investment, therefore the burden of taxation in Chile tends to fall harder than it needs to on the middle sectors. And because the Chilean welfare state has been based on a means-tested model of social expenditure, the middle class also fails to receive many benefits from the state.

Venezuela also displays the potential for microlevel explanation, given the emphasis of the Bolivarian regime's rhetorical embrace of socialism and its commitment to the advancement of the poor. Indeed, while an unmitigated failure in nearly every area, the one exception to this trend can be found in issues related to poverty. Specifically, Venezuela's reduction of poverty rates is well above the regional median. Additionally, the regime seems to have made significant progress on one of the region's most intractable challenges: inequality. Although there has not been a great deal of research on this topic, inequality does seem to drive regime dissatisfaction, at least in some circumstances (Anderson & Singer, 2008). Inequality data are presented in Table 2.4.

These data suggest a possible alternative explanation within a performance-centric framework, namely that strong performance

Table 2.4: *Inequality levels and change by country*

Case	GINI Index	Difference from Regional Average	Change Since Transition
Chile	51.8	0.9	−3.19
Venezuela	44.8	−7.3	−2.46
Difference	7.0	8.2	−0.7

Change since transition refers to the sum change in inequality during the reign of the current regime, which begins in 1990 for Chile and 1999 for Venezuela. From World Development Indicators.

within one social sector drives support despite overwhelming failure in the others. Specifically, malaise in Chile might be the result of a neglected middle class; euphoria in Venezuela may be due to the Bolivarian regime's intense focus on improving the material conditions of the poorest Venezuelans.

Neither possibility holds up to close scrutiny. The comparison with Chile rules out poverty reduction as a viable explanation, because what Venezuela does well, Chile does better. Contrary to commonly held assumptions (Posner, 1999, 2004), the material interests of the lower classes have not been completely sacrificed to the Chilean neoliberal model; indeed the means-tested welfare state that successive center-left governments have expanded halved poverty and reduced extreme poverty by two-thirds over the first six years of *Concertación* rule (Oppenheim, 2007, p. 257), and it has stayed low ever since. Chile not only ranks first in Latin America for poverty reduction, it ranks near the top worldwide (Mainwaring et al., 2010). Whatever improvements in the material conditions of the poor *chavismo* may have engendered in Venezuela (and these should not be overstated [Corrales, 2010]), they cannot compare to the advancement of the poor in Chile. Moreover Chile has actually reduced its inequality slightly more than Venezuela has over the course of each regime's respective rule (although Chile had much more room for improvement, given its sky-high inequality at the end of the Pinochet regime). Finally, poverty reduction is certainly an important metric for the poor, but it is not the only policy area that matters, and other factors that critically impact the lives of poor citizens are some of Venezuela's most egregious failures. Inflation is rampant (the informal exchange rate has increased 630 percent since research for this book began in 2012), shortages of basic goods are ever more widespread, and violent crime is completely out of control. While these ills touch all social sectors, inflation and crime disproportionately harm the poor. In sum, of four metrics of considerable concern to the popular sectors, Venezuela is slightly above average on poverty reduction, has had modest success in reducing inequality, and rests at the regional nadir on inflation and crime. On all other indicators, Chile is a resounding success and Venezuela is an unmitigated disaster.

The plight of the Chilean middle sectors survives cursory analysis in slightly better condition, but still cannot explain support dynamics in Chile without significant elaboration. Although the Chilean middle sectors certainly suffer from a number of economic problems (particularly the insecurity bred by Chile's stingy social safety net and pressures for conspicuous consumption and easy credit), they have benefited greatly from the country's macroeconomic successes. The Chilean middle class enjoys some of the highest standards of living when compared with their regional contemporaries. I discuss these dynamics in greater detail in the Chilean case study, but without some aggravating factor, it is not at all clear why relatively moderate economic grievances among middle class *chilenos* would lead to such profound discontent. Whatever its general effects, policy performance is woefully insufficient to explain patterns of support in the cases of interest here, even when the possibility of microlevel variation is taken into account. Performance may have an effect, but clearly some other factor is also in play, overriding (or, as I will argue presently, actively weakening) this relationship.

2.3   THE NEGLECTED APPROACH: PROCEDURAL EXPLANATIONS OF REGIME SUPPORT

The hegemony of output-oriented explanations of regime support fails to account for the fact that individual attitudes can be shaped by the way in which decisions are made, not merely the quality of the decisions themselves. In economics this is referred to as procedural utility (Frey, Benz, & Stutzer, 2004). However, unlike performance, where the basic metrics for evaluating success and failure are relatively uncontroversial, it is not immediately clear by which standards procedures are judged.

The comparison of interest here only muddies the waters further, because the most obvious answers do not match the cases. When looking for procedural variables in representative democracies, one might expect that the quality of representation would be a major source of regime support. There is considerable talk in Chile about a "crisis of representation," and the possibility that problems in this area may be responsible for anemic regime support has been acknowledged (Posner, 1999). As discussed in the Chapter 1, the quality of representation is primarily a function of the citizenry's ability to choose elites who actively defend their interests, and to punish representatives who fail to do so effectively (Plotke, 1997; Urbinati & Warren, 2008)[2]. Two mechanisms enhance the ability of citizens to enforce accountability: free and fair electoral competition, and a broad array of political choices (i.e. parties that offer policy platforms that span most of the spectrum of preferences in a given society). Two objections to representation-centered explanations of support can be made immediately. First, such arguments share the mediated effect of procedures that trouble performance-centered theories: procedures only matter because they shape patterns of winners and losers (Norris, 1999a, p. 219). Viewed this way, representation appears to be more of a modified performance argument, relying on intra-national distribution of quality governance rather than any intrinsic characteristics of representative procedures and institutions. Chapter 3 presents an alternative mechanism by which representation may influence regime support that is not mediated through performance: its ability to create perceptions of citizen autonomy. Chapter 6, which focuses on Chile, tests this reinterpretation and finds it wanting.

Second, the case comparison presented here rules out any such explanation. Recalling the earlier discussion of performance and poverty, no sectoral deviations from national performance trends can readily explain the paradoxes of interest here. And even if they could,

---

[2] There is also a descriptive dimension to representation (Urbinati & Warren, 2008), which may have an impact on support in certain contexts (Madrid & Rhodes-Purdy, 2016). Due to the rarity of elites who come from disadvantaged groups in Latin America, I focus on the substantive (interest-oriented) dimension of representation here. Descriptive notions of representation are addressed in more detail in the case study of Venezuela in Chapter 5.

representative institutions could not be given the credit. As Venezuela's Freedom House and Polity IV scores (see Table 2.3) indicate, those aspects of democracy most prized by liberals are far more robust in Chile. Elections in Chile are free and fair, with a large selection of parties from which voters may choose, ranging from communist and socialist to militantly neoliberal. It is difficult to argue that Venezuela, with the electoral hegemony of the *Partido Socialista Unido de Venezuela* (PSUV) and its lack of strong opposition parties, provides higher quality representation than the Chilean system. Whether or not Venezuela even qualifies as democratic any longer was a topic of heated debate even before the death of Chávez; given the turn of events under his successor, this debate can now probably be considered settled.

2.4 TOWARD A PROCEDURAL THEORY OF REGIME SUPPORT

The preceding discussion clearly shows that output-oriented arguments, including those that include procedural variation only as predictors of policy outputs, are insufficient to explain patterns of support in Venezuela and Chile. The logical conclusion is that the assent dimension of support is likely the underlying cause of these puzzling cases, and therefore it makes sense to shift focus away from those variables most closely associated with approval and turn to procedural characteristics that might directly shape legitimacy. It should be noted that nothing in the preceding discussion challenged the general relationship between performance and support. Nothing presented here could be used to argue that governance should not matter, from a logical or theoretical standpoint, but merely that in these two cases it seems performance does not matter, at least not in the simple linear fashion predicted by economistic rational choice. I point this out because, as I turn to procedural arguments in Chapter 3, it raises the bar by which alternative theories must be evaluated. It is not enough for an alternative theory to find some procedural variable that can positively impact support; the divergences observed in Chile and especially Venezuela are far too severe to be explained away by some countervailing relationship. A fully specified theory of support must, to be fully applicable to the cases of interest, propose both structural and contextual variables. That is to say, a good theory will explain under which circumstances government performance either does or does not strongly impact support.

With this in mind, I turn to the examination of intrinsic characteristics of political procedures and their relationships with regime support. This process begins with an apparent contradiction that resulted from the brief discussion of representation presented earlier (a subject to which I return in Chapter 3, after specifying an alternative mechanism through which representation may have an impact on legitimacy). If some intrinsic aspect of democratic institutions is driving the divergence between support and performance observed in Chile and Venezuela, how is it that the ambiguously democratic case is more legitimate in the eyes of its citizens? In Section 2.5, I continue to use democratic theory, combined with insights form psychology, to search for alternative procedural variables.

3   Participatory Opportunities, Efficacy, and Regime Support

Chapter 2 laid out the conceptual framework of support, and demonstrated that all explanations of the Chilean and Venezuelan paradoxes that privilege the approval dimension were suspect. In this chapter, I turn to a theoretical examination of the role of assent. The notion that the procedural concerns that epitomize the assent dimension of support are important is not novel, but theoretical work on procedures is far less developed than work on performance. The concept of procedural justice, an umbrella term that might encompass any and all the potential variables that could impact assent, has yet to be rigorously examined for ways in which it may relate to support and legitimacy (Levi, Sacks, & Tyler, 2009, p. 257).

3.1   WHAT IS DEMOCRACY FOR? PARTICIPATION IN DEMOCRATIC THEORY

Perhaps one reason why so many explanations of support, even those that include institutional variables, give priority to the approval dimension is because the standard of evaluation is so much clearer than for procedural arguments. That individuals care about their material well-being, and that they come to view regimes that fail to provide for it as illegitimate, are not very controversial hypotheses. And although it is not nearly as irrefutable that citizens care a great deal about the protection of civil rights and liberties (especially those of other people), the purpose of democracy as elucidated by liberals is nevertheless straightforward and unambiguous. But what, if any, expectations, desires, or preferences do citizens have that are intrinsic to the processes and

Portions of this chapter have been published in *Comparative Politics* (Rhodes-Purdy, 2017).

procedures of democratic rule? Conceptual (D. Collier & Levitsky, 1997) and public opinion (Crow, 2007, 2010; von Mettenheim, 1990, 1995) work on conceptions of democracy has attempted to address this question, but the democratic subtypes they tend to focus upon (e.g. liberal, electoral, substantive, or egalitarian) lack a firm *a priori* theoretical basis. There are no convincing theoretical reasons why these and only these subtypes might matter to citizens, as opposed to theorists and analysts. In addition, they tend to make the fairly heroic assumption that most citizens, including those with little education or political experience, have sophisticated ideas about what democracy should be. In other words, insufficient attention has been paid to what emotional and psychological needs might be met by certain aspects of democratic politics. This book, while not inconsistent with some of the works dealing with conceptions of democracy and regime support (e.g. Canache, 2007), offers alternative explanations of the same relationships that do not require nearly so much ideological sophistication.

In this chapter, I look to two bodies of theory that have long meditated on that very question. First, I turn to normative democratic theory, particularly its participatory or "classical" variant, as elucidated by Rousseau and John Stuart Mill, and later Pateman, Macpherson, and Barber. These theorists (and others like them) posited an altogether different purpose for democracy than liberals and those scholars inspired by them. Indeed both Pateman (1970) and Held (2007) saw this fundamental disagreement over the purpose of democracy as the critical cleavage in democratic theory, dividing it into two broad subcategories. Pateman refers to the two as "participatory" and "representative" variants, while Held refers to them as "developmental" and "protective" (2007, p. 35). Held's terminology, inspired by Macpherson (1977), is meant to apply only to liberal democracy, but participatory democracy clearly shares many assumptions of the developmental camp. Riker (1988), a partisan of liberalism, uses the terms "populism" and "liberalism," which more or less overlap with Held's terms (albeit with the normative preferences reversed). In the following discussion, I use the terms developmental and instrumental, because they match the underlying assumptions that unify each school, rather than the preferred institutional arrangements that flow from those assumptions. All of the performance-oriented theories of support described in Chapter 2 can be considered instrumental because they assume that democracy "serves a purely protective function ... it ensure[s] that the private interest of each citizen [is] protected" (Pateman, 1970, p. 20). Theorists in this group hold that democracy has no value of its own, but only to the extent to which it preserves something else of value.

3.1.1 Developmental Democratic Theory

The developmental strain of democratic theory has a fundamentally different understanding of democracy's purpose. Developmental theorists "stress the *intrinsic* value of political participation for the development of citizens as human beings" (Held, 2007, p. 35, emphasis in original). They argue that human beings have an inherent yearning for "union and communion [with other human beings]" (Barber, 1984, p. 112), which cannot be satisfied by the atomizing individualism of liberalism. Political behavior is seen, not as a chore to be engaged in only when necessary to defend or advance some other interest as in liberalism and other instrumental variants, but as essential for the "education of an entire people to the point where their intellectual, emotional, and moral capacities have reached their full potential" (Davis, 1964, pp. 40–41). There are two specific mechanisms through which democratic action can positively impact participants. The first, and least important for my purposes, is that direct political engagement morally ennobles citizens. Through their role in the construction and pursuit of the common good, they rise above their base self-interests and become more responsible and righteous through self-rule (Mill, 2009, p. 41; Rousseau, 2002, pp. 163–167). Democratic self-governance leads the citizen to "take into account wider matters than his own immediate private interests ... he is forced to deliberate according to his sense of justice" (Pateman, 1970, p. 25). While this line of reasoning has clear, interesting, and potentially testable empirical implications, it is unnecessary for the argument I propose here. My argument does not rely on any actual improvement in the ability of individuals to act as citizens. Such an argument would be just another mediated argument in favor of performance, albeit one springing from an entirely different logical font than those previously discussed. As I have repeatedly shown such mediated theories are not helpful for the question at hand. Nor does my argument rely on citizens actually *engaging* in any sort of political behavior, but only on citizens' perceptions of the political role that the regime assigns to them (i.e. if the regime provides mechanisms by which specific types of behavior would have a meaningful influence, should they choose to engage in them)[1]. I will therefore move on to the second mechanism that developmental theory suggests.

Democracy may well improve the moral character of its participants, but its direct psychological impacts are of far greater interest here. Developmental theorists have, in addition to moral considerations, examined "how the social order affects the structure of human personality" (Plamenatz, 1963, p. 440). The ingrained passivity cited so frequently by Schumpeter and his contemporaries is a part of human nature that is neither exogenous nor intractable; to the contrary it is the product of an infantilizing political system that consigns citizens to an entirely passive role in which "Politics has become what politicians do; what citizens do (when they do anything) is vote for the politicians" (Barber, 1984, p. 148). The docility of citizens in modern democracies is actually a deviation from human nature, and an acute one at that, but not an incurable one. Political regimes that allow for and encourage the active participation of citizens in self-rule can correct this departure from human nature, reversing the docility inculcated by authority and creating a new kind of citizen, one who is psychologically and emotionally ready and able to shape his or her own fate.

---

[1] I do consider it likely that, given equal participatory opportunities, those who use them will feel more empowered and connected to the political system than those who do not. This proposition is tested in Chapter 5.

Although the high aspirations that abound in normative democratic theory can make this line of reasoning seem quite fanciful, it has considerable backing in the more empirically grounded discipline of social psychology. The debate between developmental and instrumental democratic theories originates in a fundamentally different set of assumptions about fundamental drives, needs, and desires of human beings (all of which can be grouped under the less precise term "human nature"). Psychology has grappled with similar issues. Shifting between disciplines creates a considerable risk of false equivalency, but the concept of autonomy provides a sturdy bridge between democratic and psychological theory. It acts as a sort of Rosetta Stone, whereby similar strains of reasoning in each discipline can be translated into the language of the other through this shared concept. Autonomy here does not mean "freedom from" something, as it does in common parlance, but rather refers to its etymologically original definition of "self-law," or self-governing. It refers to the ability of an entity to control and shape its environment. Insights from psychology enhance this theoretical discussion in two ways. First, they provide much more firm grounding in empirical reality, giving some real-world credibility to the assumptions of democratic theory, which is more concerned with normative debates than explanation of empirical relationships. Second, the psychological literature has drawn out the implications of autonomy and its psychological necessity much more thoroughly than has democratic theory. These insights suggest a more complex, interactive, causal structure of regime support.

3.1.2 The Psychology of Popular Sovereignty: Citizen Autonomy and Regime Support

The psychological impact of an individual's real and perceived ability to shape his or her own behavior and environment has been a major question in social psychology for decades. Angyal (1941, pp. 32–38) argued that autonomy was the primary drive of all organisms, which are constantly in conflict with the heteronomous regulations that would, in the absence of self-governance, inevitably be imposed by the environment. White (1959) and DeCharms (1968), working in the field of motivational psychology, applied this logic more directly to human behavior. Both researchers argued that the basic biological drives (see Hull, 1943), which were then thought to motivate virtually all behavior, failed to explain a great deal of activity among both humans and other intelligent animals. White argued that competence, "the capacity to interact effectively with [the] environment" (1959, p. 297), was an important and analytically neglected psychological need, which could explain a great deal of play and exploration behavior among infants and toddlers. DeCharms' concept of personal causation, although differing in some minor details, served essentially the same theoretical purpose.

The concepts of intrinsic motivation (Deci, 1971, 1975) and self-determination theory (Deci & Ryan, 1985, 2000; Ryan & Deci, 2006) further clarified the role of autonomy in the human psyche, in a manner especially important given the theoretical divide at issue in this study. Specifically, Deci and Ryan's approach clarified the theoretical role of control over processes. Earlier incarnations of autonomy viewed procedural control as a clear psychological motivation; the implication being that failure to control outcomes would result in a lack of autonomy, forming a mediated argument similar to that of institutional arguments discussed in Chapter 2, and just as unhelpful. Yet later psychologists recognized that favorable outcomes were not the *sine qua non* of autonomy:

> Control refers to there being a contingency between one's behavior and the outcomes one receives, whereas self-determination refers to the experience of freedom in initiating one's behavior. A person has control when his or her behaviors reliably yield intended outcomes, but this does not ensure self-determination, for the person can, in the words of DeCharms, become a 'pawn' to those outcomes. In those cases the person's behavior would be determined by the outcomes rather than by choices, even though

the person would be said to have control ... It is true that a person needs control over outcomes to be self-determined in attaining them, but the need is for self-determination rather than for control.

(Deci & Ryan, 1985, p. 31)

In other words, the ability to influence (if not totally control) outcomes is not a need, but a necessary condition for the satisfaction of a need in the realm of goal-oriented behavior, of which politics is one. Outcomes are at the end of the causal chain, not the beginning. This distinction is crucial in the context of collective decision-making bodies, wherein an institutionally granted ability for participants as a whole to self-govern does not guarantee that any individual participant can count on getting his or her way on every decision.

Autonomy, so conceived as the satisfaction of a psychological need for self-determination through the management of one's own affairs with minimal outside interference, dovetails quite neatly with the propositions of democratic theory regarding the inherent worth of democratic politics. Just as psychology proposes the individual need for self-determination, developmental democratic theory proposes a collective version of the same need for communities of individuals. In this context, we speak of moral autonomy: the capacity of groups of individuals to make their own decisions about the common good and put them into practice (Dahl, 1989, ch. 6). It is also very similar to the concept of self-management in participatory economics, wherein decision-making power is distributed directly proportionally to the impact of the decision (Albert & Hanhel, 1991). Both these concepts represent attempts to apply ideals similar to the psychological concept of autonomy to group decision-making processes where the possibility of true individual control over a given process is vitiated, in the aggregate, by the fact that if one individual in such a process possesses complete autonomy, no one else involved in the process does. The collective nature of decision making in this version of the concept also underscores the importance of the break between outcome control and the need for self-determination discussed earlier.

Individuals may not always get what they want out of collectively autonomous processes in which they are the minority, but such processes still confer autonomy because only those who are impacted by the decision have a say in their making; even "losers" have a meaningful voice in the process. A sense of control can be conferred by such processes due to the allocation of decision-making power, without regard to outcomes in any specific instance. I use the term citizen autonomy to refer to the individual possession of a portion of this collective control over the process of collective self-governance. As Rousseau described it: "Each of us puts in common his person and all his power under the supreme direction of the general will; and in return each member becomes an indivisible part of the whole" (2002, p. 164). Given this, citizen autonomy can be defined as the ability of citizens to directly affect the course of processes by which political decisions are made.

3.1.3 Operationalizing Citizen Autonomy: Regime-Based Efficacy

The extent to which citizen autonomy exists in a given polity is only indirectly interesting to the question here; what matters is which aspects of political regimes cause widespread perceptions of citizen autonomy. Asking citizens about this issue directly via survey questions would require us to assume an unreasonably high level of awareness of competing strains of democratic theory and political processes. For empirical analysis, we require an operational substitute for actual, intellectually driven evaluations of citizen autonomy. Given that the issue of importance is the beliefs and feelings of citizens regarding autonomy, it makes sense to operationalize the concept via its "affective side," or the emotional result of the satisfaction of the need for autonomy: self-efficacy (DeCharms, 1968, p. 20; White, 1959, p. 322). The affective side has the added advantage of being frequently measured in public opinion surveys, which is an obvious requirement for empirical examination. Campbell, Gurin, and Miller defined it as "the feeling that individual political action does have, or can have, an impact upon the political processes" (1954, p. 187). Almond and Verba (1963, ch. 8), in their groundbreaking study of comparative public opinion, found that "competence" was associated with increased political participation, loyalty, and political knowledge, although the causal structure of these relationships was left unexplored. Later researchers, inspired by Bandura (1977), split the concept into two constitutive dimensions: internal and external (Craig et al., 1990; Finkel, 1987; Kölln, Esaiasson, & Turper, 2013; Madsen, 1987). Internal efficacy is related to an individual's knowledge and understanding of the political system and policy disputes, and is not of direct relevance here, as the ultimate source of variation in support in this study lies at the level of the state. External efficacy, which is sometimes (and more accurately) called regime-based efficacy (RBE), is another matter. Several authors have pointed out that citizens recognize that the utility or futility of their political action is in part determined by the extent to which regimes are willing or able to respond to such petitions (Finkel, 1987; Kölln et al., 2013; Madsen, 1987). In other words, although individuals may not understand the underlying reasons, they are capable of recognizing the extent to which their political regimes pay attention to their preferences and accede to or refuse their demands.

3.1.4   Summary: The Implications of Democratic Theory and Psychology for Regime Support

This body of theoretical and empirical work on the importance of autonomy is a major challenge to rational choice-inspired assumptions that, on the whole, citizens would rather involve themselves in politics at the minimum level necessary to defend their interests (Downs, 1957; Hibbing & Theiss-Morse, 2002). Delegation of decision-making authority may be appealing in this or that instance, but when it becomes general practice, it robs citizens of the chance to shape their own fates. In the context of modern democratic nation-states, direct control by the citizenry in all aspects of politics is impractical. Even advocates of participatory democracy generally see it as a supplement to representative institutions, rather than a replacement (Barber, 1984; Urbinati & Warren, 2008). Some participatory democrats, especially those inspired by Marxism, have theorized how participatory modes of decision making might be grafted on to existing systems, in order to minimize the difficulty of transitioning from a democratic model to another. For example, Macpherson (1977) suggests that the delegate model discussed in Chapter 1 could be implemented within political parties, rather than through the creation of new legislative bodies and supporting institutions, which would be far more taxing.

Despite these developments, participatory democracy has not, as of yet, fully accepted the (at least medium-term) certainty that mediated democratic forms cannot be replaced, and thus even hypothetical syntheses such as Macpherson's are of limited use without modification. However, it is not difficult to see that institutional variation, even in the domain of full democracies, may create considerable variation in the responsiveness of the political system and the autonomy of citizens, as I discuss in Sections 3.2.1-3.2.2. And given the psychological need for such empowerment, it is reasonable to suppose that regimes that encourage such sentiments would be viewed more positively by their citizens. In addition to this direct relationship, there is good theoretical reason to believe that support based upon citizen autonomy provides regimes a reservoir of good faith during troubled times that can further buttress their legitimacy.

3.1.5 RBE and Forgiveness of Failures

The effect of RBE is more complex and powerful than simply as a necessary precondition for personal well-being. Psychological studies on the subject indicate that intrinsic motivations and externally imposed rewards and punishments interact with one another (Deci, 1971; Deci, Ryan, & Koestner, 1999; Johnson & Sarason, 1978). Especially relevant to this study is the role that a sense of control over events plays in altering individual responses to extrinsic stimuli.

Rotter (1966) found that individuals tended to have distinct and durable beliefs about loci of control; each individual has set beliefs about how his or her behavior affects the course of events. Bandura (1977) refined this argument by emphasizing that while locus of control may be an element of personality that is relatively fixed, individuals are also quite capable of separately evaluating their efficacy depending upon the procedures by which rewards and punishments are generated. In other words, beliefs about one's ability to self-govern are partly fixed and partly contextually determined.

Although Rotter and Bandura were primarily concerned with the impact of control beliefs on learning (Rotter, 1954), psychologists later applied the same reasoning to analyze variation in psychological distress as a response to negative events. Johnson and Sarason (1978) found that a personal belief in one's control over environmental reinforcers significantly weakened the effect of traumatic life changes on levels of depression and anxiety. Orpen (1994) found a similar relationship when studying anxiety over job insecurity. Walker (2001, ch. 8) applied this logic directly to situations in which individual perceptions of control were impacted by the details of a specific process (in this case, interactions with health care providers), not just fixed beliefs, with similar findings.

The relevance of these findings for studies of regime support is fairly straightforward. Applying psychological research specifically to the political realm, it is reasonable to propose that citizens who believe that they have a meaningful impact on political decisions will be far less distressed or enraged when those decisions go awry. In other words, the much-cited relationship between regime performance and support is very likely interactive. Autonomy and performance perceptions interact with one another, with the strength of the latter's effect being partially determined by the former.

This line of reasoning is quite similar to that developed and applied to states by Hirschman (1970). In his seminal work *Exit, Voice and Loyalty*, Hirschman argues (in the context of interactions between economic firms and clients) that the choice available to individuals confronted with declining performance between immediate "exit," or termination of the firm-client relationship, and suffering in silence is a false dichotomy. He posits a third option: voice, wherein dissatisfied patrons can choose to express their frustration over declining quality in an attempt to alter the firm's behavior. Later in the book, Hirschman applies this reasoning directly to the relationship between citizens and the state. Hirschman directly addresses attitudes about political regimes when developing his theory of loyalty:

> As a rule, then, loyalty holds exit at bay and activates voice ...
> That paradigm of loyalty, 'our country, right or wrong,' surely
> makes no sense whatever if it were expected that 'our' country
> were to continue forever to do nothing but wrong. Implicit in that
> phrase is the expectation that 'our' country can be moved again
> in the right direction after doing some wrong.
>
> *(Hirschman, 1970, p. 78)*

Hirschman's theory, while intuitive, has considerable weaknesses when applied to the political realm. For one thing, it is not at all clear what "exit" from the state would look like. Would it be a quiet withdrawal of support in one's own mind, active protest or rebellion, or something else? The coercive nature of the state means that citizens cannot "leave" in the same way they can exit a relationship with a firm; whether exit is even possible (except perhaps by emigration) is debatable. The point here is that, while poor performance usually results in some form of withdrawal from the declining entity (if only in affective terms, as in the withdrawal of support from a political regime), this relationship can be broken, or at least bent. Loyalty, which is essentially the weakening of the performance–support relationship, is at least in part the product of effective voice. In the realm of democratic politics, voice can be much more than a simple statement of concern; indeed the whole point of democratic politics is that some level of influence is held by the governed.

Democratic theory, psychology, and Hirschman's work in economics all concur with one another: the relationship between performance and regime support, whose existence I conceded earlier, is not constant. Rather, governance problems lead immediately to withdrawal of regime support only when citizens feel they have little or no say in the policy process. Where citizens perceive themselves to have an important role in shaping political decisions, they are more forgiving of failures and imperfections. This dynamic very closely resembles that described by Easton (1975), where political systems manage to weather economic storms that would engulf other polities. Citizen autonomy provides a potential mechanism that can explain that dynamic: it breaks the causal chain between performance and regime support. Given that the "high support" case used here also has grave governance issues, this additional impact of citizen autonomy will be crucial in explaining national variation.

3.2 REPRESENTATION OR PARTICIPATION? THE INSTITUTIONAL DETERMINANTS OF CITIZEN AUTONOMY

With the potential of citizen autonomy shown, we can turn to an examination of what types of procedures might be expected to impact perceptions of this factor. The paradox of interest here is at the level of nations, and therefore requires institutional variables that impact individual perceptions of citizen autonomy. In the language of statistical analysis, this question requires a multilevel theoretical framework, with clear hypotheses regarding the relationships between national-level institutions and individual-level attitudinal measures. Extensive discussions of how specific institutions impact citizen autonomy and perceptions of it are left to the case studies, because it can be misleading to analyze the impact of institutional variants in isolation. Therefore, the discussion of institutional antecedents of autonomy in this section will be kept at a relatively high level of abstraction, with a focus on types of mechanisms by which institutions can influence citizen autonomy. With this in mind, I return to the schema of mechanisms developed in the Introduction (Section 1.1) which could encourage autonomy: representation (composed of accountability and choice), and participation, composed of a delegate model of representation and ease of governance, where mediated forms of politics are unavoidable, as well as participatory opportunities (which grant citizens an unmediated role in shaping policy outcomes) wherever practicable. In section 3.2, I more carefully analyze these mechanisms and their potential for explaining the Chilean and Venezuelan paradoxes. I also introduce another mechanism that, while not fitting neatly into any of the categories existing in democratic theory, must be examined due to its relevance in the Venezuelan case: charismatic bonding.

3.2.1 Representation

In Chapter 2, representation was ruled out as a possible explanation of support because it was mediated through performance, which failed to explain the discrepancies in Chile and Venezuela. The ability of representation to affect perceived levels of autonomy is an alternative mechanism through which representative institutions could have an impact, and thus it is necessary to revisit the concept through this lens. To many theorists, the ability of citizens to choose representatives is the fundamental mechanism for binding political elites to the popular will (Plotke, 1997). Although representation is often the preferred mode of governance for those who are highly suspicious of popular involvement in politics (e.g. Hobbes, 1985; Mosca, 1939; Sartori, 1987; Schumpeter, 2008), some developmental theorists accept or even embrace mediated forms of democratic politics. John Stuart Mill, for example, in his work *Considerations of Representative Government*, goes on at great length about the importance of participation in politics to the moral and psychological development of individuals. He then concludes that "since all cannot, in a community exceeding a single small town, participate personally in any but some very minor portions of the public business, it follows that the ideal type of a perfect government must be representative" (Mill, 2009, p. 87). Mill considers this so self-evident that he offers no further justification. The notion that representation can increase regime support through empowering citizens has been applied to Latin America by Singh and Carlin (2015), who argue that presidents who enjoy either too much or too little legislative power enervate citizens. Citizens' autonomy is compromised by depriving them of the ability to hold presidents accountable through rebukes during legislative elections (for the former) or by thwarting their expressed approval of the President's agenda via gridlock (for the latter).

Most developmental theorists are not nearly so sanguine about the capacity of representation to meet the needs of citizens. They argue that no mechanism for controlling representatives could ever be sufficiently binding to truly subjugate the will of elites to the citizenry as a whole. Representatives cannot be trusted or made to be trustworthy, therefore the people cannot have control in the absence of direct self-governance (Barber, 1984; Rousseau, 2002). Although this is a strong statement of this viewpoint, the notion that the principal–agent relationship, which forms the core of representative democracy, has grave potential for the distortion of popular preferences has a strong basis in democratic theory (Urbinati & Warren, 2008). In order for representation to be an effective mechanism for ensuring autonomy (as Mill suggested it could), representatives would need to be almost entirely responsive to citizen preferences, a view of the concept that Pitkin (1967, p. 4) claims is the province of only "a vocal minority" of theorists. In other words, representation would need to cease to be, and be replaced by delegation, which as the Chapter 1 specifies is a mechanism more appropriately thought of as a form of participation.

It is likely that substantive representation, and particularly variations in the level of autonomy granted to representatives, can have a significant impact on levels of citizen autonomy. Yet this particular relationship is almost certainly not relevant to the comparison of interest here. All of the criticisms based on comparison of the cases leveled against representation in Chapter 2 apply here as well: namely that any problems that may exist in Chile are at least as severe in Venezuela. Whatever its faults, Chile is a full-fledged competitive political system and citizens there are much abler to choose their rulers than are voters in Venezuela under Bolivarian hegemony. The current Chilean regime has witnessed two successful turnovers at the executive level; Venezuela has had none.[2] Chile has a perfect score on both political and civil rights as measured by Freedom House; Venezuela is counted as only partly free with a score of 5 on each. For those who are (quite reasonably) skeptical of Freedom House scores, Chile also has a perfect combined Polity IV score and (by the standards of representation) is the most democratic country in the region, while Venezuela's score of -3 indicates that it is at least a semi-autocracy, with only Cuba being less democratic. Despite the continuing existence of free elections, electoral competition in Venezuela has been stymied by a gradual increasing of the costs of being outside the dominant *chavista* coalition (Corrales, 2010). In short, substantive representation enforced by selection of elites is strong in the low-support case and weak in the high-support case, casting immediate doubt on its analytical value. With this in mind, I turn to another, more promising, autonomy mechanism.

3.2.2 Participatory Opportunities

Theories of procedural justice and utility often hold that participation (sometimes referred to as the fair distribution of decision-making authority) is a crucial aspect of just procedures (Lind & Tyler, 1988; Thibaut & Walker, 1975). Participation here refers not to individual behavioral choices but rather an institutional granting of decision-making authority to those who will be governed by the decision. I use the term "participatory opportunities," as defined in the Chapter 1, to refer to decision-making procedures that grant those individuals affected by that process's decisions a direct role in making them. In the political realm, this generally means institutionally structured procedures through which citizens can have a direct role in making policy.

---

[2] Unless one is willing to count the passing of power to a handpicked successor upon the death of the regime's founder, which I am not.

Although participation likely can, at least in certain circumstances, influence support for democracy as many analysts have argued (Almond & Verba, 1963; Finkel, 1987; Moehler, 2008), explanations based solely on actual participatory behavior have some serious shortcomings. First, they relegate the impact of participatory opportunities (a characteristic of the political regime) to a subordinate role in the causal chain: they only matter because they increase actual participation (an individual behavioral choice that may have any number of additional causal antecedents). Additionally, whatever hypothetical value direct participation may have, empirically speaking such a small number of citizens take advantage of such direct opportunities that actual participatory behavior is not a promising explanation of macrolevel patterns of legitimacy.

Opportunities for direct participation can have an impact on public opinion that reaches far beyond those individuals who actually avail themselves of such opportunities on a regular basis. Research on external political efficacy demonstrates that citizens are capable of recognizing when political systems grant or deny them the ability to affect government decisions (Finkel, 1987; Kölln et al., 2013; Madsen, 1987; Niemi, Craig, & Mattei, 1991). Both representative and participatory institutions can enforce popular sovereignty, but the former are indirect and prone to breakdown, while the latter put political questions directly into the hands of those most directly impacted by policy choices. Given the theoretical importance of citizen autonomy established earlier, participatory institutions provide a procedural variable (that is, one that describes a regime characteristic) that theory can clearly link to an individual-level perception (citizen autonomy, operationalized as RBE), which in turn may well be an important source of legitimacy.

The importance of participatory opportunities to empowering ordinary citizens is a key aspect of Bolivarian thought; indeed, it is one of the few clear tenets of a movement whose ideology is extremely ill defined. Chávez came to power on the promise to transform Venezuela into a "participatory, protagonist" democracy.

The inclusion of the adjective "protagonist," while somewhat awkward in English, is particularly telling. The idea of putting the destiny of the people in their own hands has clear echoes in the concept of citizen autonomy used here. The idea has manifested itself in Venezuela primarily in the form of direct democratic mechanisms at the national level (plebiscites, executive recall, and referenda) and more significantly in an ever-increasing plethora of participatory fora, including:

- A subset of the social welfare organizations known as *misiones* (Social Missions) (Hawkins, 2010; Hawkins, Rosas, & Johnson, 2011);
- *Círculos bolivarianos* (Bolivarian Circles): small cells of up to eleven individuals sworn to defend the Bolivarian Constitution and its principles, as well as serve their communities (Hawkins & Hansen, 2006, pp. 102–103);
- *Comités de tierra urbana* (Urban Land Committees): groups of 100–200 families in the vast barrios of the country's cities, self-managed organizations responsible for drawing up maps of their communities to be submitted to the government, at which time individual families would be granted titles to their land. The CTUs also had broad discretion to address issues of community identity, strategies for improvement, and other community issues (García-Guadilla, 2011, p. 104);
- Rural equivalents of the urban land committees;
- *Mesas técnicas de agua* (water roundtables), focused on providing water infrastructure;
- Legally recognized cooperative associations (López Maya & Lander, 2011);
- *Consejos comunales* (communal councils), umbrella organizations that serve as the voice of civil society as a whole in a given area ("Ley orgánica de los consejos comunales," 2006; "Ley orgánica de los consejos comunales," 2009).

The emphasis on direct participation in Bolivarian Venezuela provides a potential explanation for that system's unusually high levels of support. Given the near total dearth of such opportunities in Chile, and the general elitist bent of the Chilean political system, it is a promising variable in both cases. However, to contend that legitimacy in Venezuela is the result of perceptions of citizen autonomy is likely to be provocative to many readers.

Evaluating Participatory Opportunities

The proposition that participatory programs increase actual or perceived citizen autonomy is likely to be extremely controversial. Critics of these programs label them as instances of *impulsada* (Briceño, 2012) or conditioned (Triviño Salazar, 2013) participation. How can instances of participation that are shaped and directed, at least in part, by the state be autonomous? Either explicitly or implicitly, such arguments rely on the assumptions of public space theorists, who argue that genuine participation is assumed to rise organically from the political space between the state and the private sphere, without interference or direction from political elites. (Avritzer, 2002; Oxhorn, 1994, 1995).

Without taking a position on the impact such organizations may or may not have on the quality of democracy (which is beyond the scope of this book), it is simple enough to show that criticisms based on this reasoning are not compelling when applied to the Bolivarian participatory fora without substantial modification. Imagine, for the sake of argument, an ideal organization as conceived by public space theory. Citizens gather and coalesce into a movement, forming both organizations and identities that allow them to become a collective actor that can agitate or petition the state. As I discuss in detail in Chapter 5, determining the autonomy of Bolivarian participatory programs is a difficult task, because it requires sorting out countervailing forces that simultaneously grant and stifle the organizations' autonomy. Quantifying the autonomy of this hypothetical organization, however, is simplicity itself: the level of autonomy of such an organization is exactly zero.

One may recognize and admire the authenticity of such an organization, and its ability to grant its members the ability to shape their own political identity, but independence is not equivalent to autonomy. Indeed, independence of this sort is an illusion; the organization would be independent only in the sense that it was organically created by its members. It has absolutely no ability to govern itself: it operates in the context of a sovereign state, which has the final authority to make political decisions that govern the organization's members. When defined correctly, it becomes clear that independence is actually *negatively* associated with autonomy. That is to say, for an organization to be truly self-governing it must be granted that authority through a concession by the state, effectively making the organization a para-state institution, as is the case in both democratic and authoritarian forms of corporatism. This would of course represent a necessary sacrifice of independence, which could nullify autonomy were interference in its operation sufficiently severe. What is clear is that these programs are at least potential examples of participatory opportunities as defined earlier. And if they are, the sheer abundance of such programs in Venezuela would make strong perceptions of autonomy, and thus strong regime support, far less puzzling.

3.2.3 Alternative Mechanisms of Creating Autonomy: Descriptive Representation and Charismatic Attachment

At this point it is necessary to briefly discuss alternative mechanisms for generating autonomy that do not fit neatly into either category as currently defined. The first is descriptive representation, which despite its name emphasizes neither accountability nor choice, at least in the sense used thus far. As Urbinati and Warren (2008) note, descriptive representation is an alternative bond between leaders and citizens that is based upon shared characteristics (usually membership in a similar social group), rather than any set of policy preferences or interests. I raise the issue only because there is some potential for its relevance in the Venezuelan case. Chávez certainly had some phenotypical traits associated with Venezuela's marginalized mestizo and Afro-Venezuelan populations. Yet descriptive representation based on race or ethnicity is not very promising, because research seems to indicate that some level of politicization along demographic lines is necessary for the relationship to have an impact; the presence of a leader who "looks like me" is a necessary but insufficient condition (Madrid & Rhodes-Purdy, 2016).

Charismatic Attachment

A more promising alternative form of creating autonomy, or at least the perceptions of autonomy, is charismatic attachment. Charismatic attachment is a relationship between a leader and his or her followers defined by intense emotional devotion of the latter to the former (Madsen & Snow, 1991).[3] The key difference between this mechanism and those discussed earlier is that representation and participation were assumed to increase *perceptions* of autonomy by actually *creating* autonomy. Charismatic attachment, on the other hand, is somewhat illusory, creating subjective empowerment from objective subordination, even if that subordination is not total. Even if some genuine authority is truly devolved to the citizenry (as I argue has happened under Chávez), that devolution must be balanced against the concentration of power in the hands of a single individual.

This raises serious and inescapable problems from a participatory perspective. Classical democratic theory (Rousseau, 2002) holds that the "general will," meaning the preferences of a community as a collective, must be actively constructed by the participants. It does not and cannot exist without such action. When followers divest themselves of their agency and subsume themselves beneath a leader, the general will cannot be forged, only displaced by the will of the leader (Hawkins, 2009, 2010; Wiles, 1969). Yet the potential for creating the illusion of autonomy through such a relationship is clear, and as the towering presence of Hugo Chávez in one of the cases under investigation here, various forms of arguments that include charisma as an explanatory factor must be taken seriously.

Before proceeding further, we must distinguish "charismatic attachment" from "charisma" as the word is commonly used, both popularly and within academia. The former is an interaction of a leader and his or her followers, and will thus be shaped by character-

---

[3] Madsen & Snow use the term "bond," rather than attachment. I use the latter because a bond is usually seen as *mutual* attachment, whereas this book focuses on the attitudes and emotions of the followers.

istics of both parties, as well as the social context in which they operate. The latter, however, focuses exclusively on the leader. There is an implicit assumption that can easily be divined in these sorts of arguments,[4] that the personal magnetism of the leader alone is sufficient to mesmerize followers into believing their subordination to be empowerment. I refer to this mechanism as "personalism" from here to distinguish it from charismatic attachment.

Discussing Chávez is perhaps the best way to illustrate competing conceptions of how personalism or charismatic attachment may inflate perceptions of autonomy. Chávez's supporters and sympathizers see his rule as rising organically from the demands of Venezuela's long-ignored popular sectors (e.g. Ciccariello-Maher, 2013; Eastwood, 2011; Wilpert, 2005; Wilpert, 2011). Their views have considerable merit. Opponents of Chávez are quick to ignore the genuinely participatory character of the 1999 constitution, the fact that Chávez was able, mostly through inspiration, to unify the diverse threads of newly independent social organizations, which achieved a critical mass in the 1990s, and the myriad of (as I will argue) very real opportunities for participatory self-governance that Chávez's governments implemented over the course of his rule.

Yet defenders of the Bolivarian regime are often too quick to brush aside its dark side. Throughout his reign Chávez took advantage, through his rhetoric and personal background, of long-standing feelings of resentment and exclusion that had been nurtured by exclusivity and elitism to gather excluded sectors of society under his leadership (Molina, 2006). But he often made his appeals in ways that were hostile or punitive, rather than aspirational. He demonized his enemies, refused to tolerate dissent within his own ranks, and (most alarmingly) failed to distinguish between the fate of his movement and his own political fortunes. As I argue in Chapter 5, the Bolivarian

---

[4] The titles such authors use, which include such phrases as "Populist seduction" (De la Torre, 2010) or which refer to the populist as a "dragon" (Corrales & Penfold, 2015), are perhaps the clearest evidence of this assumption.

movement's trajectory is defined by participation and contestation in its early phase, and the gradual erosion of those characteristics under the steady pressure of Chávez's messianic populism. Eventually the grassroots elements of the Bolivarian movement collapsed into subservience, with their primary role being to defend Chávez from his enemies.

The personalist interpretation of this fact would be that Chávez was able, through his personal connection to the masses, to create a sense of inclusion based solely on one's membership in the Bolivarian movement, rather than through any expansion of the political role of ordinary citizens. The belief that the masses can be swayed through force of personality alone is a manifestation of the fears intrinsic to liberal democracy: that citizens are *inherently* susceptible to seduction by charismatic leaders, and only strong institutions can keep such would-be demagogues away from power.

This book recognizes the potential power of charismatic attachments of followers to leaders, but rejects the proposition that such bonds are an inherent risk of democratic politics. Charismatic attachment is predominantly the product of social, political, and economic circumstances. A broad sense of powerlessness in the face of a hostile social environment leads individuals to essentially relinquish their agency to the leader, who they see as uniquely capable of correcting society's course (Madsen & Snow, 1991); this quite closely describes the social environment immediately preceding Chávez's rise to power. This circumstantial requirement further implies that charismatic attachments do not simply happen, but must be actively forged and maintained, especially given that the circumstances that give rise to the attachment will almost certainly change as the leader's power grows. This raises the question: how can leaders accomplish this?

Although personalism must be taken seriously, it stands on fairly shaky theoretical ground. I find it incredible that such rhetoric can stand solely on the force of the populist's personality, with nothing real to lend it plausibility. Personalism driven by magnetism is an extremely fuzzy concept; so much so that it verges on unscientific. How do we measure the ability of a leader to mesmerize only with words? How could we possibly separate the impact of the leader's words from his or her actions? Charismatic attachment, on the other hand, is more plausible. As I argue in Chapter 5, populist rhetoric of grand struggles of the people against the oligarchy can give greater meaning to the actions of populists, and the populist must take actions and implement initiatives that lend credence to his or her rhetoric. In other words, rhetoric and action mutually reinforce the attachment of followers to the leader, each amplifying the effect of the other. Charismatic attachment was an important aspect of Chávez's populism, yet this fact actually *amplifies,* rather than falsifies, the importance of the mechanism that drove the support paradox in that case: participatory opportunities. This is due to the requirement that charismatic attachments be backed up with concrete actions: in Chapter 5, I argue that participatory opportunities, bounded at the local level, were the most powerful mechanism by which Chávez maintained ties with his followers, and were especially crucial in his 2006–2012 government, when his power became increasingly hegemonic as the regime's performance deteriorated.

Summary

The preceding section 3.2 specified four potential mechanisms for generating autonomy (although some only do so in the minds of individuals): representation, participation, personalism, and charismatic attachment. These are not necessarily mutually contradictory mechanisms: many democracies will have strengths in both representation and participation. And as I will argue in section 3.3 and in Chapter 5, participation was a vital element that helped to forge and maintain the charismatic attachment between Chávez and his most devoted followers. In the next section, I briefly examine the cases of interest, gauging which mechanisms (or configurations of mechanisms) have the most potential for explaining levels of perceived citizen autonomy in each case.

3.3 PARTICIPATORY POPULISM AND DEMOCRATIC ELITISM IN VENEZUELA AND CHILE

Of the mechanisms belonging to the typical categories of interest in democratic theory (representation and participation), participatory opportunities are by far the most promising source of the support paradoxes of interest here. Direct participation has a much clearer connection to autonomy as laid out by both developmental democratic theory and social psychology than any form of representation. It has the additional advantage of being the national-level independent variable upon which the two cases of interest here diverge most starkly. Chile and Venezuela represent fundamentally opposing solutions to the dilemmas posed by the simultaneous need or desire for democracy and the instability and social conflict that popular involvement in politics can create.

3.3.1 Representative Elitism

Despite their shared region, Chile and Venezuela are quite different, in terms of culture, demography, and economic structure. Nevertheless, their political histories share common episodes, albeit in different eras. Both countries adopted similar regimes after devastating democratic failures and traumatic periods of military rule. In Venezuela, a brief period of effervescent democracy ended when it was overthrown by a military coup led by Marco Pérez Jiménez in 1948. Chile's long-standing tradition of competitive politics ended in 1973 with a similar coup. In both cases, leftist governments confronted an uprising of their grassroots militants and social bases, upsurges which were viewed as risky provocations and thus contributed to the failure of democracy (Coppedge, 1994, pp. 37–39; Ellner, 2003a; Hellinger, 2003; Myers, 2006; Roberts, 1998). Years later, when democracy returned, elites in both states remembered the lessons of these democratic failures. These memories manifested as a deeply ingrained suspicion of mass politics, which was embodied in the nascent democratic regimes that came after military rule. In both cases, the ousted militaries and their supporters remained viable powers during and after transition. In Chile especially, where the loss of the country's proud tradition of democratic politics was especially traumatic and where the military remained quite powerful, fear of its return to power was widespread among the returning political elite (Constable & Valenzuela, 1991, ch. 12).

Elites in both states faced a dilemma: how to reestablish democracy, which has popular participation as a fundamental component, when such political inclusion was perceived as so threatening to stability? The solutions adopted by Chile and Venezuela differed considerably in the details (hardly surprising given the underlying structural differences), but both can be described as pacted transitions that were more concerned with limiting than expanding citizen autonomy. Venezuela limited both participation and representation, and came to embody Adam Przeworski's warning of "cartels of incumbents against contenders," wherein competition among elites was the lone form of institutionalized popular involvement in politics (Encarnación, 2005; Przeworski, 1991, pp. 90–91). Under the Punto Fijo agreement in Venezuela, authority was tightly held by a small number of elites within the system's dominant parties: the social democratic *Acción Democrática* (Democratic Action, AD) and the Christian Democratic *Comité de Organización Política Electoral Independiente* (Independent Political Electoral Organization Committee, COPEI), and to a lesser extent the *Unión Republicana Democrática* (Democratic Republican Union, URD). The mass bases of the parties had a largely subordinate role that did little to genuinely empower average citizens (Ellner, 2003a, 2003b). Distribution of benefits derived from oil revenues became key to maintaining the top-down flow of power from elites to masses, given the absence of institutionalized channels for making demands on the political system (Karl, 1987, pp. 86–89). This democratic variant, wherein free elections were held but power was monopolized by a small number of internally elite-dominated political parties, came to be referred to as *partidocracia*, or partyarchy in English; a neologism that emphasized the widespread view that such regimes were not fully democratic, as they failed to establish true popular sovereignty (Coppedge, 1994, ch. 1).

Chilean political elites likewise embraced performance-based legitimacy. Although lacking Venezuela's oil reserves, they had to rely on competent administration of the national economy, buttressed with careful expansion of the welfare state, rather than the distribution of rents. And although the institutionalization of the dominance of the large electoral pacts was more of a shotgun wedding than a consensual pact (it is largely enforced by the electoral system that the exiting Pinochet government demanded), elites from both sides of the ideological spectrum, wary of destabilizing political activity, accepted and adapted to the new rules of party politics. Unlike in Venezuela, elitist party dominance in Chile is the result of a variety of sources, rather than a single pact, including technocracy (Garretón, 2003; Kurtz, 2004a, 2004b; Silva, 1991), the electoral system (Posner, 1999), and elite preferences for top-down decision making (Huber, Pribble, & Stephens, 2010; Posner, 2004). And also unlike Venezuela, Chile was able to accomplish this limitation of autonomy despite relatively fair elections and a multiparty system, which covers the ideological spectrum from communist to far right. In other words, Chile did not vitiate autonomy by sacrificing representation. Instead, as I argue in Chapter 6, elites retained their dominance by limiting participation.

3.3.2 *Participatory Populism in Venezuela*

Both post-Pinochet Chile and *puntofijo*-era Venezuela adopted unresponsive, weakly rooted political systems that prioritized stability above all else, including democratic norms of participation and popular sovereignty. In other words, both adopted elitist representation as the sole institutional mechanism for popular involvement in politics, with Chile's being significantly more representative than that of Venezuela. It is important not to exaggerate the failings of these regimes. Both managed to consolidate, despite the very real possibility of a return to military rule. And each provided extremely significant economic benefits for considerable periods of time. In many important ways, the Chilean regime continues to thrive. *Puntofijismo*, on the other hand, demonstrated the underlying fragility of elitist representation. With the arrival of the debt crisis of the early 1980s and subsequent fluctuations in the price of oil, the system of rent distribution in Venezuela became unsustainable. I leave the details of the collapse to Chapter 5. For the present purpose it is sufficient to note that, with the pillar of economic benefits knocked out from under the regime, its minimal standard of democracy was woefully insufficient to bear the weight of the crisis. When democratic regimes stake their entire claim to legitimacy on their ability to deliver economic benefits, they more or less guarantee that economic crises will also become political crises.

It is not surprising that the regime that rose from the ashes of the failure of elitist representation under *puntofijismo* repudiated its tactics so completely, sacrificing both competitive politics and sound economics in favor of populism and direct participation. This was not predominantly a result of any political learning: Chávez had been considering such an approach to democratic politics at least as early as 1975, after observing the design of the leftist military regime of Juan Velasco in Peru (Gott, 2011, p. 35; Jones, 2009, ch. 3). Something more akin to natural selection was at work, where potential successors to *puntofijismo* were evaluated by citizens based upon the strength of their opposition to the old system. Those who made the mistake of colluding with the former dominant parties (such as the leftist movement La Causa R) fell by the wayside (López Maya, 1997). Eventually Chávez's promises of "participatory protagonist democracy" won through. The end result was a system that was the mirror image of both the *ancién regime* in Venezuela and the current democratic mode in Chile. The new constitution, drafted in a process in which Chávez had tremendous influence but did not dominate entirely, is a fascinating document that simultaneously granted a bewildering array of social and political rights to citizens, including (among other things) the right to referenda and to recall any public official (with some time constraints). It gave civil society and citizens various roles in overseeing and contributing to the public administration, such as via participation through the citizen's power branch (Hellinger, 2011). It also has as other features that are consistent with participation as defined here, including a unicameral legislature elected via proportional representation. These constitutionally guaranteed forms of participation would eventually be augmented by the bewildering array of local-level participatory fora described earlier in this chapter.

Despite this participatory focus, the constitution's only troubling provisions from a representative point of view involve the powers of the President, which were excessive even prior to the amendments pushed by Chávez in later years. Particularly troubling was Article 236, section 8, which granted the President to legislate by decree with authorization from the legislature. In other circumstances, this system, which reflected the influence of newly independent social organizations as well as that of the Bolivarian movement's military faction, might not have been such a crucial failing. However, when this provision combined with the domineering personality of Chávez, it led to a situation where a docile legislature would happily concede its functions to the executive, and Chávez often used enabling laws to make rapid changes with minimal interference from the legislative branch (Jones, 2009, ch. 17, 19). The results were predictable: representation was relegated to at best a secondary role in enforcing popular sovereignty, and was to be maintained not through competition for votes but by charismatic attachment to the populist. Instead, the direct participation of ordinary citizens was seen as the primary mechanism for binding political decisions to the popular will; this also became, as I show in Chapter 5, the principle mechanism that allowed Chávez to maintain the loyalty of his followers as a series of storms battered both his government and the regime he helped to create.

3.4   CONCLUSION

If there were two democratic theorists, one instrumental and one developmental, who observed the Venezuelan and Chilean political systems, with no foreknowledge of public opinion data in either case, they would make radically opposing predictions regarding support and legitimacy. The instrumentalist, finding a nearly ideal manifestation of his or her preferred democratic variant in Chile, would assume that substantive representation, civil liberties, and strong economic performance should be more than enough to ensure popular contentment. The developmental theorist, observing the plethora of opportunities for direct participation in Venezuela, would likely not be surprised to learn of the solid legitimacy of the Bolivarian regime, although he or she might well be disturbed by the commanding role taken by Chávez and the intensity of devotion to him. Table 3.1 presents an array of the various factors involved in such a hypothetical comparison.

As the table shows, only participatory opportunities and charismatic attachment unambiguously match patterns of support. And unless we are prepared to concede that *only* charismatic attachment can generate strong perceptions of autonomy, only participatory opportunities have any potential to explain *both* cases, given that they are part of a family of mechanism (participation) that can be applied to democracies broadly. Such a basic comparison is of course

Table 3.1: *Institutional determinants of autonomy and support in Chile and Venezuela*

	Chile	Venezuela
Representation	High	Low
Charismatic attachment	Low	High
Performance	High	Low
Participatory opportunities	Low	High
Support	Low	High

nowhere near sufficient to simply conclude that developmental theory is correct. If nothing else, a detailed examination of the Venezuelan case would be necessary to determine whether participatory opportunities, charismatic attachment, or both are responsible for the paradox in that case.

One can derive some concrete and empirically testable propositions from the preceding theoretical discussion, and through testing these against competing approaches, I demonstrate that developmental theory does in fact provide considerable leverage on the support paradox under investigation. The first proposition is that perceived citizen autonomy is a crucial source of regime support. Autonomy directly predicts support and further reinforces it through its moderation of the impact of performance; polities filled with citizens who believe themselves to be autonomous can weather economic storms that would otherwise sink them. Developmental theory suggests that participatory opportunities, rather than any form of representation, are the most powerful source of perceived autonomy. Applied to the cases here, this suggests two additional propositions. First, participatory programs in Venezuela are likely an important source of that country's unusually high levels of support (although I will argue that charismatic attachment, reinforced by these opportunities, is also important in that case). Second, it suggests that such programs could ameliorate low support in Chile. The remainder of this work is dedicated to testing hypotheses based upon these simple propositions with actual data.

4 Attitudinal Antecedents of Regime Support

A Statistical Analysis

The main argument of this book is that participatory opportunities are the key to explaining the paradoxes in Chile and Venezuela described in previous chapters. The approach derived in Chapter 3 from democratic theory and organizational justice theory suggests that the impact of participatory institutions (and characteristics of the political environment more generally) is not direct. This effect does not result from the satisfaction of conscious preferences, but from the satisfaction of psychological and emotional needs of which individuals may or may not be totally aware. This implies that in a state such as Chile wherein participatory opportunities are few and far between, citizens certainly do not withhold support because they yearn for communal councils or participatory budgeting. The lack of participatory opportunities weakens support because the Chilean state fails to give its citizens a sense of efficacy and control over their fates; there is no need to assume that Chileans *know* what institutional alternatives would make them feel more efficacious.

In short, the theory developed in Chapter 3 suggests that the impact of participatory institutions on support is indirect in most circumstances.[1] The impact of such institutions is mediated by perceptions of regime-based efficacy (RBE). Furthermore, my theory implies that participatory institutions (mediated by RBE) can also moderate the relationship between performance and support. Given this complicated attitudinal relationship structure, it would be

---

Portions of this chapter have been published in *Comparative Politics* (Rhodes-Purdy, 2017).

[1] Bolivarian Venezuela, where these institutions are an explicit part of Chávez's concept of "participatory, protagonist" democracy is an exception, as shown in Chapter 5.

premature to immediately proceed to any analyses testing the impact of participatory opportunities on regime support. Instead, I must first demonstrate that the relationships between performance, RBE, and regime support can be supported by available data. Only once these relationships are established can we turn to the institutional origins of these attitudes. In this section, I use cross-national public opinion surveys from across Latin America and the United States to test these hypotheses, before turning to the role of specific institutions in the cases of interest in subsequent chapters. I do not confine these analyses to the cases of interest; again, theory suggests that the attitudinal relationships to be tested are broadly applicable and should be evident in most populations.[2]

The statistical analyses presented in this chapter are fairly complex. Issues arising from the difficulty of accurately measuring abstract concepts like RBE and regime support; the interactive nature of the relationships between RBE, performance, and regime support; and the sampling complications presented by a region-wide, multiyear survey all preclude the use of simpler methods (such as least squares estimation). This raises something of a dilemma. This book is not intended exclusively for those possessing considerable quantitative skills; the theory and analysis I present have relevance to country and areas studies specialists, as well as students of democracy and democratic theory. However, the statistical analyses provide absolutely crucial evidence for my arguments, and in order for these analyses to be convincing, a considerable amount of mathematical specification and statistical minutiae is required. Additionally, the models presented in this chapter are adapted to different indicators, specific arguments, and datasets in later chapters. There is a serious risk that this amount of technical detail may deter readers who specialize in political theory or the comparative analysis of democracy.

---

[2] To ensure that the relationships do pertain to the cases of interest, I perform separate analyses of data from Chile and Venezuela, using the same model as the cross-national analyses, later in the chapter.

In order to provide the details necessary for readers with strong quantitative skills to evaluate the appropriateness of the models presented here and in subsequent chapters, while maintaining accessibility for readers who do not have advanced statistical skills, this chapter proceeds in three sections. The first section is an "executive summary" of the analyses, which are intended to be accessible to anyone, including qualitative scholars, area studies specialists, and democratic theorists who may have no training in or experience with statistical methods, although some familiarity with OLS regression is assumed. Modeling, measurement, and estimation choices are explained without jargon, and results are presented using visualizations and prose descriptions, rather than tables of parameter estimates. This section also specifies the three major hypotheses that will be tested throughout the remainder of this book. The first two (see Section 4.1.1) concern attitudinal relationships between RBE, performance, and regime support, and are the primary focus of this chapter. The third hypothesis addresses the elements of the political system or regime that are theoretically indicated to influence RBE, especially participatory opportunities. Section 4.1 includes a preliminary test of this hypothesis.

The second section of this chapter (Section 4.2) concludes the more substantive discussion of the results, noting that cross-national analyses are unlikely to provide the best test of the third hypothesis. It then briefly foreshadows how this hypothesis will be tested in the case-study chapters to follow. Those without considerable graduate-level statistical training should feel free to read the first two sections, and then proceed to Chapter 5.

The final part of this chapter (Section 4.3) acts as a technical or methodological appendix, and contains all necessary details for the reader to fully evaluate these analyses. In this final section, I specify hypotheses and models in equation form, and present results of estimations in full data tables and more advanced visualizations. Readers without quantitative backgrounds should feel free to pass over this section.

4.1 SUMMARY OF STATISTICAL ANALYSES AND RESULTS

4.1.1 Hypotheses

The most important purpose of this chapter is to provide evidence for the hypothesis, derived from the theoretical discussion in Chapter 3, that RBE positively influences regime support. In other words, individuals who feel that their political system grants them a substantial role in the political process will generally report higher levels of regime support than individuals who do not feel so efficacious. In the terminology of statistical hypotheses:

H1: Regime-Based Efficacy (RBE) increases regime support, controlling for other factors.

Of course the relationship between performance and regime support is also of interest here, and could be stated in similar terms (perceptions of good policy performance will generally increase regime support). As the substantive theory to be tested here is focused on RBE, I elect not to give this hypothesis a label.

Ordinarily, testing these hypotheses would be a simple matter of conducting an Ordinary Least Squares (OLS) regression, with regime support the dependent variable (DV), and RBE, performance, and a suite of demographic control variables the independent variables (IV). Several complications to which I alluded in the introduction to this chapter preclude this tactic. When using OLS, the relationship between a DV and an IV is described as a one-unit increase in the IV (say, RBE), the DV (in this case regime support) will, on average, increase by some set amount, *regardless of the value of any other variable*. In other words, the relationship between one IV and the DV is assumed to be constant.

The theory developed in Chapter 3, especially the parts derived from the social psychology of organizational justice, implies that such an assumption of a constant relationship between RBE, performance, and support is not reasonable. Recall that the theory used here predicts that individuals with a strong perception of RBE are expected to react in a more measured way to performance failures than those who feel powerless. For example, an individual who feels that he or she can effectively influence the political system will be less likely to withdraw support during an economic crisis; meanwhile, an individual in the same political system who feels politically helpless, who may have supported the regime during good times, will turn against the system much more quickly. This requires a modification of the language from linear, additive OLS to describe the relationship between performance and support used earlier: for a one-unit increase in perceived performance, regime support will, on average, increase by some set amount, *but that amount will not be constant but instead will change as the level of RBE changes.* This type of relationship, where the strength (and potentially even the direction) of a relationship between an IV and a DV is dependent upon another variable is called a moderated relationship (also called an interactive or multiplicative relationship); the variable that influences the relationship between the IV and the DV is called a moderator. To state this hypothesis specifically:

H2: The effect of performance is moderated by RBE.

Generally, moderating relationships are easy to manage; simply including a multiplicative term with the IV and its moderator is sufficient (see Equation 4.03 in Section 4.3). Including moderated relationships does make interpretation of estimation results significantly more complicated, even in models appropriate for OLS estimation, because the regression coefficient (usually specified as β or γ) attached to an IV with a moderated relationship is *not* equal to the effect of that variable on the DV (i.e. the amount by which the DV increases on average for a unit increase in the IV), as is usually the case. Instead, the effect of the IV is a composite of its regression coefficient and the coefficient attached to the multiplicative term multiplied by the value of the moderator (see Equations 4.06 and 4.07). This makes everything from gauging the relative strength of the relationship between different IVs and the DV (the strength will vary depending on the value of the moderator) to determining statistical significance (the relationship between IV and DV may be distinguishable from zero at some values of the moderator, but not at others) more complicated. Before dealing with these complications, one additional complication needs to be discussed.

4.1.2 Measurement

The concepts of interest here (regime support, performance, RBE) are complex and abstract. It is unlikely that any single survey question could accurately capture any of the aforementioned concepts accurately even if respondents could assign values accurately. The typical approach to dealing with abstract concepts (such as political attitudes) is to include multiple measures (often called "indicators") of a single concept, and then combine them. The idea is that the weaknesses and imperfections of each indicator will be balanced by the strengths of the others. This approach raises its own set of issues: specifically, how to combine the measures? The simplest solution is to simply sum them up (perhaps after adjusting each indicator to the same scale; the sum may also be rescaled to range from 0 to 1, thus forming an index). This approach is attractive for its simplicity, but has some significant shortcomings. The most serious of which is the implicit assumption that each indicator measures the concept of interest equally well. Such assumptions may be perfectly reasonable in some situations; for example, the indicators for regime support (presented shortly) all seem equally relevant on their face. In applied research one must often work with a suite of indicators where some are clearly superior to others, as is the case with both performance and RBE here. This can be resolved by weighting indicators: indicators that measure the concept more accurately can be set to influence a composite or index more than indicators that are poor. This leaves open the question of how to determine the quality of indicators, and how to calibrate the weights; I will return to this question shortly.

In addition to the difficulty of measuring abstract concepts accurately, public opinion data is plagued with measurement error.

It is reasonable to assume that respondents would have difficulty accurately assigning numeric values to their feelings, attitudes, and perceptions. Measurement error is a significant problem, one that is often given too little attention in applied research. Even if that error is entirely random, it leads to inaccurate estimation of regression coefficients; a single variable with measurement error can lead to inaccurate estimates for all regression coefficients in a model, even if the rest of the variables are measured without error.

Managing Measurement Issues: The Structural Equation Modeling Framework

To summarize, measurement of political attitudes is a daunting task, one for which OLS is often inadequate. Measurement error is virtually impossible to manage effectively using OLS, and basic regression techniques cannot provide much insight on how indicators can be combined and appropriately weighted to form a composite score. Due to this, I elect to turn away from OLS and instead use a method specifically designed to handle these sorts of problems: Structural Equation Modeling (SEM). SEM is capable of simultaneously estimating the "weights" of indicators (although the actual method is a bit more complicated than simply estimating weights) and the relationships between IVs and DVs. I do not wish to distract the reader with a lengthy explication of SEM techniques, but a brief summary will probably be useful. In the SEM framework, at least one variable (whether the DV, one or multiple IVs, or both) are assumed to exist, but are not measured directly, either because they cannot be measured or simply because we do not have access to direct measures. These unobserved (or unobservable) variables are called latent variables (or sometimes latent factors).

Although we do not or cannot observe the value of the latent variable for any individual observation, we *can* observe the values for a series of *indicators*. Indicators are observed variables (for example, responses to specific survey questions) that, while not directly measuring a latent variable, are assumed to relate to it in some way. In the

SEM framework, it is assumed that the indicators are affected by the latent variable, in a manner very similar to how IVs affect DVs in simple regression analysis. And as in simple regression analysis, that relationship is not one-to-one; the indicator is influenced by the latent variable, but also by a random error term (analogous to the residual in a regression), which is interpreted as random measurement error. Obviously it would not be possible to estimate such a regression (since all values for the latent variable would be missing). Yet, if one has multiple indicators, each influenced by the same latent variable, then it is possible to estimate both the influence of the latent variable on each indicator (called a "factor loading"; these loadings are represented by a coefficient which is analogous to both a regression coefficient in OLS estimation and the indicator weights discussed earlier) and the extent of measurement error by analyzing the covariation of the indicators. In other words, if observed variables are all being influenced by a single latent variable, then among individuals where one indicator is above the mean, we would expect all others to be above the mean as well (with random variation from individual to individual). If this pattern has few exceptions, we assume the latent variable has strong influences on the indicators; if one indicator frequently bucks the trend set by the others, it may very well be influenced by the latent factor, but likely to a much lesser degree than the conformists. SEM techniques are capable of simultaneously estimating the relationships between latent variables and their indicators (this is called the "measurement model") and "causal" or "structural" relationships between latent variables, observed variables, and combinations of the two (called the "structural model"). SEM also has the benefit of number of widely accepted rules of thumb for judging whether or not indicators are "good" measures of a particular latent variable.

For the analyses here, all three variables of interest (regime support, regime performance, and RBE) are treated as latent: all are abstract attitudes for which valid direct measures are not available (I would go further and argue that such measures would likely be impossible to craft). Instead these latent variables will be assumed to influence specific indicators, which will vary depending upon the specific data used for analysis.

4.1.3 Data and Indicators

To test H1 and H2, I use surveys conducted by the Latin American Public Opinion Project (LAPOP). LAPOP conducts surveys in every country in the region (except Cuba) at two-year intervals. I use the 2006, 2008, 2010, and 2012 waves of these surveys. Argentina did not (for reasons that are not entirely clear) have a 2006 wave, leaving 71 clusters.

Dependent Variable Indicators
Regime support is the dependent variable in all analyses. It is treated as a single latent variable, with the same three observed indicators in all models: pride in the political system (b2), respect for political institutions (b4), and support for the political system (b6). These are among the indicators used by the designers of the survey (Booth & Seligson, 2009). The measurement model used here differs from Booth and Seligson only in its omission of a question relating to the protection of civil liberties. I omit this indicator because it seems conceptually distinct, more a measure of perceived liberalism than of regime support specifically.

Regime Performance and RBE Indicators
Performance is measured by a combination of questions regarding the handling of specific governance issues: poverty reduction (n1), citizen security (n11), and general economic management (n15). It also includes a general evaluation of the economy (soct1) and approval of the President (m1). To tie the concept closer to the regime level, I also include the utilitarian-sounding but regime-level "satisfaction with the way democracy works" indicator (pn4). In models which utilize data from all waves (2006–2012), only presidential approval, approval of economic handling, evaluation of national economic situation, and

satisfaction with the way democracy works are available. For robustness, I also conducted analyses on two additional models, using data only from the 2012 wave. One model (the Full 2012 model) includes all indicators, while another model (the 2012 Reduced model) includes only those indicators that I feel have the greatest face validity for all latent concepts; in the case of performance, this means the three evaluation-of-governance questions and approval of the president. The satisfaction indicator is suspect for a number of reasons (Canache, Mondak, & Seligson, 2001), and the general economic evaluation is dependent upon outcomes that may be shaped by any number of factors in addition to policy outputs. SEM techniques include mechanisms for evaluating the appropriateness of indicators, called goodness of fit statistics (see Section 4.3.3). As discussed in that section, all indicators of performance, including those I exclude from the 2012 Reduced model due to concerns over face validity, are supported by these statistics.

Regime-based efficacy is measured by questions assessing the belief that politicians care what people like the respondent think (eff1), the belief that parties respond to the opinions of voters like respondents (epp1), and confidence in political parties (b21). This last is somewhat worrisome, but political parties are key institutions for collecting and acting on popular demands, and the analyses of the 2006–2012 and 2012 full measurement models suggest that it is significantly influenced by the RBE latent variable (see Section 4.3.3). Nevertheless, to provide greater confidence in the results, the 2012 model includes an additional responsiveness question (parties represent their voters well, epp3) to ensure that results are robust to this admittedly facially suspect indicator. The estimation results do not change with the inclusion or exclusion of indicators, and fit statistics and parameter estimates indicate that all indicators are appropriate for the latent concepts. The decision to exclude certain indicators in the 2012 Reduced analysis is merely a robustness check; results from the measurement model support the inclusion of these indicators, see Section 4.3.3.

The fact that some of the measures for RBE explicitly mention parties raises the possibility that the variable in question is more related to regime responsiveness, rather than RBE. Fit statistics cannot adjudicate disputes over the *substantive meaning* of a latent variable; that is the duty of the researcher, through conceptualization and theory. That is to say, perhaps the willingness of elites to respond to popular wishes is what most strongly impacts these measures, rather than the perceived ability of citizens to shape politics through their own behavior. Those concerns can be allayed in three ways. First, in the final chapters of this book, I show a positive impact of participatory democratic institutions, using both hypothetical and real-world examples, on RBE. This would not be the case if the measures used for RBE were actually measures of responsiveness, since these institutions allow for direct, unmediated participation. Second, as RBE and regime performance are assumed to be correlated, it is likely that any impact of responsiveness would be controlled for by the performance measure. Finally, as a robustness check, I include in the second part of this chapter an analysis of data from the American National Election Study (ANES), which is structurally identical to the LAPOP models but which use different indicators for RBE, none of which mention parties. Results from the ANES analyses are consistent with those obtained for LAPOP, indicating the LAPOP results are robust to both population and measurement differences. With these concerns allayed, and given the evidence from analysis of the measurement model, which is consistent with a well-specified measurement schema, I now turn to analyzing relationships between concepts.

4.1.4 Analysis of the Relationships between RBE, Performance, and Regime Support

If one ignores the complications introduced by the measurement model, the structural portion of a SEM is very similar to a more traditional regression model. It is composed of a dependent variable, which is influenced by series of independent variables (the strength of this influence is represented by the structural coefficients, which are identical regression coefficients in all but name), and a random error term. The only difference is that, in the SEM framework, some variables (in this case, both some of the IVs and the DV) are latent and thus indirectly measured as described in the Section 4.1. For the purposes of analyzing relationships between variables and interpretation of the meaning of the structural coefficients, latent variables are no different than observed variables, except in one respect: latent variables have no predetermined scale. A hypothetical latent variable, which influences three indicators that are all standard normally distributed (mean of zero and variance of one), could have a variance of one, thirty, a hundred, or indeed any other number, and still influence the indicators in the same proportions.[3] This problem is easily solved by specifying the scale of the latent variable, by specifying a mean (usually zero), and either fixing the factor loading of one indicator to one, or by fixing the variance of the latent factor to 1. For my analyses, I fix the scale of all latent variables to have means of zero and variances of one, as this makes interpretation of the magnitude of the IVs' effects on regime support far simpler.

To test the hypotheses listed earlier, I specify a SEM where regime support is the DV, and regime performance and RBE are the IVs. H2 also requires an interactive term; normally this is done by multiplying the interactive variables (RBE and regime performance), but because both are latent this process is considerably more complex (see Klein & Moosbrugger, 2000; Klein & Muthén, 2007 for details). Yet the interpretation of the moderated relationship is the same as in OLS estimation: the coefficient for an IV, which is usually its effect on the DV, is only equal to its effect when the moderator is zero. In other words, the coefficient for regime performance is only the effect of performance on regime support when RBE is at zero (which, in this

---

[3] This is an example of an identification problem. In addition to causing interpretation problems, it also has the much more serious consequence of making estimation of model parameters impossible without some constraints.

case, is also the mean of RBE). When RBE is *not* zero, the effect of performance becomes:

$$\gamma_{Performance} + \gamma_{RBE*Performance} * RBE$$

Where the coefficient labeled "performance" is the coefficient for the regime performance IV, the coefficient labeled "RBE * Performance" is the interaction term coefficient (i.e. the coefficient which pertains to the multiplied RBE * performance term in an OLS estimation), and RBE is the value of RBE for a given respondent.

In addition to the substantive variables of interest, I also include a suite of demographic control variables that likely impact regime support. These include:

- Income: respondent's income decile, by country-year
- Education: years of education
- Wealth: measured by the average number of a series of goods owned by the respondent (cars, refrigerators, computers, home, etc.)
- Sex
- Age
- Ideology: measured by a 0–10 left/right self-identification scale
- Urban: dummy variable for respondents living in urban areas
- Race: dummy variable for respondents who do not identify as "white"
- Dummy variable for country-year[4]

These variables are included because they very likely influence regime support, and are likely correlated with at least one of the substantive IVs of interest. Omitting them would thus likely lead to biased coefficient estimates.

Analysis of Results

The full tables of results are quite large, given the number of IVs and multiple models (multiwave, 2012 Full, and 2012 Reduced), and thus quite difficult to interpret. Given this, I present them in the more

---

[4] Technically, as described in Section 4.3, these analyses use multilevel modeling techniques, rather than dummy variables. Because there are no country-level IVs included, the model is mathematically equivalent to a single-level model that includes dummy variables for each country-year of the LAPOP survey.

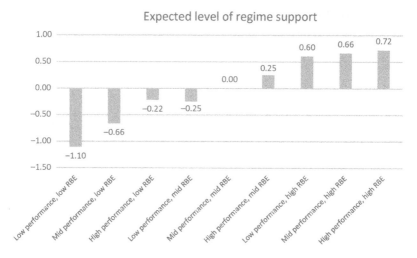

FIGURE 4.1: Expected levels of regime support for configurations of performance and RBE

detailed section of this chapter (see Section 4.3.4 for full tables). I will simply note that the coefficients for each of the substantive IVs (regime performance and RBE) are positive, statistically significant, and very large; the coefficient for the moderating term (RBE * performance) is significant, and negative (as expected), and as shown later, significantly alters the relationships between RBE, performance, and support.

Perhaps the most intuitive way to demonstrate this would be graphically. Figure 4.1 presents the expected average levels of regime support among respondents, classified as high (two standard deviations above the mean), low (two standard deviations below the mean), and mid (at the mean) for both performance and RBE.[5]

A number of elements of this graph bear commenting on. First, if the influence of RBE and performance were roughly equivalent, and

---

[5] Estimates from the multi-wave model were used for this graph. Estimates from both 2012 only models were very similar. Like performance and RBE, regime support is scaled to be standard normal and thus 95 percent of observations can be expected to fall between −2 and 2.

were those relationships constant, we would expect the right side of the graph to be high/high, high/mid, and mid/high. This is not what we observe. Instead, the three highest expected levels of support pertain to configurations with high RBE; moving from high to low performance has barely any effect on regime support at all among respondents with high levels of RBE, dropping only 0.12 points. For comparison, the decrease in expected level of regime support when moving from "high performance, low RBE" to "low performance, low RBE" is 0.88, nearly eight times greater than the previously discussed drop.

This fact is not due merely to the fact that RBE has a stronger direct impact than performance (although that is the case). Recall that the effects of both IVs of interest are not constant; because of the moderated relationship, respondents' perceptions of RBE will alter their attitudinal relationship between performance and support (and vice-versa). It is relatively easy to see this in Figure 4.1 for RBE (notice that the decrease in expected regime support is very pronounced in the first three bars, and very modest in the last three), but somewhat more difficult to see the same for performance, given the ordering. To make this clearer, Figure 4.2 presents the same information in Figure 4.1, using lines instead of bars.

As these graphs show, when one of the IVs is low, the slope of the other deepens (i.e. the other variable has a much stronger influence on support). The opposite is also true: when RBE is high, the slope of the line for performance becomes significantly shallower. This is the graphical representation of the idea, presented in Chapters 1 and 3, that individuals who feel empowered by their regimes are less likely to withdraw support in the face of poor governance than those who feel helpless and without a voice.

Although the impacts of RBE and performance are each moderated by the other, as Figure 4.2 shows, the resulting differences in expected level of support vary much more based on RBE than on performance. This is because RBE has a much higher direct effect (i.e. the effect when the moderator is at zero) than performance. This

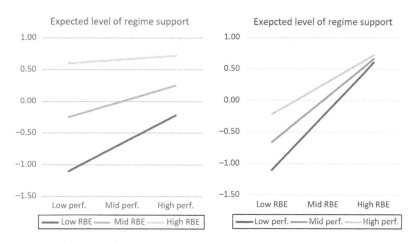

FIGURE 4.2: Line graph of expected level of regime support by RBE and performance

manifests in the graphs as relatively large gaps between the lines in the left graph (where each line represents a value of RBE, and the x-axis represents values of performance, going from low to high) than in the right (where lines represent performance and the x-axis represents RBE). The gaps between lines in the left graph are quite large, although a bit smaller on the right side (representing a slight decrease in the importance of RBE). However, the gaps between lines on the rightmost chart are smaller still, decreasing from modest on the left side of the chart to nearly nonexistent on the right side. Substantively, this represents a reduction in the influence of performance on support from modest (but still meaningful) to nearly nothing, almost a nonrelationship.

To summarize, the most important information visualized in these figures is as follows. First, RBE and performance both matter if one wishes to explain support. That said, RBE matters more. Even those with relatively high perceptions of a regime's performance will be expected to have negative (i.e. below-average) levels of regime support if they feel powerless and disconnected from their regime. On the other hand, empowered individuals will typically report higher-than-average levels of regime support, even if they believe the political system is riddled with bunglers who will never get the trains to run on time. Indeed, as Figure 4.2 showed, the difference between high-RBE respondents who feel they are governed incompetently and high-RBE respondents who believe the quality of performance to be excellent is vanishingly small.

4.1.5   Analysis of the Determinants of RBE

The evidence described in the preceding Section 4.1.4 is consistent with the theoretically suggested interactive relationship between support, performance, and RBE described in Chapter 3. Yet these analyses have little to say about what impacts average levels of RBE in a given country at a specific time. The theory discussed in Chapter 3 suggests the following hypothesis:

H3: Countries that have extensive opportunities for direct participation should have higher levels of RBE than those that do not.[6]

The most important and valid tests of this hypothesis are contained in Chapters 5 and 6, which analyze the influence of the Venezuelan and Chilean political systems on RBE and support.[7] Yet it seems appropriate to provide a cross-national test, which, while not definitive, will demonstrate the plausibility of H3 before diving into the case studies. To test this, I used the International Institute for Democracy and Electoral Assistance's direct democracy database, which contains data on whether a given country has provisions for mandatory referenda, initiatives, and provisions for recalling the President. To categorize countries as either having or lacking direct

---

[6] Participatory institutions such as those analyzed in Chapters 5 and 6 should not be confused with direct democratic institutions, which are what the IDEA dataset measures. Both institutional variants provide respondents an opportunity to have a direct role in the political process, and thus positive results using IDEA data should at least demonstrate that my theory is sufficiently plausible to warrant application to the cases of interest. It would of course be better to test the influence of participatory institutions directly, but such data is not currently available.

[7] For a discussion of the logic behind using case studies, rather than cross-national analysis, as the primary method of testing H3, see the conclusion of this chapter.

Table 4.1: *List of countries with and without direct participation*

Many participatory opportunities	Few participatory opportunities
Bolivia	Argentina
Dominican Republic	Brazil
Ecuador	Chile
Guatemala	Colombia
Honduras	Costa Rica
Mexico	El Salvador
Nicaragua	Panama
Peru	Paraguay
Uruguay	
Venezuela	

participatory opportunities, I conducted a Latent Class Analysis (LCA) of the Latin American countries included in the 2012 wave of the LAPOP study. LCA is similar to the measurement techniques used in a typical SEM, with one major difference: the latent variable is treated as categorical (in this case binary), rather than continuous. Based on the presence or absence of combinations of these three indicators, countries were assigned to one of two classes: countries with extensive participatory opportunities, and countries that do not have many such opportunities. This categorization is presented in Table 4.1.

Using the measurement scheme for the 2012 reduced model, I conducted an analysis that allowed the intercept of RBE to vary across these two groups. I then conducted a likelihood ratio difference test, comparing this model to one that constrained the mean to be equal. The difference was significant at the 0.05 level ($p = 0.048$). The mean for countries without opportunities was fixed at 0; the estimated mean of countries with opportunities was .011. This is by no means a definitive test of H3, yet it does provide sufficient evidence to delve into a more rigorous test of that hypotheses through an analysis of the cases of interest.

4.2   CONCLUSION

The analyses presented here demonstrate clearly that the relationship between RBE and support implied by both participatory democratic theory and social psychology conforms to available evidence. RBE is a crucial variable for explaining support, more so than regime performance or any of the demographic control variables. And as social psychology suggests, RBE is also capable of significantly reducing the importance of performance as a predictor of support. These results are robust to choice of indicators, differences in survey years, and differences in geographical domain.

This chapter has less to say about those factors that shape RBE. The final analysis suggests that participatory opportunities play some role, but the difference between countries that have opportunities for direct participation and those that do not is rather modest. Furthermore, a simple comparison of means cannot account for any number of potential confounding variables. However, a full regression model positing institutional antecedents for RBE would be extremely difficult, if not impossible, to specify. The sheer number of institutional variants that might play a role would quickly dwarf the number of second-level groups (fewer than eighty in even the LAPOP multi-wave model). The fact that many relationships would not be additive exacerbates this issue. Single-member districts, for example, could either enhance or inhibit RBE, depending upon the size of the district, the level of competition within the district, rules for internal party structure, and so on.

Given this, in the following chapters, I instead elect to focus on two case studies: Chile and Venezuela. I chose these cases because each has a disjunction between support and performance. I support my case that participatory opportunities are the critical factor in determining RBE in each country. In Venezuela, I show that participatory self-governance is a core part of the Bolivarian regime's strategy for winning the support of its population, and for developing an organizational base, which it can activate to defend it during its not infrequent crises.

Chile is a more difficult case, because the outcome of interest (low support despite strong performance) is attributable to the absence of something, rather than something that is present. Yet this analytical challenge is not insurmountable. In Chapter 6, I show that a lack of participatory opportunities is the root cause of Chile's democratic malaise in two ways. First, I demonstrate that issues of participation are a driving factor in the lack of confidence in the country's party system, using statistical analysis of data collected by the Center for Public Studies (CEP). Second, I show that participatory opportunities could ameliorate low support in Chile, using an experimental analysis and an evaluation of a municipal level participatory initiative in the Providencia commune.

4.3 DETAILED DESCRIPTION OF STATISTICAL ANALYSES AND RESULTS (TECHNICAL APPENDIX)

This section presents details (especially technical details that might bog down readers who are not quantitatively focused) omitted from the previous Section 4.1, and thus acts as a technical or methodological appendix to this chapter. I have, wherever possible, avoided repetition and redundancy from the prior Section 4.1, including content from that section only where I feel it necessary to remind the reader of substantive concerns that might influence their evaluation of modeling choices or statistical techniques. This section also includes full tables of coefficient estimates for both measurement and structural models; the previous Section 4.1 presented the latter graphically and omitted the former.

4.3.1 Hypotheses and Model Specification

The first and most basic hypothesis here is:

H1: Regime-Based Efficacy (RBE) increases regime support, controlling for other factors.

This hypothesis assumes the following statistical model.

$$\text{Regime Support}_i = \gamma_0 + \gamma_1 \text{RBE}_i + \gamma_2 \text{Performance}_i + \zeta_i \qquad \text{(Eq 4.01)}$$

Where i is the ith respondent, and ζ is the disturbance term.[8] With the model specified, H1 can be restated as:

$$\text{H1}_0 : \gamma_1 = 0$$

$$\text{H1}_A : \gamma_1 \neq 0 \qquad \text{(Eq 4.02)}$$

Performance is not a part of H1, but its inclusion will become clear shortly. As stated in Chapter 3, social psychology suggests that the relationship between performance and support is not constant across all individuals. Instead, theory suggests that RBE should moderate that relationship: individuals who feel their regimes provide them a great deal of say in the political process will be slower to withdraw support in the face of policy failures than individuals who feel powerless.

H2: The effect of performance is moderated by RBE.

Testing this hypothesis requires the model specified by Equation 4.01 to be respecified as:

$$\begin{aligned}\text{Regime Support}_i = \gamma_0 + \gamma_1 \text{RBE}_i + \gamma_2 \text{Performance}_i \\ + \gamma_3 \left(\text{Performance}^* \text{RBE}_i\right) + \zeta_i\end{aligned} \qquad \text{(Eq 4.03)}$$

H2 can be stated mathematically as:

$$\begin{aligned}\text{H1}_0 : \gamma_3 = 0 \\ \text{H1}_A : \gamma_3 \neq 0\end{aligned} \qquad \text{(Eq 4.04)}$$

It should be noted that with a nonadditive model such as Equation 4.03, the test of H1 presented in Equation 4.02 is no longer valid, because:

$$\frac{\partial \text{Regime Support}}{\partial \text{RBE}} \neq \gamma_1 \qquad \text{(Eq 4.05)}$$

---

[8] I use ζ following the conventions of structural equation modeling.

as it does in the additive model. Instead we have:

$$\frac{\partial \text{Regime Support}}{\partial \text{RBE}} = \gamma_1 + \gamma_3 \,\text{Performance}_i \qquad \text{(Eq 4.06)}$$

In other words γ_1 is not, in the interactive model, the effect of RBE but only the intercept of the effect (the effect when performance is at zero, which for reasons explained later is also its mean). The actual effect is different for every individual, depending upon their level of RBE. The same is true for the effect of RBE:

$$\frac{\partial \text{Regime Support}}{\partial \text{Performance}} = \gamma_2 + \gamma_3 \,\text{RBE}_i \qquad \text{(Eq 4.07)}$$

To account for nonadditivity, H1 must be restated as:

$$\begin{aligned} &\text{H1}_0 : \gamma_1 + \gamma_3 \,\text{Performance}_i = 0 \,\forall\, i \\ &\text{H1}_A : \gamma_1 + \gamma_3 \,\text{Performance}_i \neq 0 \,\forall\, i \end{aligned} \qquad \text{(Eq 4.08)}$$

In other words, H1 states that there are at least some levels of performance at which the effect of RBE is nonzero (and vice-versa). It should be noted that if zero is a meaningful value of the moderating variable, as it is here (RBE and regime performance both have fixed means of zero), then an estimate of the effect intercept (γ_1 or γ_2) that is statistically significant is a sufficient but not necessary condition for rejecting the reformulated H1$_0$.

Most estimation methods assume independence of observations; that is to say, all respondents' answers and probability of being sampled do not depend on those of other respondents. This assumption is clearly violated here, because respondents are nested within country-year survey waves. Respondents' country and year of survey may have an impact on their opinions and feelings and thus must be controlled for. Given this, I respecify Equation 4.03 as follows:

$$\begin{aligned} \text{Regime Support}_i = &+\gamma_3 \left(\text{Performance}^* \text{RBE}_i\right) + \zeta_i \,\beta_{0k} + \gamma_1 \,\text{RBE}_i \\ &+\gamma_2 \,\text{Performance}_i \\ \beta_{0k} = &\gamma_0 + u_k \end{aligned} \qquad \text{(Eq 4.09)}$$

where β_{0k} is the intercept for country-year k, γ_0 is the intercept for the sample as a whole, and u_k is the difference between the country-year specific intercept and the overall intercept. This model is equivalent to adding dummy variables for each country-year, forming a fixed-effects model (Allison, 2009).

Finally, I include a suite of demographic control variables that could conceivably impact regime support. These variables are not directly useful for testing the theory developed here, but failing to include such variables would render any estimation of the model described in Equation 4.03 suspect due to omitted variable bias. These variables include income, wealth, education, gender, ideology, race, urban/rural respondent, and age. This leads to the following, final structural model:

$$\text{Regime Support}_i = \beta_{0k} + \gamma_1 \, \text{RBE}_i + \gamma_2 \, \text{Performance}_i$$
$$+ \gamma_3 \left(\text{Performance}^* \text{RBE}_i\right) +$$
$$\gamma_3 \, \text{Income}_i + \gamma_4 \, \text{Wealth}_i + \gamma_5 \, \text{Education}_i +$$
$$\gamma_6 \, \text{Gender}_i + \gamma_7 \, \text{Ideology}_i + \gamma_8 \, \text{Urban}_i + \gamma_9 \, \text{Age}_i + \gamma_{10} \, \text{Race}_i + \zeta_{i};$$
$$\beta_{0k} = \gamma_0 + u_k$$

$$(\text{Eq 4.10})$$

Distilling the theoretical discussion of institutional antecedents of RBE (H3 from Figure 3.1) is a more difficult task than the purely individual-level attitudinal hypotheses for several reasons. First, it is not possible to specify a fully convincing model that would allow for testing of the hypothesis that participatory opportunities (created by institutions) increase RBE. Measures of "participatory institutions" are not available (although reasonable proxies may soon be available via the V-Dem project), and if they were available, cross-national public opinion data that included a sufficient number of level-2 units with comparable measures of RBE are not.

While it is not possible to construct a fully specified "causal" multilevel model that could be estimated by available data, it is possible to identify one major source of variation in RBE for the cases of interest alone. That factor is the presence or absence of participatory opportunities. This leads to the following hypothesis:

H3: Countries that provide more participatory opportunities will produce higher average perceptions of RBE.

Although the test of this hypothesis is primarily the domain of the case-focused Chapters (5 and 6), a preliminary evaluation can be conducted by comparing average levels of RBE across groups of respondents, sorted according to the presence or absence of extensive opportunities for direct participation (E.O.D.P.) in their countries of residence. E.O.D.P. is measured by the presence or absence of initiatives, referenda, and presidential recall provisions, in the respondents' countries, leading to the hypotheses:

$$H2_0 : \mu_{E.O.D.P.} = \mu_{\sim E.O.D.P.}$$
$$H2_A : \mu_{E.O.D.P.} \neq \mu_{\sim E.O.D.P.}$$

(Eq 4.11)

where $\mu_{E.O.D.P.}$ and $\mu_{\sim E.O.D.P}$ represent the population mean levels of RBE in countries with and without extensive opportunities for direct participation, respectively, assuming unequal variance across groups.[9] This test has the advantage of having only one level of analysis, that of the individual. However, it assumes equality of mean RBE within each group, which is not a very reasonable assumption, given the fact that individuals are nested within countries. To account for this, a multi-level mean structure model needs to be specified. This is done by decomposing the mean level of RBE into two components:

$$\mu_{gk} = \beta_g + e_k$$

(Eq 4.12)

where μ_{gk} is the mean RBE of country k in group g, β_g is the mean for group g (presence or absence of E.O.D.P.) and e_k is a random disturbance representing the difference of country k's mean from the mean of the group to which it belongs. Based on this, H2 can be reformulated as:

$$H2_0 : \beta_{E.O.D.P.} = \beta_{\sim E.O.D.P.}$$
$$H2_A : \beta_{E.O.D.P.} \neq \beta_{\sim E.O.D.P.}$$

(Eq 4.13)

The advantages of multilevel model estimation in this instance are significantly weakened by the small number of countries involved

---

[9] See Section 4.4.3 for an explanation of how countries were assigned to each group; for a list of countries by group, see Table 4.6.

in the region of interest here (nk = 18). Statistical tests will likely lack sufficient power to detect even sizeable differences.

4.3.2 Measurement

Measurement error leads to bias in parameter estimates. In multivariate models this error spreads to all estimates, not just those related to the variables with error. In order to have confidence in the results of analysis, this error must be accounted for in the model. I do so by using Structural Equation Modeling (SEM) techniques. SEM involves specifying two submodels that are combined to form a single structural equation model. The first submodel, often (although somewhat inaccurately) called the "structural" model, specifies relationships between variables, and is analogous to a typical regression model. The second submodel is the measurement model, which decomposes each observed response (now called an indicator) into two components. One component is affected by the underlying concept of interest, which is unobserved (latent). The other component is a random error term. The parameters of the two models are then estimated simultaneously.

Generally, the following equations define the measurement model for the kth indicator y or x:

$$y_{ik} = v_k + \lambda_k \eta_i + \epsilon_i \tag{Eq 4.14}$$

$$x_{1ik} = v_k + \lambda_k \xi_{1i} + \delta_i \tag{Eq 4.15}$$

$$x_{2ik} = v_k + \lambda_k \xi_{2i} + \delta_i \tag{Eq 4.16}$$

where y_{ik}, x_{1ik}, and x_{2ik} are indicators of the endogenous latent factor (regime support) and the first and second exogenous latent factor (performance and RBE), respectively, for the ith respondent. η_i is the value of the latent regime support variable for the ith respondent; ξ_{1i} and ξ_{2i} are the values of the latent performance and RBE variables for the ith respondents, respectively. λ_k is the "factor loading" for a given indicator and latent variable; it is analogous to a regression coefficient in OLS estimation. The lambda parameters determine how strongly the latent variable impacts the observed indicator. Finally, the epsilon and delta parameters are random measurement error terms.

v_k is the intercept term associated with the kth indicator of a given latent factor. Normally this is fixed to zero by deviating each indicator from its mean; in multilevel SEMs, the intercept must be included because it is not constant. Instead, it varies by country-year. Reexpressing Equation 4.14 in matrix notation, this leads to the following modification of Equation 4.14:

$$y_{gik} = v_{W_{kg}} + \lambda_k \eta_i + \epsilon_{W_i} \qquad \text{(Eq 4.17)}$$

$$v_{W_{gk}} = v_{B_k} + \epsilon_{B_{gk}} \qquad \text{(Eq 4.18)}$$

y_{gik} is the value of the kth indicator of the endogenous latent factor for ith respondent in country-year g. $v_{W_{kg}}$ is the within country-year intercept for the kth indicator; it is the same for all respondents within a country-year, but varies across country-years. To specify this, $v_{W_{kg}}$ is decomposed in Equation 4.18 into two components: a "grand intercept," which is the same for all respondents (v_{B_k}), and a random, country-year level error term, $\epsilon_{B_{gk}}$. This is sometimes called weak factorial invariance. It suggests that, while the latent variables impact the indicators in equivalent ways across second-level groups, the means for indicators, as well as their measurement errors, will vary from group to group. Substituting Equation 4.18 into 4.17 leads to the following:

$$y_{gik} = v_{B_k} + \lambda_k \eta_i + \epsilon_{W_{ik}} + \epsilon_{B_{gk}} \qquad \text{(Eq 4.19)}$$

Variable Measurement in the ANES Model

As a robustness check against the concerns listed earlier, I conduct an out-of-sample analysis of the 1988–2012 American National Election Study (ANES) dataset, which includes different indicators for all of the key concepts. Of particular importance, none of the indicators in the ANES dataset mention political parties, and one of the indicators (no say) does not mention elites or political actors at all. Indicators for this model are presented in Table 4.2.

Table 4.2: *Indicators for ANES models*

Regime support	Performance	RBE
Trust in Federal government	Presidential approval	Government cares about people like respondent
Government run by big interests	Congressional approval	People like respondent have no say in government
Government wastes tax money	Evaluation of economy	Government pays attention to people like respondent
Most politicians are crooked		Elections make government pay attention

Measurement Model Identification

The factor complexity in all models is one; all indicators load on only one factor. All latent factors have variances fixed at one for identification purposes. As the covariance of two variables with unit variance is equivalent to the correlation between the variables, this also allows tests of whether the latent factors are conceptually distinct (see results Section 4.3.3 for details).

In all cases except the 2012 reduced model, the measurement models are identified by the three-indicator rule (Bollen, 1989). The 2012 reduced model includes two indicators (epp1 and epp3), which both concern parties and which are part of the same question block. This means that a respondent's attitudes toward parties may impact both of these indicators, separate from their perceptions of RBE. To account for this, I allow the measurement errors for these two indicators to be correlated. This model is identified by the single-factor rules method (O'Brien, 1994).

4.3.3   Measurement Model Results

Measurement must precede analysis of relationships; without confidence in the measures of concepts, no analysis of the structural or causal relationships between concepts can be trusted. Given this, I estimated the parameters of the measurement models described earlier separately from the structural model; the results are presented in this section. The results for the measurement portions of the LAPOP and ANES models are presented in Tables 4.3 and 4.4, respectively.

Each model using LAPOP data includes eighteen countries. The 2006–2012 model includes four waves (one every two years) for each country (except Argentina, which has only three due to the lack of a 2006 wave in that country), leading to seventy-one country-year clusters. Due to the lack of multiple observations over time within a cluster, and the small number of time periods, year is treated as simply a component of the second-level data structure. There is a possibility that major events (such as the economic crisis of 2008) could lead the cluster-level errors to be correlated (for example, within a country over time, or across countries within a given year). Yet if such a problem exists, it does not appear to influence the substantive conclusions of the analyses much: both 2012-only models have very similar results to the multi-wave model. Additionally, a model that included separate categorical variables for country and year instead of using multilevel techniques produced very similar results, which are excluded for brevity. The same could be said of the structural model analyses presented later in this section.

Overall, the results presented are consistent with the measurement models developed here. First, all factor loadings are positive and statistically significant; the models include no irrelevant measures. The correlations between latent variables are high, indicating that they are related. Yet model restrictions that fix those correlations at one produce significantly poorer fitting models. This means that, while the latent factors are clearly related, they are not identical to one another. The assumption that RBE, regime performance, and regime support are all separate concepts is supported by these data.

The goodness of fit indices (GFI) also show that these models are appropriate, with the exception of the Chi-square tests, all of which are statistically significant. While this would generally indicate poor model fit, the Chi-square statistic is extremely sensitive to sample

Table 4.3: *Measurement model estimation results, LAPOP*

Loadings	2006–2012 (n = 119,054)			2012 Full (n = 29,255)			2012 Reduced (n = 29,245)		
	Est.	SE	P-Value	Est.	SE	P-Value	Est.	SE	P-Value
Regime Support									
Pride in political system (b2)	0.539	0.010	0.000	0.574	0.014	0.000	0.574	0.014	0.000
Respect for institutions (b4)	0.768	0.011	0.000	0.789	0.019	0.000	0.787	0.020	0.000
Systemic support (b6)	0.737	0.012	0.000	0.744	0.021	0.000	0.747	0.021	0.000
Performance									
Poverty reduction (n1)	-	-	-	1.327	0.041	0.000	1.332	0.041	0.000
Citizen security (n11)	-	-	-	1.353	0.039	0.000	1.364	0.039	0.000
Economic management (n15)	0.701	0.022	0.000	0.801	0.026	0.000	0.802	0.026	0.000
Economic evaluation (soct1)	0.413	0.014	0.000	0.360	0.039	0.000	-	-	-
Approval of president (m1)	0.599	0.022	0.000	0.570	0.026	0.000	0.558	0.039	0.000
Satisfaction with democracy (pn4)	0.485	0.016	0.000	0.409	0.029	0.000	-	-	-
Citizen Autonomy (RBE)									
External efficacy (eff1)	0.483	0.013	0.000	0.541	0.021	0.000	0.575	0.023	0.000
Parties respond to voters (epp1)	0.632	0.014	0.000	0.694	0.023	0.000	0.689	0.028	0.000
Confidence in parties (b21)	0.603	0.016	0.000	0.618	0.023	0.000	-	-	-
Parties represent voters (epp3)	-	-	-	0.659	0.018	0.000	0.662	0.021	0.000

Table 4.3: *(cont.)*

Latent Variable Variance/ Covariance	2006–2012			2012 Full			2012 Reduced		
	Est.	SE	P-Value	Est.	SE	P-Value	Est.	SE	P-Value
Support (residual variance)	*1.000*	-	-	*1.000*	-	-	*1.000*	-	-
Performance	*1.000*	-	-	*1.000*	-	-	*1.000*	-	-
Citizen autonomy (RBE)	*1.000*	-	-	*1.000*	-	-	*1.000*	-	-
Covariance (Support, RBE)	0.714	0.014	0.000	0.718	0.014	0.000	0.644	0.023	0.000
Covariance (Support, Performance)	0.599	0.016	0.000	0.632	0.024	0.000	0.629	0.024	0.000
Covariance (Performance, RBE)	0.682	0.023	0.000	0.775	0.014	0.000	0.780	0.015	0.000

Error Variances	2006–2012			2012 Full			2012 Reduced		
	Est.	SE	P-Value	Est.	SE	P-Value	Est.	SE	P-Value
Pride in political system (b2)	0.649	0.019	0.000	0.620	0.031	0.000	0.621	0.031	0.000
Respect for institutions (b4)	0.331	0.010	0.000	0.322	0.015	0.000	325	0.015	0.000
Systemic support (b6)	0.373	0.012	0.000	0.382	0.020	0.000	0.379	0.021	0.000
Poverty reduction (n1)	-	-	-	1.259	0.057	0.000	1.245	0.056	0.000
Citizen security (n11)	-	-	-	1.075	0.046	0.000	1.044	0.045	0.000
Economic management (n15)	0.381	0.021	0.000	0.289	0.013	0.000	0.288	0.014	0.000
Economic evaluation (soct1)	0.710	0.017	0.000	0.787	0.036	0.000	-	-	-

	2006–2012			2012 Full			2012 Reduced		
Approval of president (m1)	0.513	0.015	0.000	0.582	0.030	0.000	0.595	0.030	0.000
Satisfaction with democracy (pn4)	0.685	0.014	0.000	0.802	0.038	0.000	-	-	-
External efficacy (eff1)	0.724	0.024	0.000	0.670	0.043	0.000	0.632	0.044	0.000
Parties respond to voters (epp1)	0.549	0.024	0.000	0.474	0.474	0.000	0.482	0.036	0.000
Confidence in parties (b21)	0.594	0.017	0.000	0.598	0.030	0.000	-	-	-
Parties represent voters (epp3)	-	-	-	0.530	0.043	0.000	0.528	0.037	0.000
Covariance (epp1, epp3)	-	-	-	0.161	0.021	0.000	0.163	0.029	0.000

Statistic	2006–2012	2012 Full	2012 Reduced
Chi-square	3593	2085	607
RMSEA	0.020	0.022	0.015
CFI	0.939	0.957	0.985
SRMR	0.033	0.030	0.015

Table 4.4: *Measurement model estimation results, ANES*

	Model 1 (n = 18,104)			Model 2 (n = 18,104)			Model 3 (n = 18,102)		
	Est.	SE	P-value	Est.	SE	P-value	Est.	SE	P-value
Regime support									
Trust	1.668	0.039	0.000	1.706	0.041	0.000	1.689	0.041	0.000
Big interests	2.404	0.07	0.000	3.355	0.078	0.000	2.317	0.076	0.000
Waste	1.337	0.038	0.000	1.339	0.039	0.000	1.390	0.039	0.000
Crooked	1.422	0.033	0.000	1.409	0.034	0.000	1.419	0.035	0.000
Regime performance									
Presidential approval	0.445	0.017	0.000	0.446	0.017	0.000	0.446	0.018	0.000
Congressional approval	1.135	0.062	0.000	1.138	0.062	0.000	1.132	0.062	0.000
Evaluation of economy	0.186	0.038	0.000	0.183	0.038	0.000	0.184	0.038	0.000
RBE (Citizen autonomy)									
Government cares	2.186	0.101	0.000	-	-	-	-	-	-
No say	1.585	0.061	0.000	1.098	0.055	0.000	0.285	0.013	0.000
Government pays attention	1.553	0.067	0.000	-	-	-	-	-	-
Attention at election time	1.241	0.050	0.000	1.379	0.067	0.000	-	-	-
Variances									
Presidential approval error	1.239	0.017	0.000	1.238	0.017	0.000	1.238	0.017	0.000
Support	*1.000*	-	-	*1.000*	-	-	*1.000*	-	-
Performance	*1.000*	-	-	*1.000*	-	-	*1.000*	-	-
RBE	*1.000*	-	-	*1.000*	-	-	-	-	-

Covariances

	Model 1			Model 2			Model 3		
Support, RBE/No say	0.643	0.014	0.000	0.643	0.019	0.000	0.285	0.013	0.000
Support, Performance	0.861	0.024	0.000	0.860	0.024	0.000	0.863	0.025	0.000
Performance, RBE/No say	0.396	0.027	0.000	0.359	0.035	0.000	0.170	0.019	0.000

Statistic	Model 1	Model 2	Model 3
Chi-square	1787	719	607
RMSEA	0.055	0.040	0.015
CFI	0.940	0.968	0.985

Error variance is not a parameter for categorical indicators.
GFI statistics are not available for the multilevel ANES measurement model. The use of categorical indicators in a multilevel measurement model requires numerical integration, for which GFI statistics are not available. The statistics presented here are for the equivalent single-level models.

size; specifically, its value increases as sample size increases, regardless of fit. All of these models include tens of thousands of observations; it is unlikely that any model based on these data would produce an insignificant Chi-square statistic. Given this, it is more useful to look at GFI statistics, which are less sensitive to large sample sizes. I include three of the most frequently used statistics: the Comparative Fit Index (CFI), the Root Mean Squared Error of the Approximation (RMSEA), and the Standard Root Mean squared Residual (SRMR). Hu and Bentler (1999) show that a two-index strategy, with an SRMR cutoff of .06, and either a CFI cutoff of .95 or an RMSEA cutoff of .05, is jointly sufficient to demonstrate good model fit. With these combinations of cutoffs in mind, all the models for the LAPOP data appear to have excellent fit; all RMSEA values are below .05, and all SRMR values are below .06. The two 2012 models have CFI values over .95, although the CFI for the 2006–2012 model is slightly below that figure. As this model still passes the SRMR/RMSEA test, I still consider it to have at least acceptable fit.

The statistics for the ANES models are not as unambiguously supportive. Model 1 is exactly at the cutoff point, while Model 2 is slightly above. This seems to result from the fact that several indicators of regime support, which tend to emphasize things such as waste of tax dollars, are highly correlated with indicators of regime performance. Although Model 2 appears to have only acceptable, rather than "good" fit, I include it as a robustness check in structural analyses because of aforementioned concerns about other measures of RBE.

The GFI statistics also allow for comparison between similar models, specifically the two models for the 2012 wave LAPOP data and the two ANES models. The statistics clearly show that the reduced 2012 model fits the data better than the full model. This is likely due to the fact that the excluded indicators, while loading significantly on the latent factors, contain a larger proportion of random error than do the other indicators. For example, the latent performance factor explains only 14.1 percent of the variation in the evaluation of the economy indicator, and only 17.3 percent of the variance in the satisfaction with democracy indicator, compared with 35.9 percent to 69 percent of the variation of the other performance indicators. Generally, the evidence supports the use of the reduced model for the 2012 LAPOP data. For the ANES data, the GFI statistics are quite close for both models, but suggest that the full model fits the data slightly better. However, as the reduced ANES model allows for a robustness check of measurement issues, both are used in the structural analysis, to which I now turn.

4.3.4 Analysis of Structural Models

The results from the estimation of the measurement models show that the indicators used are valid. With this shown, I turn to analysis of the relationships between the latent concepts, which are the main subject of this chapter. To estimate the parameters specified in Equation 4.10, I specify a multilevel fixed-effects model, with observations nested within country-years to account for nonindependence of observations (Allison, 2009). The inclusion of country-year-level errors also controls for the idiosyncratic effects of those country-years, in a manner equivalent to a model with country-year dummy variables. All model parameters were estimated using maximum likelihood with standard errors that are robust to nonnormality and violations of independence of observations (MLR), with missing values. This method does not require specifying a model of missing-ness, but allows the likelihood function to be constructed observation by observation, using whatever information is available (unless all exogenous variables are missing) (Allison, 2012).

The interaction between performance and efficacy was estimated using the Latent Moderated Structural Equation (LMS) method employed by the canned procedure in Mplus (Klein & Moosbrugger, 2000; Klein & Muthén, 2007). This method is, owing to its direct treatment of nonnormality under latent interaction, likely the most precise method of estimating such relationships (Kline, 2011, pp. 346–347).

LAPOP Models

Results from the estimation of the LAPOP data are presented in Table 4.5; estimates of the measurement model parameters were very similar to those presented earlier and are thus omitted here for brevity. As with the measurement model, the structural model included eighteen countries, each of which had four waves (except Argentina, which had only three), leaving seventy-one country-year clusters.

Before discussing specific parameter estimates, model fit must be evaluated. A poorly fitting model must be rejected as a whole, or its poor fit explained and justified, before looking at any specific component of the model. At first glance, all models seem to fit poorly; none of them pass the two-index strategy discussed earlier. The GFI statistics for the measurement models indicated good fit, meaning that the problems presented here seem to stem from the structural model.

All of these GFI statistics impose some penalty for including irrelevant parameters. This is due to the fact that all of these statistics improve as the number of free parameters increases, regardless of whether those parameters have any explanatory power. As Table 4.5 shows, many of the control variables are not statistically different from zero. These irrelevant factors are a likely source of poor model fit. To test this, I estimated new models that excluded all independent variables with coefficients that were not statistically significant. All three models pass the two-index strategy with these reductions. The 2012 models pass both the SRMR/RMSEA and SRMR/CFI tests; the 2006–2012 model passes the first and nearly passes the second. This demonstrates conclusively that poor model fit is due to the control variables. I continue to use the full models throughout, because the included variables are standard in public opinion research and their omission would raise concerns of omitted variable bias. Since the poor fit is clearly the result of parsimony penalties, rather than more serious forms of misspecification, I accept the models and move on to analysis of specific parameter estimates.

Table 4.5: *Structural model results, LAPOP analysis*

Regime Support	2006–2012 (n = 119,077)			2012, Full (n = 29,256)			2012, Reduced (n = 29,256)		
	Estimate	SE	P-value	Estimate	SE	P-value	Estimate	SE	P-value
Regime performance	0.125	0.016	0.000	0.116	0.033	0.000	0.194	0.029	0.000
RBE (Perceived citizen autonomy)	0.331	0.015	0.000	0.345	0.034	0.000	0.240	0.026	0.000
Interaction term (Performance * RBE)	−0.048	0.005	0.000	−0.032	0.007	0.000	−0.026	0.007	0.000
Income	−0.005	0.004	0.166	−0.013	0.006	0.039	−0.011	0.005	0.043
Goods owned	−0.002	0.005	0.648	−0.003	0.009	0.734	−0.005	0.008	0.556
Education	0.013	0.004	0.002	0.007	0.008	0.378	0.008	0.008	0.316
Female	0.027	0.004	0.000	0.030	0.010	0.002	0.032	0.010	0.002
Age	0.025	0.003	0.000	0.024	0.00	0.000	0.027	0.007	0.000
Urban	−0.031	0.006	0.000	−0.027	0.011	0.014	−0.032	0.011	0.006
Ideology	0.010	0.005	0.058	0.002	0.012	0.874	0.016	0.012	0.181
Race	0.000	0.003	0.971	0.001	0.014	0.965	0.000	0.014	0.999
Between-level residual variance	0.130	0.007	0.000	0.154	0.012	0.000	0.180	0.013	0.000

Table 4.5: (*cont.*)

Goodness of Fit Statistics	Full, 2006–2012	No Controls, 2006–2012	Full, 2012 Full	No controls, 2012 Full
Chi-Square	24,210	3592.7	7987	2084.7
RMSEA	0.036	0.020	0.034	0.022
CFI	0.600	0.939	0.787	0.957
SMR	0.057	0.033	0.050	0.030

GFI statistics are not available for SEMs with latent interactions. GF statistics presented here are for models with interaction terms omitted. All Chi-square tests were statistically significant.

The parameters of most interest here are the coefficients for regime support regressed on regime performance, RBE, and the interaction term. Both performance and RBE have coefficient estimates that are significantly different from zero. In all three models, the effect of RBE is greater than that of performance by a significant margin. The magnitude of the effect is quite large. Both latent predictors have fixed variances of one; the dependent latent factor is fixed to the scale of systemic pride, which is standardized (along with all other indicators) to avoid estimation problems arising from wide disparities in the variances of observed indicators. Thus the dependent variable also has unit variance. This means that a unit increase in RBE produces an increase of .35, .351, and .25 in support in the multi-wave, 2012 full, and 2012 reduced models, respectively. In other words, if one considers the empirically realistic scale of a standard variable to be -3 to 3, then a move from RBE's realistic minimum to its realistic maximum would produce a change in support of 25 to 35 percent of its realistic scale. The effect of performance, while smaller, is still substantively significant, ranging from .112 to .186. This is consistent with the hypothesized impact of both RBE and performance on regime support.

The theory developed in Chapter 3 suggests that the impact of RBE on support is not confined only to its direct effect, but also includes its moderation of the impact of performance. As the interaction term is statistically detectable, the interaction must be taken into account when evaluating H1. This interactive effect is presented graphically in Figure 4.3. The graphs show the effect magnitude of the independent variable named at the top of the graph, with its values arrayed along the y-axis. This magnitude depends on the value of the other variable, arrayed along the x-axis. The curved lines are the confidence intervals of the overall effect. The dotted vertical lines represent the "zone of insignificance"; the range of values of the moderating variable between which the other variable's effect is not statistically distinguishable from zero.

The coefficient estimate of the interaction term is statistically significant and, as expected, negative. If an individual rates one factor

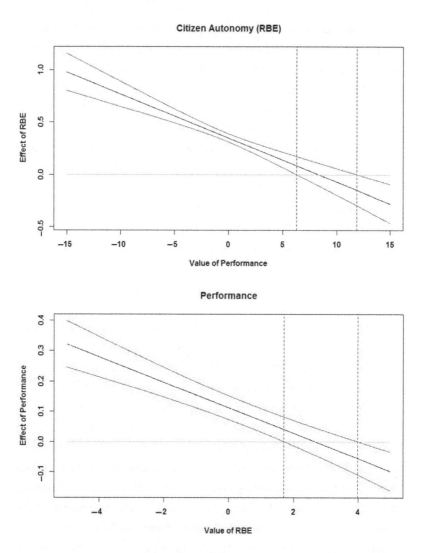

FIGURE 4.3: Interactive effects of RBE and performance on regime support, multi-wave model

highly, the other ceases to matter as much; indeed if RBE is high the effect of performance on support is essentially null. On the other hand, if a respondent is highly critical on one dimension, the rating on the other becomes critically important for determining support.

RBE, when rated very highly, can "turn off" the effect of performance evaluations entirely. The reverse is not true; positive evaluations of policy outputs can reduce the impact of RBE, but cannot entirely nullify it. As shown in Figure 4.1, performance must be more than five standard deviations above its mean for the impact of RBE to be potentially nullified (within the zone of insignificance), while the impact of performance is potentially zero with RBE at just under two standard deviations above the mean.

This result holds regardless of sample or indicators used, although both the direct and moderating effects are somewhat more modest in the 2012 reduced model. Yet even at its most modest, the estimated total effect of performance decreases from .261 to .111 as RBE moves from its lowest point (three standard deviations below its mean) to its highest (three standard deviations above), cutting the effect of performance by 57.4 percent.

These results largely hold, even if the model is restricted to the cases of interest (Chile and Venezuela) individually, rather than tested with regional data. Given the very general psychological theory from which these relationships are derived, there is no reason to believe that RBE and performance would impact support differently in either of these countries. Nevertheless it is better to test than to assume, and so Table 4.6 presents estimations of the 2006–2012 model applied sequentially to Chile and Venezuela.

These results closely match those for the regional data. In terms of the attitudinal structure of regime support, Chile and Venezuela seem to be quite typical of Latin America.

ANES Models

As mentioned earlier, some concerns over whether the indicators used for RBE actually measure the concept in question remain. Specifically these questions are worded in such a way that they measure responsiveness as well as RBE (Kölln et al., 2013). Additionally the specific mention of parties in some questions raises the possibility that attitudes toward parties, rather than beliefs about efficacy, are

Table 4.6: *Structural model results, Chile and Venezuela 2006–2012*

Regime Support	Chile (n = 6,580)			Venezuela (n = 6,010)		
	Est	SE	P-value	Est	SE	P-value
Regime performance	0.205	0.027	0.000	0.235	0.027	0.000
RBE	0.332	0.021	0.000	0.288	0.027	0.000
Interaction (RBE * Performance)	−0.092	0.009	0.000	−0.050	0.005	0.000
Income	−0.005	0.011	0.673	0.002	0.009	0.859
Goods owned	−0.018	0.011	0.089	0.005	0.008	0.521
Education	−0.024	0.010	0.023	−0.008	0.008	0.334
Female	0.016	0.016	0.298	0.016	0.013	0.214
Age	0.028	0.009	0.001	0.021	0.007	0.002
Urban	−0.033	0.026	0.199	−0.034	0.029	0.236
Ideology	0.008	0.009	0.392	−0.036	0.009	0.000
Race	−0.028	0.007	0.000	0.008	0.008	0.267
2008 dummy	−0.162	0.029	0.000	0.260	0.024	0.000
2010 dummy	−0.146	0.024	0.000	0.068	0.019	0.000
2012 dummy	−0.147	0.032	0.000	0.065	0.018	0.000

Measurement model structure is the same as for region-wide multi-wave model; estimates of measurement model parameters were very similar to those for the region-wide model, and thus are omitted here for brevity.

driving the results. As a robustness check against these issues, I also analyzed ANES data using the same model structure as used for the LAPOP data. Results of these analyses are presented in Table 4.7.

The results from analysis of ANES data are similar to those obtained from analysis of the LAPOP data. Both performance and RBE have coefficient estimates that are significantly different from zero, and the interaction is negative and significant in all models. Yet for these models the effect of performance is larger than that of RBE. This may be due to real differences in the effect size based on region, but it is likely attributable at least in part to the indicators for support

Table 4.7: *Structural model results, ANES data*

Regime Support (n = 10,356)	Model 1 (n = 18,147)			Model 2 (n = 18,147)			Model 3 (n = 15,673)		
	Est	SE	P-value	Est	SE	P-value	Est	SE	P-value
Regime performance	1.231	0.055	0.000	1.274	0.056	0.000	6.668	0.295	0.000
RBE	0.674	0.042	0.000	0.694	0.051	0.000	0.465	0.024	0.000
Interaction (Performance * RBE)	−0.158	0.024	0.000	−0.148	0.029	0.000	−0.262	0.100	0.009
Income	−0.094	0.018	0.000	−0.077	0.020	0.000	−0.060	0.020	0.002
Education	−0.069	0.019	0.000	−0.005	0.020	0.786	0.035	0.019	0.063
Female	−0.021	0.027	0.429	−0.013	0.029	0.648	−0.041	0.029	0.155
Age	0.020	0.017	0.232	0.010	0.018	0.586	0.047	0.020	0.017
Ideology	−0.018	0.012	0.137	−0.025	0.013	0.049	−0.028	0.013	0.037
White dummy	−0.139	0.062	0.025	−0.096	0.066	0.147	−0.064	0.067	0.339
African-American dummy	−0.125	0.081	0.123	−0.115	0.088	0.191	−0.087	0.091	0.339
Hispanic dummy	0.334	0.070	0.000	0.370	0.077	0.000	0.400	0.084	0.000
Residual variance	0.360	0.084	0.000	0.323	0.091	0.000	0.452	0.128	0.000

available in the ANES data. Several, including questions about wasting tax dollars and whether all politicians are crooked, are much more utilitarian than the more neutral indicators included in the LAPOP data. An in-depth examination of these possibilities is outside the scope of this dissertation, which focuses on Latin America. These data are intended to determine if the results of the LAPOP analysis are adversely impacted by the peculiarities of the RBE indicators in that survey; the fact that all three ANES models, including that which does not mention political actors at all, produce similar results suggests that one can have confidence in the LAPOP results in spite of the imperfect RBE measures.

5 Participatory Populism

Hegemony, Self-Governance, and
Regime Support in Bolivarian Venezuela

The framework developed in Chapter 3 and tested in Chapter 4 is just that: a framework. It provides a skeleton on which theories of support may be built; actual theories of support in specific cases must descend the ladder of abstraction, taking into account the idiosyncratic details of the cases they seek to explain. In this chapter, wherein I attempt to explain Venezuela's surprisingly high levels of support under the rule of Chávez, two apparently contradictory features of the institutional environment stand out as potentially crucial. The first is the plethora of participatory programs that have been initiated by the Bolivarian regime, as mentioned in Chapter 3 and elaborated upon later in this chapter. Given the preceding discussion of the importance of participatory opportunities, and the sense of efficacy and control they engender, the relevance of these programs should be clear. Here we have a potential explanation of regime support that comports nicely with the analytical framework used in this book.

The second institutional feature to which I alluded earlier complicates any argument that relies on participatory opportunities and citizen empowerment to explain support in Venezuela. Bolivarian Venezuela is hardly the ideal participatory state envisioned by Rousseau, Pateman, and Barber. While participatory self-governance may have proliferated at the local level, national politics are another matter entirely. The initial phase of the Bolivarian Revolution (roughly 1999–2005) did represent an opening of a previously elitist political system, with Chávez's rise occurring alongside that of a plethora of social organizations, newly independent as the iron grip of the *Punto Fijo* parties waned. Yet after Chávez's landslide victory (due in part to the abstention of the opposition) in 2006, the political system once again began to close. The concentration of power in the executive branch (and in the hands of the president especially), and the erosion of representative institutions and mechanisms of horizontal accountability have been the predominant features of the *chavista* regime at the national level since that time. This is part of the reason why this book focuses on the period from 2006 until Chávez's death: it is at this time that the discrepancy between support, performance, and even basic adherence to democratic norms depart from one another the most.

This contradiction of practices makes my analytical task much more challenging. Any incautious application of a participatory democratic framework, focusing on the empowerment of citizens as the primary causal variable, runs headlong into the reality of creeping authoritarianism at the level where the most consequential decisions are made. How can local level empowerment, however real, overcome the diminishment of representative institutions and competitive politics? The contradiction also exacerbates a perpetual difficulty in the analysis of other aspects of populist regimes: how can one reconcile their participatory tendencies with their hegemonic ambitions?

Both of these are core features of populism, but most analysts highlight one characteristic as the "true" nature of the concept, while discounting the other as an aberration or illusion. Approaches that see populism as a form of radical or participatory democracy emphasize the participatory nature of self-governance programs, while downplaying the role of the leader. Conversely, theoretical frameworks that define populism as personalistic, unmediated leadership (what I referred to earlier as personalism) see the authority of the leader as the sole source of support for populist regimes. As a result, they view participatory programs as little more than instruments of clientelism or other forms of social control. These one-sided assessments leave a number of questions unanswered: are self-governance programs sponsored by populist regimes truly participatory? If so, why would leaders who seek to centralize power in their own hands devolve power in some circumstances? And how do the regimes populists construct manage to maintain support, when their promises of empowerment seem to produce such limited mechanisms for citizens to influence politics? In order to answer these questions, we need a thorough analysis of how participatory fora function within the institutional environment of the Bolivarian system as a whole. Such an analysis must examine both the internal dynamics of these programs, and their interaction with other regime institutions and political actors. By so doing, I show how local participatory self-governance can dramatically enhance regime support, even amidst a crisis of governance and the erosion of representative democracy.

In this chapter, I challenge the assumption that populist tactics of power concentration and popular empowerment are theoretically irreconcilable. Instead, I chart a course between participatory democratic views of populism (e.g. Laclau, 2005; Laclau & Mouffe, 1985) and the cynical view of populism as demagoguery embraced by liberals (e.g. Riker, 1988). I argue that personalistic hegemony, charismatic attachment, and genuine participatory governance are all part of a single, unified political strategy that populists use to legitimate their regimes.

Participatory programs are a novel solution to an intrinsic problem of populism, defined as a political strategy wherein a leader wins support by promising to end the political exclusion of the masses. However, when the time comes to make good on these commitments, a problem arises: any power the leaders concede to their supporters is necessarily lost to themselves. Populists cannot afford to diminish their own authority, because the diversity and weak social roots of most populist coalitions require strong leadership to adjudicate disputes between factions and maintain unity. Yet they must find some way to demonstrate in a concrete manner their commitment to their followers; if they fail to do so, the charismatic attachments on which they rely will inevitably fade. The necessity of maintaining hegemony while empowering the masses places populists between a rock and a hard place. If they concede too much power, they risk fracturing the cohesion of their movements and thus threaten their political survival; if they concede too little, the masses will lose faith in their promises and the regime will lose legitimacy. I call this tension the populist's dilemma.

While all populists face this dilemma, solutions vary from case to case, but all involve a similar balancing act: participation must be granted, but in a form that does not threaten or diminish the dominance of the populist. Participatory programs allow populists to meet their commitment to empowering their supporters, and thus maintain legitimacy, especially among the true believers. These augmentations in participation need not be epic in actual scope. The grandiose rhetoric of the populist and the actual provision of participatory opportunities are mutually reinforcing. Opportunities for self-governance lend verisimilitude to the populist's claims to empower the people. Simultaneously, the populist's assertion that he or she seeks to usher in a new kind of politics based on the restoration of sovereignty to the people imbues these programs with greater meaning and importance than their limited nature would otherwise provide.

In addition, the organizations that sprout up or gather around these programs can provide much-needed support for mobilization during times of crisis. Yet strict limits are placed on these programs to ensure that they cannot challenge the populist. First, they are constrained to the local level; this confinement to a small scale and concrete policy issues ensures that they do not threaten the leader's national predominance. In addition, access to these programs is preferentially provided to regime supporters, inducing them to remain loyal to the leader. I call this strategy for resolving the populist's dilemma, wherein genuine participation at the local level serves to legitimate and reinforce hegemony at the national level, participatory populism. To restate in terms of the framework developed in Chapter 3, participatory populism provides locally bounded participatory opportunities to give citizens a sense of empowerment, while reducing the role of citizens at the national level through the erosion of representation. In combination with populist rhetoric and the intense emotional ties between the populist and his or her followers, supporters perceive this limited *de facto* empowerment as a significant increase in their political role, leading to increased legitimacy. This support manifests both in survey data and in the behavior of regime supporters as they mobilize to defend the populist project during times of threat.

This chapter proceeds in three sections. In Section 5.1, I briefly discuss existing approaches to the study of mass organization under populist regimes, and lay out the logic behind the populist's dilemma, which occurs due to the contradiction between the need to maintain legitimacy and the hegemonic tactics necessary to keep populist coalitions together. There are three competing approaches that can be used to interpret this dilemma: personalistic populism (personalism hereafter, for brevity), participatory democracy, and participatory populism (which combines participatory opportunities with charismatic attachment to a dominant leader). Each theory proposes distinct answers to the following questions: do participatory fora actually provide ordinary citizens an active role in making decisions that affect them? If so, are these fora independent, or is loyalty to the populist coalition a prerequisite for them to function? And finally, and most relevant to the current question, how do these programs build or reflect support for populist regimes?

In Section 5.2, I focus on the communal councils (CCs), participatory community development programs that act as umbrella organizations for civil society in a given locality, to put these competing theories to the test. I find that in both design and practice these programs conform to neither participatory democracy nor personalism. The councils do provide genuine opportunities for participatory self-management at the local level, thus allowing the regime to keep its promises of empowerment. But because these opportunities are more available to regime supporters, they also reinforce Bolivarian hegemony at the national level by strengthening the ties between the regime and civil society. These findings are drawn from public opinion data and secondary analysis of an extensive body of qualitative analysis on this topic, and from discussions with experts on the topic and my own interviews.

The extent to which programs like the councils meet objective standards of participatory self-governance is an important question. Populist regimes do not rise and fall on academic evaluations; the *perceptions* of supporters and militants are what truly matter. Whereas a great deal of qualitative work exists on this topic, quantitative analysis of the role participatory programs play in shaping public opinion, especially regime support, is extremely limited. Determining whether or not the participatory features of these programs help to legitimate populist regimes is an important question for adjudicating between theoretical approaches. In Section 5.3, I use public opinion data collected from the 2010 and 2012 waves of the LAPOP survey to test predictions generated by participatory democracy, personalism, and participatory populist frameworks regarding the relationship between the councils and support for the Bolivarian state. The results are consistent only with those hypotheses derived from the participatory populist framework.

5.1 THE POPULIST'S DILEMMA: POPULAR EMPOWERMENT AND POWER CONCENTRATION

Although this chapter focuses on how participatory programs might foster support within a populist regime, I begin by examining competing views of why populists would sponsor such programs. As I will show, the theoretical approaches see distinct motivations, and each of these motivations have deducible implications for the relationship between participatory opportunities and support for populist regimes. The theoretical divide in the literature on participatory programs in populist regimes can be distilled into a single question: why would populists sponsor participatory fora? Analysts who view populism through a radical or participatory democratic framework (e.g. Laclau, 2005; Laclau & Mouffe, 1985) generally see populism as fundamentally democratic (if somewhat illiberal), and thus take these programs at face value. They assume that these programs embody a genuine commitment to popular empowerment (e.g. Ellner, 2011; Wilpert, 2005, 2011).

Those who view populism as the domination of the masses by a single charismatic individual (e.g. Corrales, 2010, 2011b, 2014; Corrales & Penfold, 2015; De la Torre, 2010; Weyland, 2001) paint a far less rosy picture. Any "inclusionary" measures undertaken by such regimes are seen as little more than cynical attempts to divert the energies of the populace away from challenging the authority of the populist. Analysts who use this framework when studying participatory programs see them as either vehicles for clientelism (Álvarez & García-Guadilla, 2011; García-Guadilla, 2008), ways to circumvent representative institutions (McCoy, 2006), or mechanisms for enforcing loyalty at the grassroots (Corrales, 2011a, 2014).

Neither approach can satisfactorily answer the question stated earlier, as each is confronted with factors it cannot explain. The significant expansion of opportunities for participation these programs grant makes little sense within a personalistic framework, which views hegemony as the only goal of populist leaders. Participatory and radical democrats, in turn, cannot account for the dependence of these programs on the populist or their preferential treatment of groups that support the populist. A comprehensive explanation of the logic of participatory governance under populism requires a new analytical approach.

5.1.1 The Populist's Dilemma: Hegemony and Control in Populist Regimes

My analytical framework begins with a definition of populism that is inspired by two sources. First, I concur with Weyland (2001) that populism is best understood as a political strategy that leaders use to gain popular support. While Weyland emphasizes the unmediated, disorganized aspects of populist rule, I focus instead on the tendency of these leaders to divide society into two camps. Existing definitions of populism tend to emphasize the delineation of society into the wholly good people and an evil elite that has usurped the people's rightful sovereignty (Canovan, 1999; Hawkins, 2010; Mudde & Rovira Kaltwasser, 2013). These definitions have some serious limitations, not the least of which the puzzle of why an ideology or discourse that so loathes elites would be so prone to coalesce around dominant leaders. Given this, I modify this definition slightly, positing that the core feature of the populist worldview is the division of society into haves and have-nots, where what is either possessed or lacked is access to political power. This is similar to the framework developed by Laclau (Laclau, 1977, 2005), which focuses more on antagonism to power than on Manichean morality, but it refines it slightly by placing the state, and particularly the political regime, at the center of populist grievances. In other words, access to the political system creates a fundamental cleavage that shapes social conflict as much as race or class.

This definition pertains to a worldview (what Mudde and Rovira Kaltwasser (2013) refer to as a "thin ideology"), but can easily be extended to political tactics used by leaders. So modified, populism becomes a political strategy wherein a leader propagates a populist worldview, courting the masses by promising to end their political exclusion. Latin America's stark inequalities and incomplete democratization have made this an attractive strategy throughout the region's history. Yet the equally recurring instability of these movements demonstrates the inherent tension that exists when ambitious leaders promise to empower neglected segments of society to win power for themselves. By bringing previously excluded citizens into the political system, these leaders are able to gain power that would otherwise be unattainable. Once in power, they need the active support of their popular bases to survive elite counterattacks (Roberts, 2006). Without a mobilized base, Juan Perón would have likely languished in prison in 1945 (De la Torre, 2010, p. 24; James, 1988, pp. 185–186) and Chávez would not have regained the presidency after being overthrown in 2002 (Hawkins & Hansen, 2006, p. 102).

This dependence on the masses can weaken the authority of the populist, and thus threaten his or her political survival. Increasing access to the state can raise expectations of more substantive empowerment, which can quickly spiral out of the populist's control. Radical movements often rise to challenge the limitations of incorporation within a populist coalition and to demand more autonomy for their favored constituencies (James, 1988, pp. 10–11; Spalding, 1977, pp. 187–191). Even if populists were inclined to grant these demands, the diversity of populist movements would preclude such largesse. Unified only by prior exclusion, populist coalitions tend to be exceptionally diverse, aggregating many groups with conflicting interests. Lacking institutionalized methods of conflict management, only the personal authority of the populist can settle disputes (Spalding, 1977). Just as the populist depends on the people, "the people" in turn depend on the personal authority and charisma of the populist to prevent the devolution of the movement into internecine struggle. In sum, populists must balance two contradictory requirements: the need to empower their base on one hand, and the need to maintain control of that base on the other. I refer to this tension as the populist's dilemma. This dilemma flows directly from the contradictory imperatives of ending political exclusion while maintaining the hegemony of a single individual.

5.1.2   Solutions to the Populist's Dilemma: Functional Incorporation and Participatory Populism

While this dilemma plagues populism generally, solutions to it vary from case to case, depending upon the structure of exclusion to which each populist reacts. Although this paper focuses on contemporary populism, a brief discussion of the dilemma and its solutions under classical populists shows the general relevance of the populist's dilemma and provides a useful baseline for comparison.

Contemporary populists must craft new strategies for escaping the populist's dilemma because the structure of exclusion is fundamentally different from that faced by classical populists in two primary ways. First, the political exclusion to which classical populists reacted was far more severe. The classical populists generally predated the incorporation of poorer citizens into the formal political system

(Germani, 1978, p. 102). Activism outside of the institutional political processes (such as labor organization, unionization, and strikes) was frequently met with brutal repression (James, 1988, p. 171). In this context, even modest expansions of participatory opportunities could be powerful. Second, the era of classical populism coincided with the ascendance of an organized working class, which provided both opportunities and risks for leaders who could gain control over the nascent labor movement.

Reacting to these two factors, Perón in Argentina (Germani, 1978; James, 1988), Vargas and Goulart in Brazil (Spalding, 1977), and Cárdenas in Mexico (Middlebrook, 1995) resolved their dilemmas by granting the working class access to the political system through state-approved unions, reversing the repression and neglect that had characterized earlier periods, while creating new forms of control. Unionization expanded, labor demands regarding wages and working conditions were taken seriously (if not always met), union members were elected to legislatures, and relations between labor and the state became relatively cordial (James, 1988, p. 25). But these populists also marginalized more radical, autonomous labor leaders, and used state control over union funding and legal recognition to ensure that the workers' movement remained subordinate to populist authority. While the level of empowerment under classical populists like Perón is a controversial topic, especially considering their imposition of new forms of control, these regimes represented a clear expansion of the political role of ordinary citizens.

While functional or corporatist incorporation worked for the classical populists, it is far less viable in present-day Latin America. Contemporary populists react not to competitive oligarchy but to the shortcomings of liberal representative democracy. They must make their appeals to a populace that has had formal political rights for decades, and where social groups (such as organized labor) have often been incorporated through previous populist movements or political parties. In this context, previously utilized populist tactics are unlikely to be viewed as genuinely empowering, and massive, nation-wide social organizations are largely unavailable.[1] Contemporary populists must instead rely on one of the most difficult sectors of Latin American society to organize: the urban popular sector, i.e. those involved in the informal economy. And they must make their appeals in an environment where corporatist and liberal democratic inclusionary mechanisms have been tried and found wanting, reducing the populist's toolkit still further.

In short, modern populists cannot incorporate citizens along functional or corporatist lines; they must find novel forms of empowerment in order to give their appeals credibility. In this context, local-level participatory governance is an attractive alternative solution to the populist's dilemma. Participatory governance grants citizens not merely a voice in politics, but the ability to make some decisions directly. Yet these programs are inherently limited in scope to small communities due to the difficulty of enacting macro-level participatory governance. As a result, their policy domain is confined mostly to basic-needs issues and community development. In other words, modern populists can legitimate their claims of empowerment by granting opportunities for direct citizen participation in policy-making, without the need to employ heavy-handed methods of control. Such methods are unnecessary because the policy domains of such programs are by their very nature constrained; participatory fora do not touch highly contentious national issues. And such programs often provide new avenues for populists to reinforce their follower's loyalty, much as corporatist incorporation did for an earlier generation of populists. As I show later, access to participatory opportunities is granted preferentially to regime supporters, and the organizations that coalesce around these programs are expected to mobilize to defend the regime during periods of crisis.

The preceding discussion suggests that populists likely do offer genuine participatory opportunities, even if tightly constrained and controlled. Yet these opportunities are not granted out of altruism or

---

[1] Bolivia, with its large and powerful indigenous movement, is a partial exception.

any ideological commitment to participatory democracy, even if the populist in question genuinely values them. As will become clear, I believe that Chávez's commitment to deepening democracy was sincere, but his behavior and choices were often driven more by necessity than ideology. In the end it matters little what the populist truly believes; actions are what matter. And these programs, whether granted full or only partial cynicism, are most important in their function as strategic concessions, made by populists in order to ensure their survival and maintain their authority at the national level. These programs allow populists to devolve power, thus meeting their commitments to empowerment and preserving the legitimacy of their regimes. I call this strategy, where local level participatory governance is provided to legitimate national level populist hegemony, participatory populism. It is an example of a charismatic attachment by followers to leader, which is reinforced by a particular form of participation, even as those forms of participation and representation that pertain to national politics erode. This erosion is tolerated because of the trust and loyalty that followers have for the populist; both of which would not survive long without genuine empowerment at the local level to back them up.

Summary

We now have three frameworks through which to analyze participatory programs in populist regimes, and how such programs affect citizen support for those regimes: personalism, participatory democracy, and participatory populism. All three theories propose answers to the three questions raised in the introduction, as summarized in Table 5.1.

Personalism emphasizes the unmediated connection of the masses and the leader as the primary source of support for populist regimes, and thus argue that political attitudes in the presence of such a leader are nearly exclusively driven by attitudes toward the populist. As such, arguments based on personalism would answer "no" to all three questions. Participatory democracy, which

Table 5.1: *Theoretical predictions*

| | | Theory/Approach | |
Question	Personalism	Participatory Democracy	Participatory Populism
1. Do populist regimes grant genuine participatory opportunities?	No	Yes	Yes
2. Are those opportunities a crucial source of regime support?	No	Yes	Yes
3. Are those opportunities granted in a way that develops autonomous civil society?	No	Yes	No

emphasizes bottom-up empowerment, would give the opposite answers, but would have difficulty grappling with the presence of such a single, nigh omnipotent individual. The idea that the "volonté générale" could be divined and embodied by such an individual, rather than constructed by the polity itself, is antithetical to true participatory democracy. The immediate manifestation of this tension would be a failure to explain various ways, to be described presently, that such participatory fora are used for the benefit of the populist, rather than citizens.

Participatory populism agrees with participatory democracy on the first two, and personalism on the last. These predictions (which I specify in Sections 5.2 and 5.3) can be tested with quantitative and qualitative data to determine which most closely conforms to those data. From this point forward, I focus on Venezuela under Chávez, certainly the most prominent and influential instance of populism in contemporary Latin America.

5.1.3 Participatory Populism and the Bolivarian Revolution

A brief review of the history of Chávez's rise to power and the ideology of his movement shows close adherence to participatory populism. It is difficult to write anything on the topic of Chávez without generating a firestorm of controversy. Even the *origins* of the Bolivarian movement are disputed: some see it as a weakly organized collection of civil society organizations with which elements of the military joined (Ciccariello-Maher, 2013), while others see its military faction as its driving force. Although civil society groups certainly existed, and were becoming increasingly active as Venezuela's political system began to collapse, I find persuasive the view that the Bolivarian movement originated within the Venezuelan military as a reaction to endemic corruption, rampant poverty, and the state's inability to meet the challenges that arose during the economic crises of the early 1980s. The political system of this era (called the *Punto Fijo* system, after the pact that formed it) was formally democratic, but its claim to legitimacy was based more on the regularity of competitive elections and the distribution of oil rents than on any true adherence to popular sovereignty (Hellinger, 2003). Authority was tightly held by a small number of elites within the system's dominant parties (Coppedge, 1994), and the mass bases of the parties had a largely subordinate role that did little to genuinely empower average citizens (Ellner, 2003a, 2003b).

With the arrival of the debt crisis of the early 1980s and subsequent fluctuations in the price of oil, this system of rent distribution became unsustainable and eventually imploded. Although these factors certainly put enormous pressure on the system, the breakdown of representative democracy in Venezuela can be only partly attributed to the recurrent economic crises that rocked the country from 1983 through the 1990s. The inability of the political system to absorb new demands generated by these crises destroyed the legitimacy of representative institutions, leading to massive social unrest (López Maya, 1999a) and the eventual collapse of the party system. The behavior of various leaders further contributed to the loss of faith in the ability of *puntofijismo* to enforce popular sovereignty. The lack of accountability and responsiveness was perhaps most clearly embodied when Carlos Andrés Pérez, a member of the center-left and statist AD, implemented a program of neoliberal structural adjustment shortly after running against such programs during the election of 1988 (López Maya, 1999a, pp. 212–214). This about-face was only the latest in a long line of perceived slights by *Punto Fijo* elites against popular opinion. It also signaled the beginning of the system's end; Pérez was the last President from either of the two parties that had dominated Venezuelan politics for over forty years. Ten years later, both *Acción Democrática* (AD) and the *Comité de Organización Política Electoral Independiente* (COPEI) were forced to give up any ambitions of regaining power with their own candidates, throwing their support to an outsider, Henrique Salas Römer.

One major change to the Venezuelan political system during the final days of *Punto Fijo* is relevant here: the development of a truly independent civil society. The *puntofijista* parties had long dominated virtually all social organizations of any relevance, especially the labor movement (Coppedge, 1994). Venezuela's vast oil wealth enabled this patronage network, which could be funded without the kind of extractive taxation that might have pushed elites out of the pact. In other words, Venezuela was the very definition of a rentier state, with all the attendant problems (Karl, 1987; Mommer, 2003), which in Venezuela included a state-owned oil company that was nevertheless difficult for the government to control and was thus an important political actor at key phases in the country' history. The collapse of Venezuela's economy that provoked the *caracazo* in 1989 (a series of massive riots over neoliberal structural adjustment, and a key turning point in Chávez's political thinking, as I discuss Section 5.1.3) caused immense pain in the population. Yet it also had consequences that were not nearly so negative. Neoliberal adjustment tends to wrench financial resources out of state hands, and whatever influence this may have on short- or long-term economic performance, it does compromise the ability of dominant parties to use public resources to maintain hegemonic control over civil society and the state (Greene, 2009).

The neoliberal reforms intended to rescue Venezuela's faltering economy also formed a classic opening of the political opportunity structure (Tarrow, 1998) by weakening the party patronage networks, thus freeing up space for activists to adopt a more confrontational role. As a result, civil society exploded: new social organizations rose up to demand state action on issues of housing, service deliverance, and other issues related to the appalling conditions in many of the country's *barrios*, conditions that had worsened in the aftermath of the economy's collapse (Cariola & Miguel, 2005; García-Guadilla, 2003; López Maya, 1999b; Lòpez Maya, 2001; Velasco, 2015). This was a drastic change from practices during the *Punto Fijo* era, where social organizations were adjuncts of the dominant parties and served primarily as connective tissue in the networks of patronage and clientelism the parties used to maintain their oligopoly. The breakdown of these networks also enabled the rise of new political parties, such as the leftist La Causa R (López Maya, 1997). These groups and movements would eventually form a key part of the Bolivarian movement, although most would eventually leave or surrender much of their independence to the founder of the movement's military faction and its undisputed symbol: Hugo Chávez Frias.

The Rise of the Bolivarian Revolution: Participation, Populism, and Contestation

Chávez, who came from extremely humble beginnings, had developed leftist leanings since his early youth (Jones, 2009). Over the course of his military career, he became increasingly disillusioned with the elitism and corruption of the *Punto Fijo* regime, deepening over time as the regime began its steady decline in the 1980s. Disillusionment turned to disgust and hatred in February of 1989, when President Carlos Andrés Pérez of the AD, after campaigning against neoliberal reform, instead adopted an IMF package of structural adjustment. This package included an elimination of gasoline subsidies, leading to drastic hikes in public transportation prices on the morning of February 27th. Almost immediately, tensions that had been building prior to that moment exploded into open rioting (López Maya, 1999a, 1999b; Lòpez Maya, 2003). The military was ordered by the same *politicos* who had caused the crisis to violently repress the insurrection. Chávez biographers (Gott, 2011, ch. 5–6; Jones, 2009, ch. 8) cite these events as a point of no return, after which Chávez and his compatriots would give the regime no quarter.

Chávez's first attempt to overthrow the oligarchy he so despised took the form of an attempted military coup in 1992. The coup landed *el comandante* in prison, but it had two major consequences on his future political career. The first, and most crucial, is that it made him a political star in Venezuela. Or, rather, his brief statement (intended to persuade his co-conspirators to surrender) did. In this statement, Chávez accepted responsibility for the coup's failure; this alone would have been stunning, given that Venezuela's political class enjoyed buck passing nearly as much as they enjoyed burgling the country's treasure. His now famous (or infamous) statement that the conspiracy had ended *por ahora* (for now) became a profoundly meaningful signifier instantaneously. Social organizations that had adopted a more critical stance in the wake of neoliberal adjustment would now have a banner under which they could rally; clearly there was an appetite for a figure who would throw out the oligarchs, by fair means or by foul. The second consequence was the beginning of Chávez's wariness and mistrust of the civilian contingent of the Bolivarian movement. Chávez seems to have blamed the collapse of the coup in part on the failure of civilian groups, particularly those organized by the nascent La Causa R movement, to turn up, although those groups dispute this version of events (Jones, 2009, ch. 10).

Chávez, released from prison due to popular pressure, was obviously aware of the opening discussed earlier. Sensing weakness, he abandoned armed insurrection in favor of electoral challenge, facing Römer (along with Irene Sáez, a former mayor of the well-to-do district of Chacao) in the 1998 presidential elections. All candidates attempted to mobilize voters around the banner of anti-elite resentment, with all running on anti-party platforms. Chávez's victory and rise to power can be attributed to two strategic sources: unwavering opposition to all elements of the partyarchy of the *Punto Fijo* era (Molina, 2006, p. 170) and the unification of excluded sectors under a single political banner (Myers, 2006, p. 13). In particular, his insistence on consigning not only the parties but also the constitution that supported their dominance, to the dustbin of history, in favor of a new system based upon principles of "participatory, protagonist democracy," aided his victory. Chávez's militant insistence on a new institutional framework resonated with an electorate that had become disillusioned by the inability of representative politics to bind elite decisions to the will of the people. Empowerment of the excluded is perhaps the central source of legitimacy for the Chávez regime; promises of political inclusion had to be fulfilled in order for the movement to survive. Once in power, the newly ascendant Bolivarians found, as have many politicians throughout history, that promises are far easier to make than to keep.

The First Phase of Bolivarian Rule (1999–2006): Excising the Oligarchy

Chavismo, like most populist movements, tended to cast the political exclusion around which they coalesce not as a problem to be resolved through politics as usual, but as the intentional design of an implacable elite foe determined to deprive the people of their rightful sovereignty. To the Bolivarians, steeped in resentment toward every aspect of the old regime, the "elite" included all those actors who had any significant role in the *Punto Fijo* party system. The "elite" or "oligarchy" so defined included not only the leaders of AD and COPEI, but also their largely subordinate social organizations, such as the national labor confederation, and in what was to become the first priority for the new government, the constitution that perpetuated the system. Destruction of *la oligarquía* and continuous struggle to prevent its return were seen as a necessary precondition for ending the exclusion of the masses. This theme is apparent in *chavista* rhetoric, which emphasizes movement unity and solidarity above all other concerns, lest the old elite take advantage of intra-factional conflict (Yepes, 2006, p. 251).

Concerns over infighting were more than justified. The Bolivarian coalition had included a wide variety of groups and social sectors. By basing his electoral appeal on resentment toward the crumbling party system, Chávez drew significant amounts of support at different times from the urban poor, intellectuals, the military, social movements, and even the private sector (McCoy & Myers, 2006, ch. 2–5). Clearly, these groups have many contradictory interests and historical antagonisms, but they unified around the promise to end their political marginalization, a unity that largely held during the drafting of the Bolivarian constitution, which was approved by the electorate in 1999. Yet once the initial task of bringing the new regime into being concluded, and the much less glamorous job of governing the country under the new rules began, cracks began to appear quickly. Populist movements are, in a sense, inherently self-defeating: victory destroys their primary point of grievance. The leftward tilt of Chávez's actual political platform immediately drove away those in the business sector and a substantial portion of the middle class that had initially supported the *Movimiento Quinta República* (MVR) (Corrales, 2011b, p. 75).

Latent conflicts were further exacerbated by the heavy-handed tactics seen as necessary for uprooting remaining traces of the *ancien régime*. Whatever the attitudes of Bolivarian elites, grassroots *chavistas* tend to be fully committed to the principle of a direct political role for the masses (Hawkins & Hansen, 2006; Ramírez, 2005). The tactics required by the drive to destroy all vestiges of the old system further eroded support for Chávez among those sectors who had been co-opted under *Punto Fijo* and for whom emancipation from party dominance was an especially potent draw. Chávez's need to maintain almost militaristic discipline, driven by his ambitious plans for the transformation of Venezuelan society, began to conflict with social organizations and activists who had awakened during the opening of the *Punto Fijo* system.

Chávez's opponents also share considerable blame for the polarization that escalated during the run up to the 2002 coup attempt. There were signs of trouble to which they could point to justify their intransigent refusal to accept the new President, chief among them the brief closure of the legislature and the courts by the constituent assembly tasked with drafting the new constitution. And although Chávez's rhetoric was certainly inflammatory ("rancid oligarchs" was a favorite phrase), what sprung forth from *el comandante's* notoriously loose lips was the most provocative element of the first phase of his rule. The constitution, produced by a national constituent assembly dominated by a coalition of *chavistas* and independent social organizations, was thoroughly democratic and almost uniquely participatory (although the powerful executive was some cause for concern, especially given its lengthy term of six years). Opponents, decrying the imminent loss of their civil liberties, constantly appeared on private television stations to openly call for the violent overthrow of the President. As many supporters, including Chávez biographer Bart Jones (2009, preface, paragraph 9) have pointed out, no advanced democracy would tolerate nightly demands for the removal by force of the government on national television. The fact that the opposition eventually (if ineptly and only briefly) made good on these threats demonstrates their gravity. Finally, we cannot ignore the role of the United States, whose President at the time enthusiastically embraced militaristic regime change and whose diplomatic personnel for Latin American affairs included a number of Regan-era cold warriors who saw in Chávez another Castro in the making. In this environment of bitter antagonisms and paranoia, each side tended to overreact to the provocations of the other, leading inexorably to a crisis. This downward spiral would eventually bring the first phase of Bolivarianism, characterized by Chávez's outsized role (which should have made any true democrat uncomfortable) but also by contestation over the new power dynamics, participation in crafting a new political system, and a genuine opening of the Venezuelan political system. This gave rise to the second phase of Chávez's rule, where the hegemony of the populist would gradually destroy the independence of civil society, and where participatory access came only through loyalty to Chávez.

Nowhere was this clearer than in the 2002 coup that briefly deposed Chávez, and the subsequent work stoppage of 2002–2003 and recall referendum of 2004. The protests that led to Chávez's short-term ouster and the effort to hoist Chávez on his own constitutional petard by recalling him from office were both led by a worker–business coalition, although which controlled the other is a matter of intense dispute. The lack of common interpretation even extends to the term used to describe the stoppage: opposition supporters favor "strike," which implies worker direction, while *chavistas* call it a lockout, reflecting their belief that management (i.e. "the elite") was the driving force. This odd political union was forged by *chavista* attempts to expand their influence in the national labor federation through a new labor law and union election procedures, and their attempts to bring the state-owned (but not controlled) oil company PDVSA to heel by firing most of the company's upper-level executives. In fairness to Chávez, PDVSA had a degree of autonomy that would not be tolerated by most states, and its upper-tier executives were actively attempting to undermine his government (Ellner, 2003b, pp. 170–173). The coalition was joined by those sections of civil society groups that were dissatisfied with *chavista* policy toward autonomous social movements (García-Guadilla, 2003, p. 181). A number of prominent intellectuals who had supported Chávez mostly out of antipathy toward the old oligarchy also parted company as the hegemonic tendencies of the regime became more apparent (Hillman, 2006). Even after the coup fell apart almost immediately, the opposition and *chavistas* each dug in for the next fight, which would come in the form of a 2004 recall initiative and which also failed.

Although the Bolivarian movement survived all this turmoil, it did not do so unscathed. Among less committed sectors, support for Chávez had cratered, leading to significant defections of both prominent elites and large swathes of the movement's popular base. Participatory protagonist democracy was difficult to reconcile with the movement's heavy-handed attempts to dominate independent civil society. When a movement that promises empowerment shows more interest in establishing hegemony over every aspect of society than in actually providing a meaningful political role for its core constituency, the result is inevitable: a major crisis of legitimacy is a foregone conclusion. Survey data from the period confirms this: regime legitimacy, measured by satisfaction with the way democracy works, reached its lowest ebb in 2004 (Latinobarómetro, 2008).

The Second Phase of Bolivarian Rule (2006–2013): Charismatic Attachment and Participatory Populism

And yet from this nadir, Chávez would rise again, in many ways stronger than ever. Immediately after the coup, the relationship between Chávez and civil society changed. The actual cause of the coup's disintegration is, unsurprisingly, a contentious issue. The fact that the interim President, Pedro Carmona Estanga, took the drastic step of shutting down all institutions of government (including congress and the courts) alienated many of the coup's supporters (Cannon, 2004, p. 296), who had justly criticized the constituent assembly for the same action. Chavez's supporters saw events quite differently. To them, Chávez's return to power happened because of their efforts, specifically the counter-protests that immediately followed the coup. One cannot help draw parallels to the liberation of Juan Perón from prison by throngs of adoring protesters. In their groundbreaking work on charismatic attachment, Madsen and Snow (1991) argue that the protests that led to Perón's freedom was the critical moment when the charismatic attachment between the populist and his followers truly formed. Of course Perón had supporters and admirers prior to those events, but with two differences. First, dramatic events where supporters rescue the populist from his enemies give the former an enormous sense of efficacy and power, the lack of which drives charismatic attachment in the first place. The second, equally crucial factor is that the power of the followers is not truly their own; it becomes fused and inextricably linked to the fortunes of the populist.

Such a bonding would explain why the role of independent but allied civil society declined after the coup and recall fiascos. The opposition was left grasping for any way to delegitimize a president they saw (with some evidence, but less than they believed) as an authoritarian demagogue. Citing controversies with the national elections commission during the recall (Hellinger, 2007) and other alleged irregularities, the opposition pulled out of the 2006 parliamentary elections at the last minute. The result was predictable: Chávez's MVR (as his electoral vehicle was known at the time) and allied parties took all seats in the legislature, leaving Chávez virtually unchecked. After handily winning reelection in 2006, Chávez simultaneously moved in two somewhat-contradictory directions. First, as described in subsequent paragraphs, he attempted to create more durable organizations among his base supporters. Second, he began pushing to expand his own authority, most notably by attempting to amend the constitution to allow indefinite reelection of the executive.

To summarize, the Bolivarian movement's commitment to expanding the political role of its constituents exists in constant tension with its not entirely unjustified paranoia. The movement's military origins shape this dynamic: supporters are seen as soldiers who must do their duty to protect the movement from omnipresent threats, and the struggle against the enemies of the people must take precedence over proactive inclusion of the masses. Meeting commitments of popular empowerment in this context is extremely tricky. Traditional institutions, such as political parties and elections, are unattractive mechanisms because they are marred by their association with the old regime. The situation is further complicated by the need for movement unity: any devolution of political power must be done in such a way that it does not ignite latent conflicts. And yet, it should be reemphasized, empowerment was not optional: the legitimacy of the Bolivarian regime, already tarnished by intense conflict and repeated power grabs, rested on it. In short, *chavismo* contained mutually contradictory drives that created what could be termed a populist's dilemma: the need to devolve power to maintain legitimacy, which coexists with the need to centralize power in order to eliminate the remnants of the old regime and maintain movement cohesion.

Overcoming the Populist's Dilemma: Organization and Attachment

The earliest participatory fora in Bolivarian Venezuela, in place as early as 2000, demonstrated a potential escape from this dilemma. As it waged its campaigns against the perceived enemies of the revolution at the national level, the Bolivarian movement was experimenting with a number of local-level organizations aimed at deepening ties with its popular base through the provision of participatory self-management. One of the earliest and most important of these were the Bolivarian Circles, which were formed in small cells of up to eleven individuals sworn to defend the Bolivarian Constitution and its principles, as well as serve their communities (Hawkins & Hansen, 2006, pp. 102–103). There is some dispute as to the grassroots bona fides of these organizations. Some scholars (López Maya, 2003) argue that the circles date from the post-coup aftermath of 1992, and rose mostly organically from the various social organizations that had risen up to challenge the *Punto Fijo* system in the wake of the *caracazo* and the attempted coup. Others (García-Guadilla, 2003; Hawkins & Hansen, 2006) argue that the circles were the result of deliberate encouragement by Chávez and the Bolivarian elite during the run-up to and aftermath of Chávez's brief expulsion from the presidency in 2002. What is clear is that, whatever their status before these events, the circles took on new importance as the possibility of extra-institutional political combat became more likely in the early 2000s.

As the opposition moved away from military options and toward the ballot box, the circles lost relevance. They were later replaced by Electoral Battle Units, which were responsible for contesting the 2004 recall (Hellinger, 2007).

Not all participatory organizations have their roots in the need to defend the Bolivarian Revolution from its opponents; some were designed to use participatory mechanisms to solve intractable social and economic problems, particularly those in Venezuela's *barrios* (shantytowns where most housing is self-help, analogous to the *favelas* of Brazil or the *poblaciones* of Chile). In 2002, Chávez issued a decree (in response to an earlier opposition demand for land titles for *barrio* residents) to form Urban Land Committees (CTUs) in groups of 100–200 families in the vast barrios of the country's cities, where (as in most large Latin American cities) self-help housing is the rule and many residents lack any legal rights to their property (Holland, 2006). The CTUs were organized as self-managed organizations responsible for drawing up maps of their communities to be submitted to the government, at which time individual families would be granted titles to their land. The CTUs also had broad discretion to address issues of community identity, strategies for improvement, and other community issues (García-Guadilla, 2011, p. 104). Other organizations, such as rural equivalents of the CTUs, Water Roundtables, and legally recognized cooperative associations, were also established during Chávez's first term (López Maya & Lander, 2011).

The potential of these organizations to reinforce the faltering Bolivarian movement became apparent during the response to the 2002 coup and the recall election of 2004. The Bolivarian Circles played a key role in organizing the protests that returned Chávez to power after his brief removal (Hawkins & Hansen, 2006, p. 102). The battle units, CTUs, and other organizations were extremely effective in mobilizing support for Chávez during the recall elections (García-Guadilla, 2011, pp. 94–98). These institutions proved capable of organizing large numbers of citizens from the popular groups, which the movement relied upon for support, even when the Bolivarian elite was in total disarray, as it was during the coup. That these organizations could be redirected toward defense of the revolution at times of extreme threat was no less important: as will be shown later, citizens involved in these organizations who might otherwise have preferred to maintain a focus on community issues felt compelled, either by a sense of duty or direct pressure from *chavista* elites, to do their part in defending the revolution in a time of peril.

Throughout the tumultuous period between the passage of the Bolivarian constitution and the movement's multiple existential crises through 2004, the drive to expand participation was undeniable, but was almost entirely reserved for the community level. This was no accident: devolution of power to local-level self-management organizations was a uniquely attractive tactic because it avoided many of the inherent risks that populist movements face when devolving power to their bases. Participatory organizations would concern themselves primarily with basic issues of community development, decided among groups of individuals with common social status and backgrounds. This left thorny policy questions that might cross the social cleavage lines that constantly threaten to become active fault lines within the *chavista* coalition in the hands of Chávez himself, relying on his personal charisma to settle disputes and adjudicate conflicts in a controlled manner. The patchwork of multiple programs, often with overlapping mandates and goals, prevented them from fulfilling their full potential, both for deepening local democracy and defending the national movement.

Clearly local participatory fora, especially in a state with access to extensive funds from petroleum sales, represent an attractive way out of the populist's dilemma. From this point, I will focus my analyses on a new set of institutions that were given legal recognition in 2006 as the voice of civil society and the other participatory organizations discussed earlier: the communal councils. Whether or not the communal councils actually fulfill this role is an empirical question that must be investigated. In Section 5.2.1, I use qualitative and public opinion data to determine whether or not the councils are truly participatory, and if so, whether that participation is truly democratic.

5.2 LEGITIMATING POPULISM: PARTICIPATORY GOVERNANCE AND REGIME SUPPORT

Before investigating the councils' practices, a clear standard for evaluating their participatory bona fides must be put forward, and potential violations of that standard posited. Participation is an extremely broad term that can include anything from signing a petition to running for office, depending on how the concept is defined. Many populist movements involve a substantial degree of mobilization, although this often takes the form of predominantly symbolic activities (such as rally attendance). This is a critically important distinction for the theory presented herein, as I will argue that the communal councils provide much more genuine participatory opportunities than those provided by classical populists. Given the importance of genuine participatory access to my argument, a stricter standard is necessary here, one wherein the political action of common citizens has a meaningful and relatively direct effect on governance. I borrow a concept from participatory economics to serve as this standard: the concept of self-management, which requires that decisions be made by those who are governed by those decisions (Albert & Hanhel, 1991). This concept overlaps a great deal with the top three rungs of Sherry Armstein's "ladder of participation, especially "delegation of power" (1969, pp. 219–223). Applying this to the CCs specifically, decisions regarding policies and projects must be made by the assembly of citizens (wherein the citizenry as a whole has final authority), without undue interference from outside actors. Potential violations of this standard include higher-level government organizations dictating policy to the councils (which would then be reduced to little more than a rubber stamp), or the hijacking of council governance by their administrative personnel, especially the *voceros*, or spokespeople.

The legal framework that establishes the council is clear: the assembly of citizens in the council is the "highest instance of deliberation and decision making for the exercise of community power." Decisions in this body must be made by majority vote of at least 20 percent of community members to have legal force ("Ley orgánica de los consejos comunales," 2009, art. 20–22). The councils determine community development priorities, and may implement projects based on those priorities using resources transferred from municipal or regional governments, or from funds (such as *Fundacomunal*) managed by the central government. Often projects involve working with other Bolivarian organizations, such as the social mission for housing or the *chavista* union for construction workers, especially for major projects such as housing construction (Caripa, 2012). Types of projects include housing, organizing sports teams, and developing basic infrastructure such as electricity and water.

The rules of procedure set out by law, supported by evidence from survey data, are sufficient to dismiss concerns that *voceros* may exercise undue dominance in their councils. As José Machado of *Centro Gumilla*, a Jesuit-aligned research institute in Venezuela, points out, *voceros* are subject to recall at any point; those who usurp the assembly's authority can be easily dismissed (Machado, 2009, p. 17). An analysis that relied on extensive interviews with council leaders found that the election of *voceros* was not a significant problem (Triviño Salazar, 2013). Concerns over hijacking of the councils by their administrative personnel seem unfounded. The importance of funding from the central government is a more serious potential violation and thus requires closer analysis.

Although funds for council projects can, by law, come from a number of sources (including municipal and regional governments), in practice most of the funds for projects come from the national government, especially in poor communities where municipalities lack resources (Briceño, 2012; Liendro, 2012a). This dependence on external funding raises the question of whether the funding decisions of the central government reflect stated community priorities or unilateral impositions. If national elites ignore or pre-shape the will of the community, participation cannot be considered genuine. Deepening this concern, the ministries often submit project proposals to the councils. For example, two *voceros* whom I interviewed mentioned that their councils were currently working on projects proposed by the central government (Liendro, 2012b; Ripley, 2012).

Although these objections are serious, neither proves common enough to abrogate the authority of the councils to make decisions. Both the *voceros* who mentioned government-proposed projects (one of whom is an opposition supporter) denied that there was any undue pressure to accept the government proposals, although councils usually do accept government proposals because they tend to be easier to implement. Relations between the councils and the central government were not always cordial, often due to conflict with the ministries over funding delays and a lack of transparency. Nevertheless a survey of 1,000 council members collected by *Centro Gumilla* (Machado, 2009, p. 29) indicate that 71 percent of respondents felt that the community as a whole consented to all council projects in their community; only 7 percent felt that "official entities" (i.e. the central government) had the last word in council decisions. The ministries may not be entirely responsive to the stated priorities of the communities, but deliberate violations seem to be the exception rather than the rule. This undermines the suggestion that the existence of government proposals represents a violation of participation. In the normal course of things, the assemblies appear to work largely as intended, at least in the planning phase: they set community priorities, and create proposals for development projects based on participatory decision making.

The design of the councils in law clearly establishes them as participatory organizations, and no compelling evidence exists in either qualitative or public opinion data that the state or political actors intervene in the councils' business in a manner sufficiently systematic to represent a violation of participatory norms. This is not to say that the councils function exactly as designed. Like everything else in Venezuela, serious problems of corruption, inefficiency, and outright incompetence create all manner of problems for the day-to-day functioning of the councils. Whether or not the participatory opportunities provided by the councils are also democratic is another question entirely.

5.2.1 Who Are "the People?" Participation and Democracy in the Communal Councils

While the councils are clearly participatory, this does not address the question of whether or not they deepen democracy, as adherents of participatory democracy would expect (Burbach & Piñeiro, 2007; Wilpert, 2005, 2011). To investigate this, following Dahl (1971) and Schedler (2002), I focus on the importance of universality to democracy: that is, the requirement that whatever political rights should be available to all citizens, both in law and in practice, and that citizenship be fairly universal. The qualities of political rights and privileges are an entirely separate matter from the breadth of those rights; citizenship can provide extensive access to political power while being denied to substantial portions of the population.

Such restrictions would be quite in keeping with the Bolivarian worldview of its opponents as would-be usurpers of the legitimate sovereignty of the people, but contrary to the predictions of participatory democracy, which sees participatory self-governance as a mechanism for the development of the an autonomous and politically effective civil society (Biaocchi, 2001). In short, if it can be shown that access to participatory opportunities (no matter how genuine) is granted preferentially to regime supporters, it would provide evidence against the applicability of participatory democracy and in favor of participatory populism.

As mentioned before, the dependence of the councils on state funding raises the real possibility of deliberate politicization, wherein government allies may be given unfair access to resources. This dependence ties the effectiveness of councils to the central government, reinforcing delegative tendencies of the political system (Lovera, 2008). With few safeguards for ensuring that funding decisions are apolitical, serious potential for abuse exists

(Álvarez & García-Guadilla, 2011, p. 177). There is further cause for concern because not all projects are funded, although ministry personnel involved in funding decisions claim that sufficient resources are available to fund major priorities for all councils (Araujo, 2012). *Centro Gumilla* found that only 57 percent of councils had their projects funded, and of those 47 percent experienced significant delays in funding (Machado, 2008, pp. 37–38). *Centro Gumilla* further found that a plurality of individuals dissatisfied with their council cite the fact that the councils do not function at all, and this tendency is especially marked among opposition councils (Machado, 2009, p. 16). These findings concur with studies of other *chavista* programs, such as the social missions (Hawkins, 2010; Hawkins et al., 2011).

While direct and intentional violations of democratic norms are difficult to conclusively show given available data, there is considerable evidence for another form of discrimination, more nebulous but nonetheless crucial. This violation of universality follows directly from the Bolivarian worldview, wherein political power is the sole right of "the people," membership in which is synonymous with membership in the movement and support of its revolution. This close identification of political access and movement loyalty was written into law in 2009, wherein the purpose of the councils was rewritten to include "the construction of a ... socialist society" (art. 2). The inclusion of the term "socialist," which occurs throughout the document, might seem relatively innocuous, but in the Venezuelan context (wherein the term has become a rallying cry for the Bolivarian movement) it sends a clear message: the councils and other participatory forums do not represent universal democratic rights, but are tightly intertwined with the struggle against those whom the Bolivarians view as enemies of the people.

This association between the councils and *chavismo* has become so close that in some circumstances the distinction disappears entirely (Handlin, 2012). One professor, trying to get a list of council participants in a given municipality was directed by the mayor's office to another location where the list was available; the location turned out to be local headquarters for United Socialist Party of Venezuela (PSUV) (García-Guadilla, 2013). Occasionally the lack of distinction between these programs and their political creators leads lower-level functionaries to engage in demonstrably undemocratic activity. An employee in the complaints department of *Fundacomunal* reported, shortly after the new organic law for the councils was enacted (which required all councils to reregister and demonstrate their compliance with the new laws), that a local official was refusing to certify the founding documents of councils whose *voceros* were not PSUV members (Bowman, 2013).

This partiality manifests itself not so much in what the state provides but in what it fails to provide: political education and organizational support for citizens, many of whom are new to political participation of any kind, much less direct deliberative participation. One ministry employee cited the lack of organization as the reason why opposition councils have trouble gaining funding; these councils often submit dozens of contradictory, underdeveloped proposals that require months of revision with ministry technical teams to become ready for action. *Chavista* councils, by contrast, tend to be high functioning, submitting proposals that demonstrate feasibility of the work proposed and have clear priorities already in place when they arrive at the ministries (Araujo, 2012).

The reason that *chavista* councils are so much better organized is not entirely clear. Within the councils, the result is that many citizens who would prefer to focus on community priorities exclusively feel compelled to take a more active role in *chavista* politics in order to get the support their councils need. Many *voceros* reported feeling compelled to join PSUV in order to "be heard" (Álvarez & García-Guadilla, 2011, pp. 199–200; García-Guadilla, 2008, p. 139). Even if there is no deliberate discrimination at the ministerial level, the crippling inefficiency of the central government means that a strong connection within the PSUV is a considerable advantage in getting through administrative bottlenecks.

This would mirror the experience of other participatory programs, where active work in *chavista* campaigns is expected of participants in government-sponsored participatory programs, especially when the revolution was seen as facing an existential threat (García-Guadilla, 2011). In times of great need, the Bolivarian elite has on occasion thrown out all pretense of impartiality and demanded that the councils fulfill their "duties" to the movement. In 2009, the Minister of Participation directly ordered the councils to campaign for the *chavista* side in the constitutional referendum (López Maya & Panzarelli, 2013, p. 257).

To summarize, discrimination against opposition councils is likely a mixture of direction from upper leadership, sporadic acts by individual *chavistas*, and reflexive adherence to a populist view of opponents as enemies. Whatever the relative proportions of each, the councils clearly fail to encourage the kind of autonomous civil society that participatory democracy would envision. Instead the councils are an instance of what one author who conducted extensive interviews with council participants called "conditioned participation" (Triviño Salazar, 2013). Self-governance in local matters is a real aspect of the councils, but it is granted in such a way that it encourages movement unity and allows the councils to be turned toward defense of the regime when the need arises. This finding is consistent with what other researchers have found when studying other Bolivarian social organizations (Hawkins, 2010; Hawkins & Hansen, 2006).

It should be reemphasized that this does not cast any doubt on the reality of participatory governance within the councils; discrimination can be thought of as an unacceptable restriction on democratic citizenship, which is an entirely separate issue from the content of rights conferred by that citizenship upon those who possess it. This distinction is important, because it further supports the view of Bolivarianism as an instance of participatory populism. Partiality in the provision of access to functioning councils is clear, but that partiality does not extend to the principles of participatory decision making within the councils. This combination fits poorly within a framework influenced by personalism or participatory democracy, but is entirely consistent within a worldview that sees direct participation, and the empowerment it brings, as essential political rights, but which reserves political rights for those who prove themselves worthy through support of the struggle against an oligarchical class constantly scheming to usurp the authority of the people.

5.3 COUNCIL PARTICIPATION AND REGIME SUPPORT: A QUANTITATIVE ANALYSIS

Although the level of entanglement of the state and the councils shown through qualitative analysis casts immediate doubt on participatory democracy as an appropriate framework, such analyses cannot adjudicate between the two varieties of populism so conclusively. The mere existence of participatory programs does not favor one form of populism over the other: rather the disagreement between the two rests on their role in building popular support for the Bolivarian system. Quantitative analysis of public opinion data has the potential to reinforce the qualitative findings by addressing this. Personalism suggests that support for the populist is the primary determinant of regime support. Participatory populism, on the other hand, predicts that the populist's dilemma is resolved via the councils (and other programs like them) by fulfilling the movement's promises of empowerment and inclusion.

The preceding statements can be refined into hypotheses that can be tested with survey data. Personalism suggests two hypotheses:

- **H1a: Support for Chávez should have a positive effect on regime support, all other things being equal.**
- **H1b: Any association between council participation and support for Chávez and his regime should consist of a strong positive impact of regime support and support for Chávez on council participation.**

Participatory populism suggests two hypotheses, both of which require a bit more explanation. Recall that the populist's dilemma is resolved through a trade-off: national hegemony of the populist for local self-governance. This satisfies the promises of empowerment upon which Chávez staked his movement's legitimacy. While this proposition is not directly testable, it does imply two subsidiary hypotheses that are. First, because the effect of the councils is dependent upon the satisfaction of a desire for participatory access, it suggests that the effect of council participation is not constant, but rather will be much stronger among those who have strong participatory preferences. Conversely, if personalism is correct and the "participatory" nature of the councils is illusory, then one would expect citizens with strong participatory preferences to become disillusioned and withdraw support. This hypothesis can be refined as:

- **H2: The effect of council participation varies with the respondent's preference for participatory modes of governance. The effect should be significantly stronger among those with strong participatory preferences.**

In other words, a significantly positive interaction term supports participatory populism; a null or (especially) a negative one would provide strong evidence against it. Finally, while the satisfaction of the regime's promises suggests a direct effect of council participation, the importance of empowerment described earlier also suggests an indirect effect. The councils should have an additional impact on regime support through their impact on a respondent's sense of their ability to influence the political sphere. This hypothesis can be refined as:

- **H3: Council participation should have a strong positive impact on external political efficacy. External efficacy should in turn have a significant impact on regime support.**

This hypothesis is the most direct application of the framework developed in Chapter 3; it is therefore appropriate that it shares a label (H3) with the corresponding hypothesis specified in Chapter 4. Participatory institutions are hypothesized to impact regime-based efficacy (RBE), which in turn effects support. H1a is consistent with both frameworks, but H1b cannot be true if either H2 or H3 is true. A chart of these relationships is presented in Figure 5.1. Note that only the substantive variables of interest are included in the chart; control

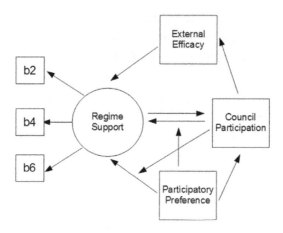

FIGURE 5.1: Relationship chart

variables (including instruments which identify the model) are omitted for clarity and ease of use.

H3 can be further modified based on relationships theoretically predicted by the populist context in which participatory governance programs operate, allowing us to further discriminate between the two participatory explanations of support in the Bolivarian regime. Specifically, participatory populism predicts that the impact of council participation on RBE will not be constant across all individuals for two reasons. First, qualitative analysis suggests that these programs (and the support necessary for them to function effectively) are not equally available to all; regime supporters have far greater access. Second, Chávez's participatory rhetoric, and his supporters' fervent belief in that rhetoric, likely inflates the perceived importance of these programs, as they are not merely mechanisms for participatory local governance but part of a broader attempt to restore the people to their rightful sovereignty. In other words, the impact of these programs on participants' perceptions of their efficacy will be amplified by their charismatic attachment to Chávez. This leads to the following corollary to H3:

- **H3a: The effect of council participation on RBE will be significantly stronger among *chavistas* than among opposition supporters.**

5.3.1 Data and Variables

To test these hypotheses, I use data from the 2010 and 2012 waves of the LAPOP survey in Venezuela. LAPOP is one of the most frequently used and highly respected regional public opinion survey projects. Each wave includes roughly 1,500 respondents per country. Sampling is conducted using subnational clusters to ensure a representative sample is obtained; details can be obtained from LAPOP's website (www.vanderbilt.edu/lapop/ab2012/AB-2012-Tech-Info-12.18.12.pdf).

Dependent and Independent Variables

The following models include three dependent variables: regime support, council participation, and regime-based efficacy (RBE). Endogenous SEMs are, in my experience, extremely prone to estimation failure. That is, the algorithms for maximizing the likelihood function tend to break down with such complex models. The quantitative model used in Chapter 4 thus provides a basis for this model, but the additional complication of a reciprocal relationship between council participation and support caused the estimation routine to fail, no matter what tweaks were made (e.g. different starting values, parameter constraints). As such I will here describe how the models in Chapter 4 are altered in this chapter; equations specifying these differences can be found in Section 5.5, the technical appendix to this chapter.

The dependent regime support variable is measured in the same fashion as described in Chapter 4, using systemic pride, respect for institutions, and systemic support. Regime performance and RBE are both measured as they were in the 2012 Reduced model, but instead of estimating the measurement model simultaneously with the structural model, I estimate the former first in order to get predicted scores on each latent variable, then use those scores as observed variables in the structural model. Second, I exclude the interaction between RBE and performance. This is troubling given the importance of that interaction to the framework here, but Chapter 4 established that relationship conclusively, and no version of the model with that interaction in place could successfully be estimated. It is more important here to exclude it and analyze the variables of interest that pertain specifically to Venezuela.

Participation in the communal councils is measured via a four-point scale of frequency of participation (cp15). The last of the substantively interesting variables, participatory preference, is measured via a seven-point scale question, which asked respondents if they agreed that the people should govern directly (pop107). Council participation, confidence in Chávez, and participatory preference are rescaled to have a minimum of zero and a maximum of one, for ease of interpreting the interaction term. In addition to these, I include a number of standard demographic control variables: income, education, ideology, sex, race (a dummy coded zero for white respondents and one for all others), urban/rural, and a dummy variable for survey year. Finally, I include latent variable measured by frequency of attendance at a variety of social organizations as a measure of individual "social capital." This variable predicts council participation, and is included as an instrument to identify the model-estimating antecedents of council participation; it has no bearing on the theoretical debates discussed here. Results from the measurement model analyses are presented in Table 5.2.

5.3.2   Results of Analysis

To briefly review, the primary hypotheses of interest here are: that council participation increases regime support, and that relationship will be stronger among those with participatory preferences; and that RBE is also increased by council participation, but only among *chavistas*. Results of the structural component of analysis are presented in Table 5.3.

The first important result is that *chavismo* has an extremely strong positive impact on regime support. This is not very surprising. It does cast further doubt on participatory democracy as a reasonable framework for analysis (although it was already discredited by the qualitative analysis), but says little about which type of populism best fits the Bolivarian state. The results for council participation are far more enlightening. Council participation has a substantial positive impact on support, but only among those with strong participatory preferences.

Table 5.2: *Measurement model estimation results*

$n = 3{,}000$	Factor loadings			Error variances		
Regime support	Est.	SE	P-value	Est.	SE	P-value
Pride in political system (b2)	1.091	0.033	0.000	2.234	0.062	0.000
Respect for institutions (b4)	1.750	0.030	0.000	0.887	0.044	0.000
Systemic support (b6)	1.728	0.030	0.000	0.870	0.043	0.000
Regime performance	Est.	SE	P-value	Est.	SE	P-value
Management of poverty (n1)	1.677	0.032	0.000	0.986	0.045	0.000
Management of crime (n11)	1.684	0.029	0.000	0.762	0.036	0.000
Management of economy (n15)	1.807	0.029	0.000	1.405	0.035	0.000
Loadings for RBE	Est.	SE	P-value	Est.	SE	P-value
External efficacy (eff1)	1.508	0.061	0.000	1.850	0.165	0.000
Parties respond to voters (epp1)	0.801	0.072	0.000	2.148	0.129	0.000
Parties represent voters well (epp3)	1.053	0.071	0.000	2.002	0.129	0.000

Table 5.2: (*cont.*)

n = 3,000	Factor loadings			Error variances		
Loadings for social capital	Est.	SE	P-value	Est.	SE	P-value
Attendance, religious org. (cp6)	0.168	0.029	0.000	1.405	0.037	0.000
Attendance, school parents' org. (cp7)	0.292	0.030	0.000	0.807	0.026	0.000
Attendance, community improvement org. (cp8)	0.772	0.064	0.000	0.169	0.098	0.000
Attendance, workers org. (cp9)	0.112	0.014	0.000	0.223	0.006	0.000
Latent variable covariances	Est.	SE	P-value			
Support, performance	0.757	0.010	0.000			
Support, RBE	0.712	0.028	0.000			
Support, social capital	−0.183	0.024	0.000			
Performance, RBE	0.768	0.029	0.000			
Performance, social capital	−0.191	0.024	0.000			
RBE, social capital	−0.254	0.030	0.000			

Goodness of fit indices all indices (RMSEA = 0.024, CFI = 0.992) indicate excellent fit.

Table 5.3: *SEM analysis of regime support*

n = 3,000	Regime Support			Council Participation		
	Est.	SE	P-value	Est.	SE	P-value
Council participation	−1.295	0.097	0.000	-	-	-
Participatory preference	−0.502	0.044	0.000	-	-	-
Interaction (council participation * participatory preference)	2.174	0.152	0.000	-	-	-
External efficacy	0.186	0.026	0.000	-	-	-
Confidence in Chávez (*chavismo*)	0.905	0.044	0.000	0.563	0.047	0.000
Regime support	-	-	-	0.537	0.039	0.000
Regime performance	0.056	0.023	0.016			
Social capital	-	-	-	0.225	0.006	0.000
Income	0.001	0.011	0.947	0.002	0.007	0.761
Education	−0.008	0.010	0.449	-	-	-
Female	−0.046	0.018	0.011	-	-	-
Age	0.027	0.009	0.004	-	-	-
Urban	-	-	-	0.018	0.005	0.000
Ideology	−0.016	0.010	0.126	-	-	-
Race	0.063	0.019	0.001	-	-	-
2012 dummy	−0.072	0.019	0.000	0.039	0.012	0.001
Intercept	*0.000*	-	-	0.498	0.037	0.000

Goodness of Fit Statistics	Statistic	P-value
Chi-Square (REF)	3130	0.000
RMSEA	0.091	
CFI	0.860	
SRMR	0.042	

Table 5.4: *SEM analysis of RBE*

RBE (n = 3,000)	Est.	S.E.	P-value
Council participation	0.183	0.066	0.006
Confidence in Chávez (*chavismo*)	1.299	0.037	0.000
Interaction (council participation * chavismo)	0.262	0.088	0.003
Participatory preference	0.231	0.034	0.000
Income	−0.008	0.013	0.556
Education	0.006	0.012	0.610
Ideology	−0.103	0.012	0.000
Age	0.013	0.011	0.252
Urban	0.019	0.009	0.041
Female	0.044	0.022	0.044
Race	−0.058	0.023	0.010
2012 Dummy	0.060	0.022	0.066
Intercept	−0.952	0.053	0.000

Goodness of Fit Statistics	Statistic
Chi-Square (REF)	262
RMSEA	0.087
CFI	0.892
SRMR	0.032

Among those who do not prefer direct participation,[2] the effect is actually negative −1.295), which may reflect dissatisfaction with some of the operational problems that impact many councils. Among those with strong participatory preferences,[3] the impact of council participation rivals that of *chavismo* (0.879 compared to 0.905), which is remarkable given the overwhelming dominance of Hugo Chávez in the Venezuelan political system. The results for efficacy further support participatory populism; results for the analysis of RBE are presented in Table 5.4.

These results are consistent with participatory populism and inconsistent with the other two approaches. Opposition supporters

---

[2] Participatory preference at 0.   [3] Participatory preference at 1.

who participate regularly in the councils actually feel *less* empowered compared to those who do not, although the difference is not statistically significant. On the other hand, *chavistas* who participate in councils have a much higher predicted level of RBE than those who do not. *Chavistas* who engage with the communal councils frequently have a predicted support level of 0.792, while those who do not have a predicted level of 0.347.[4]

The findings most directly inspired by the framework developed in Chapter 3 also find strong support here. Support for Chávez has a massive impact on efficacy; this is unsurprising given the Bolivarian regime's previously discussed tendency to grant greater political rights to supporters and to diminish the rights of everyone else, and in light of the argument here that empowerment was part of the charismatic attachment to Chávez. Of the remaining variables, no variable has a greater impact on RBE than council participation except ideology (again, not surprising in such a polarized political environment).

Interpreting effect magnitudes from data tables can be difficult, especially with all the complications (interactions and mediated relationships) in play here. A graphical representation can help simply interpretation. Figure 5.2 presents the predicted level of regime support, taking into account the values of four variables: confidence in Chávez, council participation, participatory preference, and RBE.

The columns are formed by varying the first three predictors mentioned earlier, from their minimums (0) to their maximums (1). RBE, as an endogenous variable, assumes its predicted score based on the values of *chavismo* and council participation. A few things about the graph immediately stand out. First, and not surprisingly, is that *chavismo* has an enormous influence on regime support; all of the largest predicted values belong to *chavistas*. The second is that, unless they are both high, neither participatory preferences nor council participation improve support; in fact they negatively influence it, although their influence on RBE moderates this somewhat.

---

[4] Assuming all other variables fixed at zero.

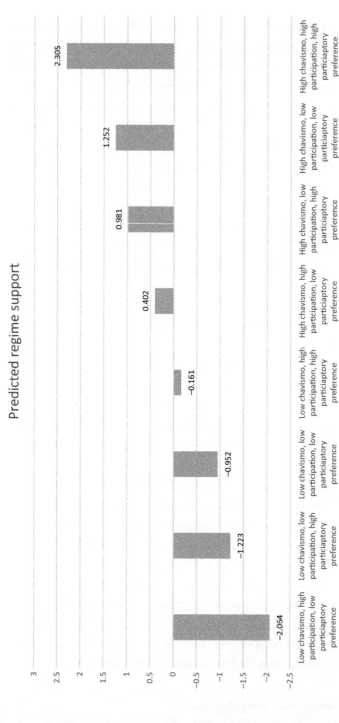

FIGURE 5.2: Predicted level of regime support by *chavismo*

The most crucial element of the graph for my argument, however, is what occurs when both participatory preference and council participation are high. Even among those who have no confidence in Chávez, this configuration has an important influence on regime support, bringing it closer to the support mean (zero), from -.952 (for the low/low/low configuration) to -.161. Although these individuals will never support the Bolivarian system that Chávez created and co-opted, the participatory features of the councils seem to make them less critical. The effect is much more dramatic among Chávez loyalists. Among them, those with participatory preferences and council participation report nearly twice the levels of support (2.305), compared with the next most supportive category (1.252).

In sum, these analyses demonstrate that the councils allow the Bolivarian movement to convince its militants that its most important promise is being kept: that those who were long excluded from democracy as practiced during the *Punto Fijo* era are finally allowed to exercise power directly and collectively within their communities. They further show the importance of this promise to the legitimation of a regime that might otherwise have alienated its base with its authoritarian practices. With this contention supported, the view of *chavismo* as a straightforward incarnation of personalism becomes difficult to maintain. It would be foolish to deny that Chávez's political style and personalism are similar in many ways, but the type of participatory self-management shown to exist in the councils, and the reliance on same to legitimate the regime, simply do not fit within a framework defined by the complete dominance of the leader, who utilizes his personal charisma and emotional connections with followers, rather than genuine empowerment, to maintain his position.

5.4 CONCLUSION

Personalism and participation are both readily apparent features of the Bolivarian political system, and theories that deny one or the other are incomplete. The fact that participatory populism, with its combination of authoritarian and democratic practices, was[5] so successful at maintaining support for the populist regime raises some interesting questions. Many students of participatory democracy experiments hope that such organizations can improve the quality of democracy (Biaocchi, 2001). Following Rousseau (2002) and others, advocates argued that microlevel participation could train citizens to become more assertive and active in the political process at higher levels, challenging entrenched power-holders and thereby enhancing representative institutions (Avritzer, 2002; Barber, 1984; Pateman, 1970).

The case of Venezuela demonstrates an important caveat: that participatory governance can exist outside a liberal democratic framework. Participatory experiments do not exist in a vacuum, but are nested within a broader political system, and their effect on that system is not always straightforward. In the Venezuelan case, participatory governance actually serves to reinforce the ties between the masses and a dominant leader (Lovera, 2008). Given the undeniable incompetence of the Bolivarian elite, such reinforcement was absolutely crucial for the movement's survival. The inherent constraints on participatory self-governance programs, particularly their confinement to local-level issues, make it an attractive choice for populists seeking novel ways to empower citizens without vitiating their own dominance. And yet, the high levels of support in Venezuela that I sought to explain in this chapter demonstrate the power of such limited participatory access in a political context long defined by the enervation of the people. In such circumstances, a small amount of participatory empowerment can cover a multitude of sins.

5.5 APPENDIX: EQUATIONS AND TECHNICAL DETAILS

This section includes some technical detail that readers may not need to evaluate the overall argument of the chapter. The model

---

[5] Recall that this strategy requires both participation and the charisma of the populist to function. With the death of Chávez, the latter has been lost and systemic support has cratered under the weight of the regime's failures. This is discussed in greater detail in the Conclusion (Chapter 7).

analyzed in Section 5.3 is based upon those used in Chapter 4. Given the introduction of several new variables, some with complex relationships, I choose to write out the equations underlying analysis in detail here, rather than simply relying on those listed in Chapter 4 with modifications explained in the text. The primary relationship of interest here is the relationship between regime support and council participation, controlling for support for Chávez. Personalism predicts that support for Chávez, the Bolivarian regime, or both should determine council participation. Conversely, participatory populism and participatory democracy both predict that council participation should predict regime support. This leads to the following set of equations:

$$\text{Regime support}_i = 1\,\gamma_{10} + \beta_{11}\text{Council Participation}_i$$
$$+ \gamma_{11}\text{Support for Chávez}_i + \zeta_1 \qquad \text{(Eq 5.01)}$$

$$\text{Council Participation}_i = \gamma_{20} + \beta_{21}\text{Regime Support}_i$$
$$+ \gamma_{21}\text{Support for Chávez}_i + \zeta_2 \qquad \text{(Eq 5.02)}$$

The participatory frameworks both make two additional predictions. First, the *participatory opportunities* provided by the councils drive the positive effect on regime support, rather than the resources they provide or any other factor. Therefore it is reasonable to presume that the effect will be stronger among those with participatory preferences. Second, council participation is assumed to have an indirect effect on regime support through its relationship with external (regime-based) efficacy. This leads to the following modification of Equation 5.01, and a new equation for external efficacy:

$$\text{Regime support}_i =$$
$$\gamma_{10} + \beta_{11}\text{Council Participation}_i + \beta_{12}\text{Efficacy}_i$$
$$+ \gamma_{11}\text{Participatory Preference}_i + \gamma_{11}\text{Council Participation}_i{}^{*}$$
$$\text{Participatory Preference}_i + \gamma_{13}\text{Support for Chávez}_i + \zeta_1$$
$$\text{(Eq 5.03)}$$

$$\text{Efficacy}_i =$$
$$\gamma_{30} + \beta_{31}\text{Council Participation}_i + \gamma_{31}\text{Participatory Preference}_i$$
$$+ \gamma_{32}\text{Support for Chávez}_i + \zeta_3$$
$$\text{(Eq 5.04)}$$

Three additional modifications must be made to make the model complete. I include a suite of control variables in Equation 5.03. Second, there is a clear potential endogenity problem in the model specified by Equation 5.03. Regime support may well be driven by council participation, but council participants self-select, and support for the regime that sponsors those participatory fora likely increases individuals' likelihood of participation. Given this, I specify in Equations 5.05 and 5.06 a simultaneous SEM, where regime support and council participation impact one another. To identify the model, I exclude several demographic variables (such as education, income, gender, and age) that seem unlikely to influence council participation from the equation predicting council participation. I include two variables in the equation predicting council participation in order to identify the model via the rank and order conditions (Bollen, 1989). First, I include a dummy variable for urban respondents, although this turns out to be a weak instrument at best. A better instrument is the measure of "social capital" to which I alluded during the measurement discussion. It stands to reason that individuals who show a general propensity for participating in social organizations will be more likely to participate in the councils, which are a form of social organization. This variable turns out to be a much stronger instrument, and thus the model is identified.

Finally, to test H3a, I include an interaction term in Equation 5.03, with confidence in Chávez moderating the impact of council participation on RBE. This leads to the following:

Regime support$_i$ =
$\gamma_{10} + \beta_{11}$ Council Participation$_i$ + γ_{11} Participatory Preference$_i$
$\quad + \gamma_{11}$ Council Participation$_i$*Participatory Preference$_i$
$\quad + \gamma_{13}$ Support for Chávez$_i$ + γ_{14} Income$_i$ + γ_{15} Education$_i$
$\quad + \gamma_{16}$ Female$_i$ + γ_{17} Age$_i$ + γ_{18} Ideology$_i$ + γ_{19} Race$_i$
$\quad + \gamma_{1,10}$ 2012 Year Dummy$_i$ + ζ_1

$$(Eq\ 5.05)$$

Council Participation$_i$ =
$\gamma_{20} + \beta_{21}$ Regime Support$_i$ + γ_{21} Support for Chávez$_i$ $\qquad$ (Eq 5.06)
$\quad + \gamma_{22}$ Urban$_i$ + γ_{23} Social Capital$_i$ + ζ_2

$\text{Efficacy}_i =$
$\gamma_{30} + \beta_{31}\text{Council Participation}_i + \gamma_{32}\text{Participatory Preference}_i$
$\quad + \gamma_{33}\text{Support for Chávez}_i + \gamma_{34}\text{Support for Chávez}_i{}^*\text{Council}$
$\quad \text{Participation}_i + \gamma_{35}\text{Income}_i + \gamma_{36}\text{Education}_i + \gamma_{37}\text{Female}_i$
$\quad + \gamma_{38}\text{Age}_i + \gamma_{39}\text{Ideology}_i + \gamma_{3,10}\text{Race}_i + \gamma_{3,11}\text{Urban}_i$
$\quad + \gamma_{3,12}\text{2012 Year Dummy}_i + \zeta_3$

(Eq 5.07)

Estimation of model parameters was conducted in MPLUS version 7.2 (data and code are available on request), using Maximum Likelihood with Missing Values (MLMV). MLMV builds the likelihood function one observation at a time, using whatever information is available for each observation, without requiring the specification of a measurement model (Allison, 2012). Because communal council participation is likely predicted in part by systemic support and *chavismo* (as personalism suggests), I allow participation to be endogenous in order to avoid bias. This requires treating the council participation variable as continuous, which is risky given its four-point scale; treating it as ordinal using a WLS estimator did not substantially alter the results. The measurement model is identified via the three-factor rule. Since efficacy is not impacted by support, I conducted analysis of that model separately. This allowed the inclusion of all relevant control variables without concerns over identification issues.

6   The Other Liberalism

Laissez-Faire, Protected Democracy, and Support in Chile

Of all the terms that have been applied to anemic regime support in Chile (crisis of representation, dissatisfaction with democracy, etc.), none fits better than "malaise." Like malaise, Chile's legitimacy issues are chronic, rather than acute; something is clearly amiss, but the malady does not appear to be fatal. Although waves of contentious politics and increasing electoral abstention are cause for concern, no one expects the system to collapse anytime soon. And like physical malaise, the underlying source of the problem is maddeningly difficult to pin down. It is easy enough to find potential causes, both in the academic literature and the general conversation on the topic: neoliberalism, authoritarian enclaves, and the party system are all commonly cited reasons why Chileans express little affection for their state. Due to a lack of theoretical clarity and methodological rigor, there is still much we do not understand about why the best-governed state in Latin America has produced a detached and apathetic citizenry. Which of the variables listed above matter? Do some matter more than others? Do they all impact support directly, or are the effects of some factors mediated through others? If poor support is caused by neoliberalism or the party system, what specific characteristics of these abstract concepts are to blame? None of these questions can be entirely settled by the existing literature.

This chapter seeks to provide answers to all these questions by applying the theoretical model developed in Chapter 3 (see also Figure 1.1), and tested in Chapters 4 and 5. The most crucial aspect of this framework is the proposition that intrinsic characteristics of democratic procedures shape support directly and separately from performance. This suggests that, in order to truly understand the roots of Chile's legitimacy troubles, we must disentangle the impacts of economic factors from those of political procedures. The first step in this separation is to recognize that not one, but two liberal[1] revolutions were initiated by the Pinochet regime and bequeathed to the democratic system that replaced it: one economic, the other political. In this chapter, I seek to analyze which of these revolutions is most responsible for patterns of support in modern Chile. In Section 6.1, I review the economic dimension, briefly summarizing the story of Chile's turn to laissez-faire economics after decades of economic statism. And while this turn is cited by many commentators as the immediate source of Chile's lack of support, available evidence does not bear this out.

It is the second, political transformation that has had the greatest effect on Chilean political attitudes. The military dictatorship, responding as much to the rapid incorporation of new social groups into the political system as to Allende's socialist experiment, left behind a tutelary, protective[2] democratic system of the sort commonly associated with liberal conceptions of the proper role of the state in society. This system confined the political role of citizens to the periodic selection of leaders. And it placed severe constraints on the potential of those electoral choices to translate into significant policy changes. Restated in terms of the mechanisms of autonomy discussed in the Chapters 1-3 of this book, the Chilean political system excels in both governance and representation, but reduces participation to the lowest level possible in a full democracy. The evidence presented here shows that this rejection of participation is the most important source of democratic disaffection in Chile.

---

[1] From this point forward, I use the term "liberal" in the classical sense of the word, as described in Chapters 2 and 3, in place of "neoliberal." The latter term is normatively loaded and usually applied exclusively to economic (rather than political) systems.

[2] These terms are frequently used synonymously in the Chilean context; this is an error. Tutelary and protective characteristics of the Chilean state can be distinguished from one another. And as I will show, while the former have been eradicated, minimal progress has been made on the latter.

The chapter proceeds as follows. First, I review the existing literature on Chile's modern economic transformation from statism to liberalism, including works that cite that transformation as the source of weak support. Yet available data do not support such theories. I then propose an alternative explanation, which posits that the protective elements of Chile's democracy, installed by a military government[3] whose principal goal was to prevent the return of social politicization of the sort that erupted prior to its seizure of power, influence support separately (although not independently) from economic variables.

I then test this theory in three ways. First, following Carlin (2014), I attempt to break down the various standards by which individuals may evaluate parties to determine which is most important for determining confidence in parties. I demonstrate that concerns over participation, rather than representation or economic performance, drive citizen attitudes toward both the state and Chile's least popular institution: its party system. These findings are consistent with my argument, but they are somewhat indirect. Although the theoretical framework presented in earlier chapters allows evaluation of the Chilean regime as it exists, my argument must still contend with the inherent difficulty involved in proving that the absence of something (participation) is the cause of an outcome. To overcome this, I use a series of laboratory experiments conducted among Chilean university students to test the counterfactual argument that a Chile with extensive participatory opportunities (institutionally guaranteed mechanisms for citizens to make political decisions without intermediaries) would gain more support from its populace, regardless of policy outcomes. This test has the advantage of providing additional evidence for the hypothesized impact of participatory institutions on support (see H3 in Chapters 3 and 4).

---

[3] It should be noted that the Chilean political class, for the most part, accepted the limitations on popular engagement with little protest and with some enthusiasm.

Experiments, like all social science methods, have their weaknesses. The question of external validity is particularly worrisome: it is difficult to evaluate if the highly controlled context of a lab experiment accurately reflects real-world dynamics. To increase confidence in the findings, I also conducted a qualitative program evaluation of one of the rare opportunities for direct participation in Chile: the participatory process by which the municipality of Providencia created its communal development plan. I show, through the evaluation and a survey conducted by the municipality (designed in consultation with the author), that this program significantly reduced tensions between the municipality and social movement activists, which had been endemic prior to the program. This is precisely what the theory developed here predicts. None of these pieces of evidence alone would be sufficient to prove that my framework is correct and that a lack of participatory opportunities is to blame for Chile's lack of legitimacy. When taken together, with the weaknesses of each method compensated for by the strengths of the others, the findings presented here provide convincing evidence of my theory.

6.1 ECONOMIC LIBERALISM AND SUPPORT IN CHILE

Despite its objective successes in the democratic era, Chile's economic model is not popular among ordinary citizens (Angell, 2010). It is therefore a reasonable proposition that the model may be related to poor support, as many scholars (not to mention nonacademic social commentators) have argued. Theories of support in Chile that blame economic liberalism vary considerably in the details, but a general theory can be summarized by reviewing the literature on the subject, although not all cited authors would agree with every element.

A thorough rehash of the move from statism to liberalism in Chile is beyond the scope of this chapter, and would only cover extremely well-trodden ground. As I ultimately conclude that economic liberalism does not provide much insight on the question of support in Chile, this summary will be brief. Prior to the military takeover in 1973, the Chilean state had a major economic role (Bitar, 1986; Garretón, 1989b; Oxhorn, 1995; Stallings, 1978). Even before the Marxist Popular Unity (UP) entered government, the state controlled 47 percent of GDP, a staggering proportion even by Latin American standards (Stallings, 1978). Control of the state was thus of paramount importance for all social groups in pursuing their economic interests. This situation only intensified as the political system began to challenge the entrenched interests of the elite, first with the Christian Democratic (PDC) government of Eduardo Frei, and later with the election of Socialist Salvador Allende. The Frei administration, in part due to coaxing by the United States (A. Valenzuela, 1978, p. 35), embarked on a program of land reform that directly threatened the interest of the landed aristocracy.

The UP government of Salvador Allende drastically accelerated the pace of reform. The fall of Allende's government had many causes, but the core economic dispute that triggered the constitutional crisis was the dramatic and rapid expansion of the state-owned enterprises, achieved largely through the expropriation of private businesses.[4] The infringements on private property were too much for the economic elite to bear. Previously the state's role had largely been protective of domestic capital, as Chile followed an import-substitution-industrialization (ISI) model (Garretón, 1989a, ch. 1; A. Valenzuela, 1978, p. 13). The result was a political impasse that would tragically be resolved with bombs and bullets rather than ballots, ending with the overthrow of the UP government and the suicide of its leader.

Nevertheless, the military did not immediately embark upon a new economic project.[5] Although the junta did reverse many of Allende's reforms, the fundamental restructuring of the economy did not begin immediately. Instead the military hithered and dithered with piecemeal changes (Fontaine Aldunate, 1988) for several years.

---

[4] The mass mobilizations that drove this process were probably even more crucial; see Section 6.2.1 for a more detailed discussion.

[5] As I will show later, this indecision was because the transformation of politics, not economics, was the first priority of the dictatorship.

In 1975 a group of liberal economists called "the Chicago boys" gained influential posts in the regime. Beginning immediately with anti-inflationary measures and accelerating rapidly in 1977, the regime pushed full speed ahead with the adoption of an almost fundamentalist liberal model, the result of which was a massive withdrawal of the state from its historic role in the Chilean economy. This included the privatization of state-owned enterprises, reduction in taxation and social spending, limitation of labor organization, and elimination of protectionist measures. With the adoption of the "seven modernizations," the logic of laissez-faire was extended to even more areas of society, include healthcare, pensions, and education, among other areas (Foxley, 1983, ch. 4).

The economic model survived the transition to democracy, which began with the plebiscite of 1988, relatively unscathed, and persists to this day (albeit in modified form). This is somewhat surprising, given the severe economic pain it inflicted upon much of society. Although the model produced significant macroeconomic gains over much of its existence, during the transition the economy was under severe strain due to an eleventh-hour spending spree by the dictatorship (Angell, 2010) and the poverty rate was an abysmal 45.1 percent (Oppenheim, 2007, p. 257). Scholars point to a number of factors to explain the durability of economic liberalism into the contemporary era. Liberal economics tend to create an atomized, highly individualistic society wherein collective action is difficult, especially for the poor (Garretón, 1989b; Roberts, 1998). The electoral system devised by the regime during the transition process led to overrepresentation of the right, which could thus block reforms (Polga-Hecimovich & Siavelis, 2015; Posner, 1999), although this point is contested (Zucco, 2006). Finally, the parties that emerged from the crucible of dictatorship were fundamentally different from those that had operated in earlier democratic eras (Oxhorn, 1994, 1995). Specifically, ties to the grassroots, especially among the socialist parties, the Socialist Party (PS) and the Party for Democracy (PPD), had not survived repression and the exile of much of their leadership. And given

the continuing threat that the military might emerge from its barracks again if the political system deviated too much from its economic legacy, these parties were ill disposed to renew their ties with
society.

According to those who cite Chile's economic liberalism, the
end result is a system wherein the economy remains largely
decoupled from the political system (Garretón, 2003; Kurtz, 2004a,
2004b). Economic policy has become technocratic, outside the realm
of political contestation (Silva, 1991, 2008). This leaves issues of
pressing interest to the poor and working classes effectively off the
political table, as no political actor is willing and able to fight for
them; this lack of interest attendance ultimately produces low
support (Posner, 1999; Santos, 2005).

The economic liberalism explanation of poor support in Chile is
intuitive, given the model's unpopularity, and sounds perfectly plausible. Indeed, I will point to many of the variables mentioned in the
preceding discussion when I develop my own approach, although the
underlying theoretical logic will be very different. It is also a perfect
example of why social science theories must be rigorously tested, as
its predictions simply fail to hold up to data. Before showing this, it is
necessary to clarify the causal story a bit. A graph of the theory is
presented in Figure 6.1.

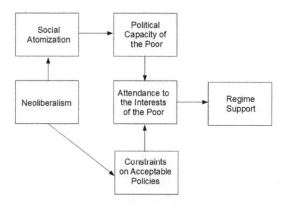

FIGURE 6.1: Graph of economic liberalism theories of low support

This graph should feel familiar: it is yet another example of a performance-centric theory that, while including input-oriented variables, places them toward the beginning of the causal chain. The immediate source of discontent, in other words, has little to do with politics and everything to do with policy outcomes. This suggests an important prediction: those who suffer most (or benefit least) from laissez-faire economics should be the least supportive of the Chilean state. In other words, low support should be concentrated among the poor and working classes.

This prediction does not hold up to available data. The Chile-specific analysis presented in Chapter 4 (see Table 4.6) contains three separate measures related to socioeconomic status: income, wealth (goods owned), and education. The first two have no significant effect on support. And while education does have an effect, it is in the wrong direction: more educated respondents were less supportive of the Chilean regime. Evidence from other surveys also contradicts the economic theory of weak support put forth by critics of the laissez-faire model. Figure 2.4, summarizing data from Center for Public Studies (CEP) data found that the middle sectors, rather than the poor, were the least supportive of the regime. Analyses presented later in this chapter find no relationship at all between socioeconomic status (SES) and support.[6]

Why the discrepancy between theory and evidence? Theories go awry when they rest on invalid assumptions, and the assumption that the Chilean system neglects the interest of the poor is highly dubious. While the liberal model certainly wreaked havoc on subaltern sectors during the dictatorship, successive center-left governments have in fact substantially modified the model, softening its rougher edges. Chile does extremely well by regional standards on issues such as

---

[6] This holds regardless of whether support is regressed on SES in combination with other variables. When regressed alone, the highest social class (ABC1) is more supportive than the poorest, but there are no significant differences between any of the other classes.

inflation, employment, poverty reduction, and public security, all of which are of paramount importance to the poor (Mainwaring et al., 2010). Regardless of the various obstacles the poor face in forcing elites to attend to their interests, those interests have not, in fact, been neglected. The Chilean left (especially the PS and PPD) have abandoned their doctrinaire Marxism, but charges that they have entirely left the poor to the vicissitudes of the market are untrue and unjust. By many metrics, Chile's poor do better than their counterparts in any Latin American country. Of course problems still exist among Chile's poor, and many scholars would dispute that the neoliberal model has been as successful as macroeconomic data suggest. A strong preponderance of the evidence, however, is inconsistent with the suggestion that economic issues are the primary source of democratic disaffection in Chile.

Despite the contradictory evidence, I too place the blame for Chile's legitimacy woes at the feet of liberalism. Yet liberalism in Chile is not confined to the economic sphere. The military regime also initiated a liberal[7] revolution in the political realm, and this revolution has been altered considerably less than the economic variety. This political liberalism, and the institutions which embody it, circumscribe participatory opportunities to the bare minimum required of a full-fledged democracy. The absence of such opportunities is responsible for the weak legitimacy of the Chilean regime.

6.2   TUTELARY PROTECTIVE DEMOCRACY AND REGIME SUPPORT IN CHILE

As the framework developed in Chapter 3 shows, the widespread assumption that what regimes do is the primary criterion citizens use to evaluate them is unfounded. Individuals also have attitudes

---

[7] Although explained in detail later, it is worth noting here that "liberal democracy" is often used to mean "full democracy," encompassing everything from the United States and Chile to the Nordic social democracies. I will use it here in a much narrower sense.

about the procedures and institutions that produce decisions. Whether or not such decision-making processes allow ordinary citizens to have a meaningful say is of paramount importance. This framework has considerably more potential to explain support patterns in Chile than economic liberalism. While the Chilean economic system has departed significantly from doctrinaire laissez-faire in a manner that produces positive (if not ideal) outcomes across the social spectrum, those aspects of the political system that inhibit the ability of citizens to exert influence over the political process largely remain.

In this section, I outline the changes in the Chilean state, from the time leading up to the Allende era to the present day. Although this material is not absolutely necessary for my argument, it provides useful contextual information for those readers not familiar with Chilean politics. Additionally, it further emphasizes a major theme of this research, namely that political forces are often powerful causal variables in their own right, and independent of the economic outcomes they produce. The political history of Chile should not be understood as a solely as a struggle between workers and capitalists, or between landlords and peasants. Of course these struggles matter, but political science has long recognized that the influence of class struggle on political outcomes can be mediated through political variables (R. B. Collier & Collier, 2002; Pierson, 2000; Skocpol, 1979, 1985). Another element must be considered in tandem with class struggle: the story of conflict between politicians, often reformist presidents and intransigent parliaments. The political sphere was opened to new groups, many from the subaltern sectors, by political actors seeking to gain advantages over their opponents. This rapid incorporation of the lower social strata, and the chaos it wrought, contributed to the crisis of the Allende government. The political system developed by the military, which still exists (albeit in modified form), reflects the lessons of this history, and was deliberately designed to prevent political actors from resorting to mobilization to resolve political disputes in the future.

6.2.1   The State and Society in the Pre-Allende Period

The assumption that economic liberalism must be the source of support is a grave but predictable error. Political science often gives undue precedence to socioeconomic factors; the literature on regime support is, as discussed in Chapter 2, particularly prone to this sort of mistake. This is a particularly grave error for students of Latin America, where the state has historically had a crucial role in economic development and management. As stated earlier, the economic role of the Chilean state from the consolidation of democracy in 1932 until the Allende era was enormous even by regional standards. This caused the state to take a leading role in shaping the economic destiny of the country. The state did not simply reflect social dynamics, but fundamentally altered them at key points in history.

Political parties, through control of the state, determined which social groups would become political actors. The political incorporation of new groups, particularly those belonging to the so-called popular sectors (i.e. the working class, the peasantry, and the urban informal sector) significantly outpaced any underlying economic changes (Oxhorn, 1995; Pinto, 1996). This discrepancy occurred because economic change did not propel new actors into the political arena; instead existing actors reached out and pulled new groups in, often as a strategic method of overcoming gridlock. This process of politically driven incorporation was accomplished through two mechanisms: changes to suffrage and electoral rules, and organization and mobilization of new groups.

Changes to voting rules and the incorporation of new social groups by political elites were not the result of bottom-up demands, but rather initiated by existing political actors attempting to win influence by expanding suffrage to potential supporters. The first major move to incorporate subaltern groups occurred during a period of intense struggle between a conservative parliament and the reformist President Arturo Alessandri, who was also supported by groups within the military. The expansion of the electorate was intended to provide additional political backing to Alessandri's modernization program, and to break his dependence on the military. This fundamentally altered the dynamics of political competition, but not necessarily in the way Alessandri hoped. The Communist Party and other Marxist groups, which had been quite radical, now had a viable chance to compete for power through elections, and Marxist parties managed to seize a sizable portion of the working-class vote from Alessandri, who primarily catered to the middle sectors (Boeninger, 1997, pp. 98–99).

While these reforms gave a formal political role to miners and laborers, they had little impact in the countryside. The rural peasantry remained under the control of their landlords, and agricultural areas remained conservative bastions until well into the twentieth century (Lapp, 2004; Roberts, 1998). This changed due to two factors. The first was the return to power of populist reformer (and former dictator), Carlos Ibáñez; the second was the rise of the Christian Democratic party (PDC). Ibáñez was a reformer along the same lines as Alessandri, although the two were bitter political enemies by midcentury. And like Alessandri, his reform program faced intense opposition from Chile's landed aristocracy, who controlled a sufficient proportion of legislative seats to block most reforms. In an attempt to marginalize his opponents, Ibáñez attempted to break one of the primary sources of the right's electoral strength: the domination of peasants by landlords (Baland & Robinson, 2006, p. 21). Control of the peasantry was critical to the electoral survival of the right, which represented a constituency that was great in wealth but small in numbers.

Although the secret ballot had been implemented prior to 1958, the dominance of the right in rural areas, and the weakening of that dominance after the introduction of the Australian ballot, suggest that secrecy rules were ineffective. Rural oligarchs had several tools to ensure that peasants could vote where other, more autonomous subaltern groups could not, and to force those peasants to cast their ballots for the right. Landlords frequently circumvented Chile's ban on voting by illiterates by teaching peasants to sign their names (Millar, 1981). And because Chilean parties printed their own ballots, landlords could easily determine if a peasant voted against the right and punish them accordingly (Loveman, 2001, pp. 221–223). The electoral reform of 1958 broke this control by introducing an Australian ballot that included all party slates, depriving landlords of information regarding individual voting choices. The reform had its desired effect: eventually conservative dominance in rural areas diminished considerably (Baland & Robinson, 2006; Hellinger, 1978). As a result, demands for land reform and other issues of importance to the peasantry would become contentious political questions with which future governments would have to grapple.

This change did not occur instantly: in the election immediately following the reform, conservative Jorge Alessandri won the presidency, showing that voting behaviour among the peasantry would not respond automatically to the reformed electoral rules. Simply allowing peasants to vote as they chose was not sufficient to ensure their defection to the center or left. The peasantry, long subject to domination by landlords and lacking political experience, could not simply transform itself into an effective political force independently, at least not in the short term. Yet reform did create opportunities for parties to organize and mobilize the peasantry. The Christian Democratic Party (PDC) was the first party to seize this opportunity. The PDC, although originating in the Conservative party, eventually developed its own communitarian ideology as an alternative both to traditional oligarchic conservatism and Marxism (Garretón, 1989a, pp. 13–15; A. Valenzuela, 1978, p. 34). This political project required the party to expand beyond its core constituency in the middle sectors by wooing groups that might otherwise support the Marxist left. The newly liberated peasantry was a pool of support previously untapped by centrist and leftist parties that held great promise for the PDC. Yet incorporation of the peasantry also required the PDC and the parties of the left to more firmly embrace land reform, something rural elites found particularly threatening.

The PDC also looked to the cities for support. They particularly sought to organize individuals who belonged to the informal sector.

These voters had been largely ignored by the left, which focused mostly on the industrial working classes (Garretón, 1989a, p. 29; A. Valenzuela, 1978, pp. 5, 26). The urban informal sector had also been impacted by the reform of 1958, which introduced true compulsory voting by making registration mandatory and stiffening penalties for nonvoting (Lapp, 2004, p. 60). Given the tendency of lower-income voters to abstain from voting at higher rates than wealthier voters, this reform ensured that parties that could successfully mobilize the subaltern sectors would have the largest possible gains for their efforts. The PDC's courting of newly politically relevant social groups was largely successful; by 1964, the PDC had grown in power and influence to the point where the right, in a strategic move to prevent the left from eking out a plurality, threw its support to PDC leader Eduardo Frei. By the end of Frei's term in office, the party would have cause to rue its rapid introduction of the poor into the political system. The failure of the PDC to translate its incorporation of new groups into victory in the 1970 Presidential elections began a trend that would ultimately lead to the fall of democracy in Chile. Conservative forces, which despite the reform could still mobilize large numbers of peasants to their cause, could not be entirely vanquished. The fact that Chile's electoral districts had not been reapportioned and thus failed to reflect the extreme urbanization of the preceding decades gave these conservative bastions a disproportionate level of influence in democratic politics (McDonald, 1969; A. Valenzuela, 1972). Newly included groups could not always be controlled, particularly when expectations were high and the pace of reform was insufficiently rapid. Many of the groups organized by the PDC defected to support Salvador Allende and the UP in 1970 (Kurtz, 2004b, pp. 102–103). Despite his victory, Allende soon found himself in a similar situation to that of the PDC.

If forced to point to a single policy battle that contributed most to the military coup of 1973, the creation of a socialized sector of the economy (the Area of Social Property, or APS) is the most likely candidate. Although the policy of the state entering into economic arenas previously reserved to the private sector was bitterly contested in and of itself (Boeninger, 1997, pp. 177–180; A. Valenzuela, 1978, p. 59), the way in which the program came to be implemented was far more destructive to Chilean democracy. The UP never gained control of the legislature, and made the disastrous choice to circumvent that institution in its creation and expansion of the APS. One mechanism for expropriation that had particularly unfortunate unintended consequences was a law, dating back to the twelve-day socialist regime of Marmaduke Grove in 1932, allowing the state to seize an enterprise that was suffering from production problems, especially those caused by labor disputes. The use of this provision would come back to haunt Allende. UP militants in the labor movement, who were already predisposed to accelerate the pace of social transformation through the use of factory seizures, were encouraged to intensify their efforts by taking factories without approval from the government; this often led the government to expropriate enterprises it otherwise would have left in private hands, if only for the time being (Winn, 1986). Essentially the UP, by making use of a decades-old law in ways never intended by its authors, unintentionally invited UP militants to radicalize even further. By doing so, the UP set in motion an escalating series of mobilizations and countermobilizations, which quickly spun out control. The resulting chaos, exacerbated by international antipathy and severe economic problems, led directly to the military coup of 1973.

Summary

One major point from the preceding discussion is worth restating before proceeding further, which is the causal primacy of the political realm. Between 1925 and 1973, political changes were the driving force behind the activation of social groups that eventually led to attempts at radical restructuring of the economy, and incorporation occurred from the top down, rather than the reverse. The base-level demands for economic restructuring that arose during the UP government were a historical exception, and resulted in part from the strategic behavior of UP leaders. The norm in twentieth-century politics was for members of the political class, including charismatic figures like Arturo Alessandri and Ibáñez, as well as party leaders such as Frei and Allende, to use expansions of political rights and mobilization to further their own ends and break political deadlocks. These expansions would occasionally be accompanied by economic reforms intended to entice the newly enfranchised to the banner of this or that party, but in all cases Chilean governments and political parties directed the course of economic and social transformation, not the other way around.

Tragically this process of rapid incorporation led mostly to frustrated expectations at the mass level, and not a few strategic blunders at the elite level, which together caused militants to engage in forms of activism that destabilized the entire system (Garretón, 1989a). This led to intense conflict, which the democratic system could not survive. This is worth noting, because while the Chilean political class certainly soured on the idea of statist socialism in the economic realm after Allende's overthrow, this historical process also inculcated an intense fear of popular mobilization and political engagement, which first developed on the right and later spread to a renovated left. This context is crucial for understanding the legacy of the military government and transition to democracy.

6.2.2 Chilean Democracy in the Modern Era: The Legacies of Authoritarianism

Many Chileans in 1973 hoped (or even assumed) that the military would seize power, take immediate steps to calm the political situation and right the course of the economy, and promptly return the reins of power to civilians. This was not unreasonable; periods of military rule in the twentieth century had been infrequent and brief. Yet the military regime that took power in 1973 sought not simply to calm society, but to transform it. The leaders of the new junta were not ignorant of the historical process I described earlier. They, and the armed forces in general, had come to believe that the political class had been criminally irresponsible in mobilizing the popular sectors to further their ambitions, and that this process of top-down incorporation led directly to the intense class conflict and deep politicization of society that preceded the fall of Allende. As a result, they sought to create a new political order that could depoliticize and discipline society through political and economic institutions (Foxley, 1983). The new regime was not about to return power to the same feckless politicians who had caused the crisis in the first place; a new political order had to be established prior to any return to civilian rule.

The 1980 Constitution: The Foundations of Tutelary, Protective Democracy

The military's political vision can be seen in the constitution that institutionalized its rule. Although the transition process brought a number of amendments in 1989, the system of government remained fundamentally the same. The 1980 constitution laid the foundation for a transition back to civilian rule under what might be called a tutelary, protective democracy. While the tutelary features have since been eliminated, the protective features, which severely circumscribe the political role of the citizenry, remain largely in place. The formally democratic and substantively elitist processes created under this document are the principal source of Chileans' disaffection with their regime.

Tutelary democracy has philosophical roots in Plato's Republic, and its conception of the guardian state. Plato envisioned a state governed by a class of philosopher kings whose duty would be to guard and guide the polity, which was seen as incapable of responsible self-governance (Dahl, 1989, ch. 4). A tutelary democracy is essentially a guardian state where power is directly held by the representatives of the people, but where exercise of that power is overseen by a guardian class. In the earliest versions of this concept as applied to modern politics, the guardian was a colonial power (Shils, 1962); as Latin American countries began to emerge from dictatorship in the 1980s, militaries assumed guardian roles in many states (Przeworski, 1988).

Several institutional features of Chile's 1980 constitution can be classified as tutelary. The National Security Council (NSC) served as the official organ of military guardianship. The NSC included the President of the Republic and the presidents of the Senate and the Supreme Court, but in practice would be dominated by the four heads of the armed forces who were also members (Constitution of Chile 1980, art. 45). The NSC had significant powers: it had to be consulted on foreign and domestic security policy (Constitution of Chile 1980, art. 40), appointed two members of the Constitutional Tribunal (Constitution of Chile 1980, art. 81), and appointed four former heads of the armed forces to the Senate (Constitution of Chile 1980, art. 45.d). In short, the military, through its majority in the NSC and its guaranteed seats in the upper chamber of the legislature, had the ability to insinuate itself into the business of all three branches of the Chilean regime. The tutelary features of the Chilean regime have since been removed, albeit in a process that was far too slow for many;[8] in a 2010 article Patricio Navia proclaimed that all "authoritarian enclaves" in the Chilean system had been eliminated (2010). These were not the only mechanisms the military included in the constitution to secure its political legacy. The constitution also includes a number of features that, while not tutelary, serve to inhibit the pace of political change.

While Chilean democracy is no longer tutelary, it remains protective. The protective conception of democracy was discussed in some detail in Chapter 3 as it relates to instrumentalism, but it is worth reviewing it here. The protective view of democracy sees competitive politics as a means to ensure the survival of some other social or political goal (Held, 2007, p. 35; Macpherson, 1977, ch. 2). Liberalism is often associated with protective democracy. Liberals see

---

[8] The constitutional reform that fully removed the last vestiges of the guardian state occurred in 2005, fifteen years after the first civilian president took office.

democracy as the best form of government for protecting individual rights and the pursuit of private interests. Popular sovereignty is not the goal of such a democracy; indeed protective democracy includes a suspicion of the unchecked powers of the masses and the fear that politics will devolve into a tyranny of the majority (e.g. Madison, 1952; Sartori, 1987; Schumpeter, 2008). Therefore, while protective democracies allow the populace to select its rulers, they also place a considerable number of hurdles into the policy process in order to slow the pace of change and ensure that minorities can block changes that infringe upon their rights. The result is a system in which popular opinion has only a weak and indirect role in shaping policy.

The Chilean democratic system has many protective features, and unlike its tutelary characteristics, most of the protective elements remain in force. The basic structures of government, with separation of powers between the legislature and the presidency, as well as the bicameral structure of the legislature, are common features of protective democracies inspired by classical liberalism, but all of these features are typical in Latin America. The military placed additional veto points in the Chilean regime. Originally, nearly half the Senate (at least ten out of twenty-three members) were to have been appointed by the President, the Supreme Court, or the NSC (Constitution of Chile 1980, art. 45), although the number of elected Senators was increased during the transition process (Constitution of Chile 1980, art. 45). This meant that the Senate would, for at least eight years, be significantly influenced by individuals who had never faced election and would therefore would have had little need to consider popular opinion.[9] The 2005 reforms abolished all appointed Senatorial seats.

The electoral system, established by organic law as required by Article 43 of the 1980 Constitution, is another major protective

---

[9] These appointed Senators blur the line between tutelary and protective features. As these Senators were given seats based on positions to which they came during the dictatorship, they also formed part of the guardian class, and thus had a tutelary role.

feature.[10] As stated previously, the binomial system creates a district magnitude of two for both the Chamber of Deputies and the Senate. The first and second place electoral pact each win a seat unless the first-place pact gets twice as many votes as the second-place pact. There is some dispute as to how much this system gives an unfair advantage to the political right, which usually gets about one-third of the vote but half the seats (Polga-Hecimovich & Siavelis, 2015; Zucco, 2006), but the fact that this system limits the impact of voters' choices is undeniable. Imagine a district in which the vote split in an election at time period 1 is 60–40, but shifts at period 2 to 40–60. It is difficult to imagine any electoral system except for the binomial system wherein a difference of this magnitude would cause absolutely no change in the winners; such an outcome would be rare even in first-past-the-post systems like that of the United States and the United Kingdom. Whatever its impact on the left-right balance of power, it is clear that this system minimizes the ability of voters to determine who wields legislative power. Large shifts in voter preferences do not produce concomitant shifts in the composition of the legislature, and building large legislative majorities is all but ruled out.

The impact of this system is exacerbated by the fact that other features of the Chilean system require large majorities, which the binomial system virtually precludes, to make all but the smallest of policy changes. Although it is the most discussed, the electoral system is not the strongest protective feature of the Chilean state. That prize goes to the various supermajority requirements for specific areas of legislation. The Chilean constitution and corresponding organic laws go into considerable policy detail in areas such as labor organizing and education, to name but a few. Amendments to these

---

[10] The electoral system was replaced with a multi-district PR system in 2015 ("Tie breaker: a new voting system should liven up politics," 2015). Since this event occurred outside the time period under analysis here (which ends roughly in 2014), it will be discussed as though it were still in place. See Chapter 7: Conclusion for a discussion of this repeal.

policy areas require significant supermajorities in the legislature: depending upon the issue area, either two-thirds, three-fifths, or four-sevenths of each chamber must approve changes to policies that are encoded in the Constitution or organic law (Constitution of Chile 2005, art. 66). In 2014, Michele Bachelet returned to La Moneda promising to reform the electoral system and abolish private secondary education. Despite her massive popularity, she was not able to obtain the three-fifths majority necessary for the former nor the four-fifths necessary for the latter.[11] The *Concertación* came nowhere close to the two-thirds majority that would be necessary to replace the constitution entirely, another demand that seems to be gaining in popularity in Chile.

Consequences of Tutelary, Protective Democracy: Representation without Participation

To summarize, the Chilean political system has gradually been cleansed of the stain of authoritarianism, but remains riddled with countermajoritarian features and veto points. These have served their intended purpose: they drastically reduce the efficacy of ordinary *chilenos*, confining their role to the periodic selection of leaders. Many scholars have noted that a culture of elitism has taken hold in Chile's political class. Party leaders generally prefer intra-elite negotiation to mass contestation to advance their agendas (Huber et al., 2010). There can be no doubt that the Chilean left went through a process of renovation during military rule and transition to democracy that made them wary of popular mobilization (Roberts, 1998). The Chilean political class has, for the most part, come to embrace this system. Yet to those who stridently criticize this elitist turn, one must ask: what else could the left have done?

---

[11] Again, there has been progress on both these issues very recently, but since these changes could not have influenced the public opinion data presented here, this section ignores them. See Chapter 7: Conclusion for a discussion.

The values, beliefs, and preferences of the political class vis-á-vis popular mobilization and inclusion are irrelevant. Even if the elite had been committed to revitalizing the social roots of parties, it is unlikely that such a renewal would have taken place. There was simply nothing to gain (and much to lose) by adopting such a strategy. Mobilization is risky and, given the view of Chile's history common among the right, extremely threatening; any gains of such a strategy would have had to override the danger of provoking the military. Revitalization of grassroots links would have been an exercise in futility. The *Concertación* could have put all of its resources and energies into mobilizing its base and it would have made very little difference. The electoral system, which prevents large voting majorities from translating into large majorities in the legislature, combines with supermajority requirements to completely stymie any mobilization strategy for massive institutional change. And such an aggressive political strategy would have driven the right even more securely into the arms of the armed forces. As it happens, the slow, negotiated reform strategy of the center-left was the best strategy for reform. Indeed, recent history bears this out. During her first campaign and administration, Michele Bachelet ran on promises of a more inclusive, participatory style of governance, only to abandon these promises once the strategic realities of governing in a protective democracy became clear (Weeks & Borzutzky, 2012).

Nevertheless, individuals do not form political attitudes with an eye toward what might have been; they respond to what exists before them. And what exists in Chile is a system with extreme protective features designed to limit the exercise of popular sovereignty. In other words, despite fears of a crisis in this area, representation is strong in Chile: all the criteria discussed in Chapters 1 and 3 are more than met. Yet participation is thwarted at every turn by the mutually reinforcing combination of the electoral system and supermajority requirements. In tandem, these two features make mobilization of the electorate an impractical tool for settling political disputes, and elites must exercise considerable independence

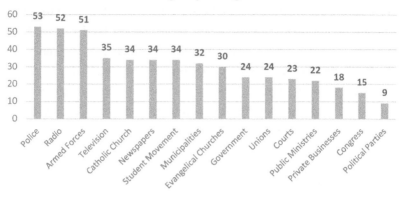

FIGURE 6.2: Confidence in Chilean institutions
Source: CEP

from their constituents in order to accomplish anything at all. Chile is undoubtedly a democracy, but due to the institutional features it is one in which the only formal mechanism for participation is political parties that have little interest in developing strong social roots. Political parties seem to be bearing the brunt of the blame for this state of affairs. Figure 6.2 below presents data on confidence in various institutions from a 2012 study of political attitudes.

While none of the representative institutions of Chile cover themselves with glory here, political parties are the least loved of all, with only 9 percent of individuals expressing confidence in them. To drive this point home, I note that the armed forces, who killed at least 2,000 civilians, tortured and sent into exile thousands more, ruled with an iron fist for nearly twenty years, and created the current political regime, are *five times* more trusted than political parties. Given the power of parties and their failure to give a voice to ordinary citizens, this should not come as a surprise. Indeed the elitism of Chile's parties has led some scholars to conclude that Chile has become not a polyarchy (Dahl, 1971) but a partyarchy (Coppedge, 1994). One recent work on regime support in Chile, concluding that concerns over representation are not the cause of democratic dissatisfaction, speculates that this development of partyarchy may be responsible (Siavelis, 2009), given the pronounced antipathy toward parties and the party system in public opinion data. And Carlin (2011) cites a lack of trust in parties as a crucial factor in driving the student movement to contentious politics. Within the analytical framework used here, we should expect such a system to have anemic support at best, because while the system may meet the material needs of its citizenry, it severely neglects their need to have a voice in the political processes that impact them.

6.3   ANALYZING THE TWO LIBERALISMS

The previous Sections 6.1 and 6.2 demonstrated that Chile underwent two liberal revolutions under the Pinochet regime: one economic, the other political. Both have been subsequently altered by democratic governments, but the essential legacy of military rule remains: a laissez-faire economy and a protective democracy. This raises an important question: which matters more for support? Should we look to performance, or to procedures? The theoretical and empirical work presented so far suggests that, while performance issues probably matter, we cannot afford to neglect the independent impact of participation, which has been compromised by protective democracy and the partyarchy it created and enforces. In this section, I test that assertion with data. First, I perform statistical analyses of data relating to regime support, as well as to attitudes toward the party system. This data shows that concerns over participation, rather than performance (or its close relative, interest attendance), drive lack of support for the Chilean regime and its party system. I then use experimental analysis, buttressed by a program evaluation of a participatory initiative in Providencia, to further demonstrate that participation, or rather the lack of same, is responsible for the woes of Chilean democracy.

6.3.1   Testing the Impact of Protected Democracy: Analysis of CEP Data

Two hypotheses can be derived directly from this logic. The first is that lack of support for the party system is driven by the failure of parties to encourage participation. The second is that this lack of faith in the party system is a form of depressed regime-based efficacy (RBE); citizens who express disaffection with the party system do so because parties no longer enable ordinary Chileans to impact the course of politics. This implies that confidence in the party system should have much the same effect that RBE does in previous models (see Chapter 4).

I test the latter hypothesis first, using the "Audit of Democracy" study, conducted in 2012 by the Center for Public Studies (CEP). This model is very similar to the model defined by Equation 4.11 in Chapter 4, with a few small differences. Regime support is measured by a latent variable that impacts four indicators, all measures of institutional confidence. Those institutions are: government, the Congress, the public ministries, and the courts. Booth and Seligson (2009) have shown that, although individuals can have idiosyncratic attitudes toward one institution or another, when specified as indicators of a single latent variable they form a measure of "broad institutional confidence," which is highly correlated with regime support. Performance is measured by evaluation of the economy, which is the only indicator of the concept available. Confidence in political parties is used in place of regime-based efficacy (RBE); this substitution will be justified with additional tests. Given Chile's homogeneity, no variable for race is included. Finally, socioeconomic status is measured via respondents' registered social category. Results are presented in Table 6.1.

Several of these results are important here. First, note that confidence in parties works exactly as it should if it is a reflection of parties' role as enablers of popular engagement in politics. Confidence in parties significantly and strongly impacts regime support; furthermore,

Table 6.1: *Analysis of CEP data on regime support*

Measurement (n = 1,481)			
Regime Support	Est	SE	P-value
Factor loadings			
Confidence in government	1.000	-	-
Confidence in Congress	1.046	0.039	0.000
Confidence in courts	0.663	0.038	0.000
Confidence in public ministries	0.819	0.038	0.000
Error variances			
Confidence in government	0.398	0.023	0.000
Confidence in Congress	0.340	0.022	0.000
Confidence in courts	0.735	0.030	0.000
Confidence in public ministries	0.595	0.027	0.000
Courts * ministries	0.157	0.021	0.000
Structural (n = 1,481)			
Regime Support	Est	SE	P-value
Evaluation of economy	0.161	0.035	0.000
Confidence in parties	0.582	0.056	0.000
Interaction	−0.126	0.064	0.049
Social class			
ABC1	0.049	0.044	0.257
C2	0.012	0.056	0.830
C3	−0.027	0.083	0.748
D	−0.075	0.083	0.369
Education	0.033	0.035	0.353
Age	0.111	0.028	0.000
Female	−0.012	0.025	0.638
Urban	−0.064	0.026	0.015
Ideology	0.235	0.035	0.000

it moderates the impact of economic concerns, just as RBE did in Chapter 4. Additionally, note that none of the SES dummies have a significant impact; this is evidence against the economic liberal theory of low support in Chile.

I freely admit that the interpretation of confidence in parties as a measure of RBE is questionable, even in light of the results presented here. Party confidence was used in models in Chapter 4, but only in tandem with other variables that relate directly to RBE. Happily, no assumption is actually necessary on this point, as the CEP study also included a suite of questions related to party system attitudes directly. By analyzing the relationship between these specific questions and general attitudes toward the party system, I am able to show more directly that problems of participatory access are the most important factor. I conduct two analyses: one analyzing the sources of discontent with existing parties, and another which analyzes more abstract views of the necessity of parties to democracy.

Table 6.2 presents an analysis of the antecedent attitudes that lead to a lack of faith in political parties. CEP includes several questions that can shed light on whether participatory or representational

Table 6.2: *Sources of confidence in parties*

Confidence in parties ($n = 1,481$)	Est	SE	P-value
Parties give alternatives	0.066	0.027	0.014
Parties encourage participation	0.160	0.026	0.000
Parties only divide people	0.103	0.027	0.000
Participatory preference	−0.087	0.036	0.016
Evaluation of the economy	0.145	0.027	0.000
Social class			
ABC1	0.288	0.221	0.193
C2	0.127	0.195	0.515
C3	−0.009	0.171	0.960
D	−0.003	0.168	0.985
Education	0.019	0.035	0.583
Age	−0.024	0.028	0.387
Female	−0.077	0.052	0.135
Urban	0.088	0.060	0.144
Ideology	0.017	0.037	0.638

issues are responsible for low confidence. These include two measures of participatory preference,[12] and three questions about specific aspects of parties in Chile: whether parties encourage participation, whether they provide voters with real alternatives (an evaluation of the parties' representative function), and whether they serve only to divide people. The analysis also includes the same control variables as the earlier CEP model.

Although the evaluation of the representative function of parties does influence party confidence, assessments of parties' role as facilitators of participation matters twice as much. This is consistent with the argument that problems related to participation, rather than representation, drive negative attitudes toward parties. The fact that individuals with strong participatory preferences have much more negative party system attitudes is likewise consistent with the argument. This seems to suggest that, while concerns about representation (such as those raised by the economic liberal argument) may have an impact, the lack of participatory opportunities that parties are expected to offer is far more important.

This is even clearer when analyzing beliefs about the necessity of parties for democracy. Results are presented in Table 6.3. Belief in the necessity of parties has been shown to more directly reflect attitudes regarding the party system than confidence in political parties, which tends to be impacted both by party system attitudes as well as assessments of specific, individual parties (Bélanger, 2004; Poguntke, 1996). In other words, someone who generally admires political parties but *really* despises one specific party (perhaps the Communist party or the far-right UDI) may appear to have negative party system attitudes based on their confidence in parties; such individuals' lack of systemic animus tends to be clearer when the question concerns the necessity of parties for democracy.

---

[12] These are measured by a belief that each of the following is important: "For politicians to take the opinions of citizens into account when making decisions" and "Allowing citizens to have more opportunities to participate in the making of public policy (politicas) decisions."

Table 6.3: *Sources of the belief that parties are necessary for democracy*

Necessity of parties (n = 1,481)	Est	SE	P-value
Parties give alternatives	−0.018	0.028	0.517
Parties encourage participation	0.169	0.027	0.000
Parties only divide people	0.156	0.027	0.000
Participatory preference	0.202	0.039	0.010
Evaluation of the economy	0.044	0.028	0.114
Social class			
ABC1	−0.005	0.237	0.982
C2	0.095	0.213	0.657
C3	0.034	0.191	0.861
D	0.026	0.188	0.889
Education	0.086	0.036	0.017
Age	0.144	0.029	0.000
Female	−0.045	0.053	0.391
Urban	−0.048	0.063	0.442
Ideology	−0.040	0.040	0.324

Here there is little doubt about which factors shape attitudes toward parties. Neither the performance metric, nor measures of SES, nor evaluation of parties' representative function matter for determining this attitude. Evaluations of the participatory function of parties, on the other hand, matter more than any attitudinal or demographic variable present. Together these analyses paint a fairly clear picture: systemic support in Chile is driven down by negative attitudes toward the country's party system. And the party system is despised because political parties should serve as the primary link between citizens and the state, and Chile's parties have abdicated that role.

While the preceding analyses all support the hypothesis that a lack of participatory opportunities is responsible for the weak legitimacy of the Chilean state, these tests are somewhat indirect. They require considerable inferential leaps about the relationship between party system attitudes, regime attitudes, and question interpretation. Additionally, observational statistics cannot demonstrate causality, due to the inability to control for all conceivable confounding variables. Fortunately, I need not rely on these tests alone; in Section 6.3.2, I provide a more direct and rigorous test of my framework using laboratory-style experiments.

6.3.2   Participatory Institutions and Support in Chile: An Experimental Analysis

To provide a more conclusive test of H3, I conducted a lab experiment in Chile among 147 students in six classes at Catholic University and Diego Portales University, which formed experimental blocks. The questionnaire (in Spanish) is available in the appendix to this chapter. Students in each block read a short news article about a decision-making process at the municipal level, involving a grant from the national government to be spent on community security. The issue of security was chosen because it was likely to have equal salience across demographic groups. The news article stated that municipalities could spend the money on security cameras or hiring private security personnel. Respondents were asked about their preferred option prior to being informed of the outcome. The outcome of the decision-making process remained constant across groups: the municipality chose to spend the money on cameras.

Students were randomly assigned to one of two treatments. In the first treatment, the municipal government consulted a group of security experts before making their decision. In the second treatment, the municipality held a series of participatory town-hall meetings (cabildos) wherein residents of the municipality debated and voted directly on the issue, choosing the cameras. Two treatments were applied without a true control group (which would entail divulging only the choice of policy with no explanation of how the choice was made) because such a control would make the actual choice the sole criteria for evaluation. Explicating the expert-led process allowed for a point of comparison that is similar to how decisions are commonly made in Chile.

The subjects were then asked a series of four questions regarding their support of the municipality and its handling of the issue: whether they approved of the way the municipality handled the process, whether they thought the process was fair, whether they thought the process was undemocratic, and if they thought the municipality should use the method for future decisions whenever possible. I constructed two scales of these questions (differences on individual questions were also tested). First, I constructed an unweighted index by adding all items (with democratic-ness recoded to match the others) and rescaled the sum so that the index has a value from zero to one. This assumes that all questions have equal importance, which is not reasonable. To relax that assumption I estimated the parameters of a Confirmatory Factor Analysis (CFA) model, which posits that answers on these questions are caused by a latent "support" variable. I used the estimated factor scores from this analysis, which is a continuous variable with a mean of zero and standard deviation of one by construction. I analyzed the effect of both experimental treatments (technocratic and participatory method of choice) in two ways. I conducted simple t-tests (with unequal variance assumed) for differences across treatments for each question and both indices. This approach left two issues unaccounted for. First, it did not control for whether or not the subject agreed with the chosen outcome. Second, it cannot account for the fact that the experimental subjects were not independently selected, but were nested within the classes in which the experiments were administered. I conducted a multilevel regression analysis, with subjects nested within classes, which included a dummy variable for agreement with outcome, to account for these complications. Results are presented in Table 6.4.

Even when accounting for satisfaction of a subject's preference, the mode of decision making had a significant and substantively large impact on municipal support. Subjects in the participatory treatment

Table 6.4: *Results from experimental analysis*

Measurement

Indicator (n = 147)	Parameter	Estimate	S.E.	P-value
Approval	Loading	0.617	0.059	0.000
	Error	0.620	0.073	-
Fairness	Loading	0.929	0.041	0.000
	Error	0.137	0.075	-
Democratic-ness	Loading	0.705	0.051	0.000
	Error	0.503	0.071	-
Future use	Loading	0.584	0.064	0.000
	Error	0.659	0.074	-

Goodness of Fit Statistic	Value	P-value
Chi-square	2.007	0.367
RMSEA	0.005	
CFI	1.000	

T-tests

Item	Mean for mode of decision		Difference	S.E.	P-value
	Technocratic	Participatory			
Approval (n = 147)	2.987	3.625	0.638	0.206	0.002
Fairness (n = 144)	3.247	4.169	0.922	0.193	0.000
Democratic-ness (n = 145)	2.419	4.085	1.670	0.208	0.000
Future use (n = 143)	3.108	3.884	0.776	0.219	0.001
Index, unweighted (n = 140)	0.488	0.736	0.248	0.040	0.000
CFA predicted index (n = 147)	−0.420	0.443	0.863	0.148	0.000

Multilevel regression

Predictor (n = 147)	CFA predicted index		
	Estimate	S.E.	P-value
Intercept (grand mean)	0.186	0.078	0.017
Participatory method	0.408	0.070	0.000
Agreement with outcome	0.371	0.078	0.000

group were, on average, more supportive of the municipality by .863 units. This is equivalent to an increase of roughly 20 percent of the CFA predicted index's empirically observed scale. Results were similar for the unweighted scale and all of the individual questions; in all cases the participatory treatment group had higher levels of support than those in the technocracy treatment.

The multilevel regression, which controls for agreement with the actual outcome (installation of cameras) and accounts for the fact that experimental subjects were not independently selected (due to nesting within classes), shows a similar impact. The multilevel regression used factor effects coding for the independent variables (1 for present and -1 for absent); this means that the intercept is the grand mean, and the coefficients for method of decision and outcome agreement represent the difference between the participatory treatment group and those who agreed with the chosen outcome and the grand mean. Both participatory method and outcome agreement had a significant impact on subjects' reported support, albeit somewhat smaller than that estimated by the t-tests.

Due to the relatively small number of respondents and constraints on the time students could spend on the experiment, I did not directly model the mediated relationship between participatory opportunities, RBE, and support in this experiment. The impact of participatory opportunities on support is analyzed directly. Yet the breakdown of results by individual questions conforms to the notion that RBE is the underlying causal mechanism. Note that the differences across conditions for fairness and democratic-ness, which are procedural evaluations, are somewhat larger than those for the more utilitarian approval question and the largely neutral future use question.

The experimental results demonstrate far more conclusively what the statistical analyses presented earlier cannot: that institutions that allow for a direct role in decision making produce greater support for the sponsoring actor, even when controlling for agreement with chosen policies. These results do have some significant limitations. Since all participants were university students, extrapolating these findings beyond the student population is risky, as nonstudents may have different attitudes regarding participatory governance. The fact that students are the most vocally dissatisfied group in Chilean society allays such concerns to some extent. But taken in combination with the statistical analyses presented earlier, the evidence provided here strongly confirms my theoretical framework.

The results of experiments are always subject to concerns about their external validity. The price one pays for the ability to randomize and control possible independent variable values is an abstraction away from real-world dynamics, which could contaminate the results in unpredictable ways. In short, the question remains: would participatory programs have the same impact if implemented in a real-world setting? In Section 6.3.3, I analyze one such program to bolster these experimental results.

6.3.3 *Participatory Governance in the Real World:* Piensa Providencia

This section will show that a real-world participatory program, similar to that envisioned in the experiments described in the previous Section 6.3.2,[13] produced increased support for the municipal administration by significantly reducing tensions between the government and social organizations. This section proceeds in two parts: first, I review the design and implantation of the program, relying on interviews with municipal staff and my own observations, to demonstrate that the program was truly participatory. I then present evidence from a program evaluation survey, administered by the municipality and designed in consultation with the author, to show that the program had the predicted effect: namely that it improved relations between the municipality and its citizens.

---

[13] This similarity is not coincidental; the experiment was inspired in part by this program.

Before diving into a description of the program, a brief explanation of the context in which it was implemented is necessary. Providencia is a *comuna* (municipality or commune) lying just to the east of downtown Santiago. It was once a middle-class area, but has rapidly increased in affluence over recent years. Despite the increasing socioeconomic position of its residents, it is not one of the bastions of the elite, who live in municipalities further to the east such as Las Condes and Vitacura. Social organizations grew as the city's profile became increasingly upper-middle class. This was especially true in Bellavista, a neighborhood that sits at the foot of Cerro San Cristobal. Bellavista was once a district of bars and nightclubs, but the increasing number of upper-middle class residents led to the proliferation of social organizations, including many associated with the student movement, as well as strong community organizations.

This rapid development of left-of-center social organizations was not, for many years, reflected in the composition of the municipal government. For sixteen years, from 1996 until 2012, the municipality's chief executive (*alcalde*, or mayor) was Cristián Labbé. Labbé was a member of the far-right Independent Democratic Union (UDI), who had served as a member of the armed forces and the notorious spy agency DINA; he would later be arrested in 2014 for his role in the violence perpetrated by the regime immediately after the 1973 coup ("Difunden lista completa con 1500 ex agentes de la DINA que incluye a alcalde Cristián Labbé," 2012). Needless to say Labbé had little love for the nascent social movements that took root in the municipality after 2006. His administration paid them as little attention as possible (Bica, 2013), except when they engaged in disruptive politics. He used a heavy hand to end student takeovers of high schools during the 2006 student protests ("Estudiantes del liceo Lastarria se reintegran mañana a clases," 2006). Eventually, independent leftist Josefa Errázuriz, with support from social movements in general and the student movement in particular, ousted Labbé from the mayor's office. In this sense Errázuriz identified with a broader trend within the Chilean nonpartisan left toward a more socially rooted political strategy (Fuentes, 2013). In short, Errázuriz came to office at a time when municipal relationships with organized civil society were defined by mutual mistrust and animosity. Her election certainly raised hopes that relations would improve, but a certain amount of suspicion among activists was inevitable. After sixteen years of opposition, the municipality would have to prove its commitment to greater inclusion and participation.

The *Piensa Providencia* (PP) program analyzed here was the first major initiative under the new administration that attempted to introduce a new kind of politics into municipal governance. The program concerned the development and implementation of the Communal Development Plan (PCD, *Plan Comunal de Desarrollo*). These plans are stipulated by Chilean law, and govern the joint administration by the municipality and the national government of investment and implementation of projects to promote health, well-being, education, and public services, among other things ("Ley orgánica constitucional de municipalidades," 2006). Municipal governments have the discretion to develop their own plans, which they then submit to the national administration.

PP, implemented in 2013, specified that the PCD would be developed through a series of three town-hall meetings (*cabildos*), with a separate meeting held in each neighborhood of the municipality. The first meeting introduced the program and, through working groups on various specific policy areas, developed proposals for the plan. Those proposals were then submitted to the relevant experts on the municipal staff, who converted them into actionable items that could be included on the development plan. At the second meeting, the *técnicos* (experts such as architects, engineers, and urban planners) met directly with participants, explaining any changes or omissions of proposals. For example, many proposals were rejected because they concerned issues (such as rules for bicycling on sidewalks) that pertained not to the PCD, but rather the regulatory plan, which is analogous to a municipal code in the United States. At the end of the second meeting, participants voted on the priority of the various proposals. The municipal staff then wrote the PCD according to these priorities, and the final plan was presented at the third set of *cabildos*.

The program was designed to maximize participation and transparency throughout the process. The municipal staff identified two major potential stumbling blocks: the ingrained passivity of a citizenry that has few opportunities for direct involvement in politics, and the possibility that the social organizations would dominate the process for their own ends (Bica, 2013; N. Valenzuela, 2013). To address the former, the municipal staff designed aspects of the program to encourage the free expression of ideas. The first round of *cabildos* began with an exercise called "dreams of my neighborhood," where participants were asked to write their hopes for their neighborhood on a card and place it on a wall; some of these were read aloud. Observing this, I found the exercise a bit vapid at first. It was only as the meeting progressed that I understood the purpose (and effectiveness) of the exercise. Chileans are simply not used to such direct participation; multiple participants at the first round of meetings asked where the *técnicos* were. This exercise was in fact a very effective ice-breaker, essentially welcoming participants to express their ideas and to ease them into a political role with which they had little experience. This was especially crucial for individuals who were not members of social organizations. Another key tactic for managing this issue was the training of facilitators, volunteers who answered questions about the process. These individuals went through three separate training sessions, which focused on ensuring that facilitators would only give necessary procedural advice, without interjecting their own ideas into the process. Finally, the municipality attempted to promote the program to the broadest possible audience, for example by advertising at large concerts where many individuals not affiliated with social organizations were likely to congregate (Bica, 2013). These attempts to encourage participation seemed to work. In an evaluation of the program, seventy-five respondents out of seventy-nine who attended at least one cabildo reported that they were able to express their opinions at the meetings (Rhodes-Purdy, 2014).

Although the program's architects were concerned about the natural passivity many Chileans have developed over years of dictatorship and protective democracy, they also had to contend with another potential problem: the domination of the process by social organizations. This concern was particularly acute in Bellavista, where social organizations were especially strong and more accustomed to using contention and protest than collaboration when dealing with the municipal government. That these organizations might attempt to push their own goals at the expense of unorganized individual participants was a very real possibility (Bica, 2013; N. Valenzuela, 2013).

Nor was this concern unfounded. Another participatory CDP program, this one in Santiago, conducted meetings similar to the first *cabildos* in Providencia, although after that first meeting the process was very different from what occurred in PP. In Santiago, after proposals were elaborated, instead of the constant open participation enacted in Providencia, the neighborhood associations (in consultation with the municipal administration) were given responsibility, shutting out citizens who did not belong to such organizations. This was precisely the sort of domination by social organizations that the architects of PP sought to avoid.

This did not go over well at first. At the second *cabildo* in Bellavista, an older man took the microphone during the opening meeting to denounce the municipal government for shutting his organization out of the process. Yet over the course of the program, the municipality was able to balance admirably the need to include nonorganized individuals and the demands of social organizations. The administration held separate consultations with social organizations to assuage their concerns that they were being ignored (Bica, 2013), and participation was indeed broad; according to statistics collected, over 1000 people attended at least one *cabildo*, and of those, 58 percent were not affiliated with any social organization (*Informe cabildos abril 2013, etapa 1: sueños, diagnósticos y propuestas*, 2013). Even the relatively militant organizations in Bellavista seemed to come around, eventually. At the third meeting, participants presented municipal staff with flowers and a poem of thanks to Errázuriz. The municipal staff also reported that interactions with previously antagonistic social movements had improved considerably (Equipo de Planificación, 2013).

Piensa Providencia and Municipality–Society Relations

Although the example from Bellavista is a particularly dramatic example of PP's role in thawing relations between the municipality and social organizations, more data are needed to conclude that this trend was general. The municipality collected such data in January of 2014 at a series of meetings intended to review and evaluate the program as the administration prepared to implement further participatory programs. These meetings included a survey, which I helped to design, intended to collect data on the support for the program. This survey was entirely self-selected, so no parametric tests can be done and caution is warranted on extrapolating the collected data to the municipal population as a whole. As my own observations show, social organizations who were (early in the process) dissatisfied with the program used such meetings to make their views known; if dissatisfaction were widespread, one might expect they would again take the opportunity to express their views.

No such dissatisfaction is apparent in the data collected. The program evaluation survey indicates that participants felt their voices were heard and were supportive of the program. Only 5.3 percent of respondents answered "no" when asked if they felt their opinions were taken into account during the process, 74.4 percent reported that their interactions with *técnicos* were either "good" or "very good," and 88.8 percent had a positive evaluation of participatory spaces offered during the program. Respondents were nearly unanimous (94.3 percent) in their belief that the municipality enabled participation through PP. Perhaps the best evidence of the program's support can be seen in respondents' attitudes about future use of similar programs. Nearly all respondents (97.7 percent) agreed or strongly agreed that the municipality should make future decisions using participatory programs like PP when possible, and 96.7 percent reported that they would probably or very probably participate in such programs in the future. Caution should be taken in extrapolating from these results to the population of participants, given the self-selection. However, one would expect that organized social groups would take these evaluation meetings as an opportunity to register their displeasure if such antipathy existed, as they did in early *cabildos*. The data collected show no such evidence; indeed, the results strongly point to a highly successful participatory initiative that bridged a deep chasm between civil society and the municipal government.

The qualitative evaluation of one program in a single municipality would not, in and of itself, be sufficient to conclude that participatory programs improve support for the sponsoring entity. Yet this program, and its clear impact on previously strained relationships between social organizations and the municipal administration, provide a real-world example of the causal dynamics established experimentally in the previous Section 6.3.2. The conclusion is clear: participatory programs, when carefully designed to include all citizens, can and do improve relations between government and citizens.

6.4   CONCLUSION

Despite the economic benefits the Chilean center-left has managed to wrest from the liberal economy, the framework I apply here suggests that the exclusivity and elitism which the protective features of the Chilean state encourage put a significant damper on any enthusiasm for the regime. I have presented statistical, experimental, and qualitative evidence, all of which is consistent with this conclusion. The Chilean state and its party system are loathed by many not because of the policy choices they make but because of *how those choices are made*. In short: procedures matter, no matter how good the policy they produce may be.

In this chapter, I have shown that, since the 1930s, the Chilean state took a leading role in shaping the economy and society. Mobilization and politicization of society was not driven by economic transformation but by political elites seeking to escape the constant conflict between reform and conservatism. This, along with some strategic blunders during the Allende years, was what goaded the military out of its barracks. This fear, that feckless politicians might attempt to mobilize the electorate in dangerous ways, was encoded into the 1980 constitution, which governs Chile to this day, albeit with significant modifications. That document placed Chile's nascent democracy under military guardianship, yet even when the guardianship was entirely lifted in 2005, the countermajoritarian elements embodied by supermajorities and the binomial system remained. These institutions, along with elite preferences for negotiation versus participation, have drastically limited the political role of the citizenry. Mobilization of the electorate cannot, as in pre-1973 Chile, break political deadlocks or settle policy debates. Negotiation with opponents has become the only viable path to reform, a path which the *Concertacíon* has navigated with admirable results. Despite policy successes that are the envy of the region, in the absence of a more meaningful political role for ordinary citizens, political malaise is unlikely to abate.

6.5 APPENDIX: SURVEY INSTRUMENT FOR EXPERIMENTAL ANALYSIS

Public security is an issue of widespread concern in this country. Recently, Chilean municipalities were given generous grants to encourage the development of new ways of combating crime and insecurity on the streets. Municipal governments were allowed to spend the money as they saw fit, and the process for making that decision was also left to the municipalities. The grants could be spent on one of the following:

Hiring and training additional security patrols
Installing cameras, lights, and other surveillance equipment
Before proceeding to the next page, please answer the following question:

Q1. Which option do you prefer?
Q2. How strongly do you prefer the option you chose? (10 point scale).

In the municipality of interest, the municipal government [Treatment 1 text: commissioned a panel of experts on crime and security issues | Treatment 2 text: instituted a series of town meetings, wherein residents of the comuna were allowed to discuss and debate the options] in order to decide how to spend the money. After considerable discussion and debate, [Treatment 1 text: the expert panel | Treatment 2 text: the majority of participants at the town meetings] decided that installing cameras and other surveillance equipment was the best option for improving security in the comuna. The municipal government concurred with the [Treatment 1 text: panel's | Treatment 2 text: town meetings'] recommendation and approved the proposal. The installation of lights and cameras will begin next year.

QUESTIONS:

(All questions use 7 point Likert scales)

Q3: Do you agree or disagree with the decision to spend the money on cameras?

Q4: Do you approve or disapprove of the way in which the municipality made this decision?

Q5: Are you satisfied or dissatisfied with the way in which the municipality handled this decision?

   Please read the following statements and indicate your degree of agreement or disagreement (where 1 is "totally disagree" and 5 is "totally agree") with each.

Q6: The process by which the decision was made was fair.

Q7: The process by which the decision was made was undemocratic.

Q8: The municipality should make as many decisions as possible using the process described above.

7 Conclusion

I conclude this work by discussing some of the major theoretical implications of this analysis, pointing out areas for future research, and by analyzing what these findings can tell us about normative debates about participation and stability in democracies. Before doing so, I will briefly summarize the major findings of this research and the evidence used to support them.

This project sought to test competing predictions made by liberal and participatory democratic theory regarding factors that encourage regime support. To do so, I created a general model of regime support based upon the competing assumptions that these theories make about why democracy is valuable or desirable, ideal relationships between citizens, civil society, and the state, and whether democratic participation is intrinsically valuable to citizens, or merely a means to protecting private ends. I further refined this framework by synthesizing it with social psychological theories of organizational justice, which include both performance and procedural variables, as well as subjective evaluations of these variables, into its causal framework (see Figure 1.2 for a graphical representation). This framework hypothesized that subjective evaluations of procedural justice, specified as citizen autonomy and operationalized as regime-based efficacy (RBE) impact support in two ways: both directly and by diminishing the influence of poor governance.

I first evaluated the individual-attitudinal relationships using data from across Latin America, collected by LAPOP; data from the ANES in the United States were used to test the generalizability of the framework, as well as its robustness when using different measures of performance evaluations, RBE, and regime support. All analyses, with minor differences, were consistent with the framework specified in

Figure 1.2 (see Chapter 4). By comparing average levels of RBE in countries that have extensive opportunities for direct participation to those that do not, I also provided preliminary evidence of the importance of participatory opportunities to regime support.

The most important evidence for the proposition that participatory opportunities shape support came from the case-focused Chapters 5 and 6. The chapter on Venezuela (Chapter 5) laid out a theoretical explanation of support in that regime that could account for both its participatory and populist-authoritarian features. I argued that Chávez practiced a political strategy, which I call participatory populism, wherein the regime legitimated its hegemonic politics at the national level using a mutually reinforcing combination of charismatic attachment and participatory self-governance at the local level. This stands in contrast to personalistic theories of support, which see no role for participatory programs, and participatory democratic theories, which underestimate the importance of Chávez in maintaining the legitimacy of the regime he founded. Quantitative analysis showing that council participation has a positive effect on regime support, but only among those with strong participatory democratic beliefs, ruled out personalism; the fact that a positive relationship between council participation and RBE only existed among regime supporters was inconsistent with participatory democracy. Qualitative analysis of the council's practices, including discrimination against opposition supporters and the use of the councils as a Bolivarian "reserve army" at election time further contradicted the assumptions of participatory democratic approaches. Only participatory populism made predictions that were consistent with all findings.

I then turned to the paradox of anemic support in Chile. Using quantitative analysis of survey data collected by the Center for Public Studies (CEP), I sought to understand the sources of antipathy toward Chile's least popular political institution: its party system. Evidence from these surveys indicated that Chile suffers from a crisis of participation, not representation: concerns over parties' failure to encourage citizen participation were far more important than concerns over their representative function in determining party system attitudes.

Finally, I presented experimental and qualitative evidence that participatory opportunities could improve support in Chile, were they available. The experimental analysis served two purposes: in addition to offering evidence regarding the roots of weak support in Chile, it also provided a test of the general impact participatory governance programs have on support, unsullied by concerns over the idiosyncratic details that complicate analyses of real-world programs such as the CCs in Venezuela. The fact that the impact of participatory programs can be shown by analyses from the real world and the laboratory is powerful evidence in favor of H3 (see Figure 1.2). However, experimental analyses always risk being undermined by external validity issues. To overcome such concerns, I conducted a qualitative evaluation of an actual participatory program in Chile: the *Piensa Providencia* program. I found this program to be genuinely participatory; interviews with municipal staff and a survey of participants showed that participants were extremely satisfied with the program, and that their engagement with it significantly reduced the historic tensions between the municipal administration and social organizations.

To summarize, all of the evidence presented here is consistent with the theoretical framework I developed in Chapter 3, and its proposition that participatory opportunities are a key source of regime support. Now that the major findings of this book are fresh in the reader's mind, I will discuss the broader theoretical and empirical implications of these findings.

7.1   LIBERALISM AND THE PRIMACY OF PERFORMANCE

The primary purpose of this project was to explain support paradoxes in Chile and Venezuela. Yet this research also has another, arguably more important purpose: to put the competing claims of liberal and participatory democratic theory to the test. Normative theories are often thought to be beyond the realm of empirical investigation; the conflicts between such philosophies often hinge upon what one values or believes to be morally right. Yet it is possible to adjudicate between theories with data when they rest upon implicit or explicit assumptions about "human nature." Such assumptions can, with a bit of deduction, imply a myriad of testable hypotheses. And if the premises on which a theory rests are found by empirical analysis to be wanting, the theoretical precepts based on that foundation are called into question.

In their original forms, neither body of democratic thought lends itself well to this kind of empirical adjudication. Classical liberals never presupposed that most citizens would *prefer* the liberal regime they sought to construct. In fact, they assumed the opposite: in their minds the greatest threat to the limited government they envisioned was the inevitable clamoring for the state to become involved in an ever-widening set of policy areas. Each such intrusion might well contribute to the interests of some group of citizens, but the aggregate result would be a state powerful enough and with broad enough reach to violate the rights and liberties such thinkers held dear. To liberal theorists, the popular will must be frustrated in the short term in order to preserve the greater good: a government that could not destroy the liberty it was designed to protect. In short, the conscious preferences of the people are of minimal consequence, and the fact that such preferences are unsatisfied has little bearing on the theory's validity.

A new wave of scholarship, inspired most directly by rational choice theories but making (if only implicitly) many of the same assumptions as the classical liberals, transgressed the bounds of purely normative theory by imputing liberal preferences or political orientations to individuals. Political theorists like Downs (1957) argued that, contrary to the assumptions of participatory democrats, citizens prefer *less* participation, not more. In fact, under the doctrine of rational self-interest, we should expect that citizens prefer their

regimes function effectively with the least amount of civic involvement possible; essentially Downs presumed that citizens wanted only
to periodically select elites through voting. When citizens do enter the
political arena, it is only because such intervention is necessary to
protect or advance their private interests; they gain nothing from the
participatory process itself, and the time, effort, and foregone opportunities associated with political activism leads to a view of participation as costly, rather than beneficial.

Thus the overriding concern with performance, with what
regimes do, was born. The literature on regime support has
extremely weak theoretical grounding; the major works on the issue
(Crozier et al., 1975; Easton, 1975; Norris, 1999b; Pharr et al., 2000)
make no reference to the vast body of democratic theory described
here. Many of these works are simple extensions of earlier theories
that sought to explain variation in the quality of governance.
These works uncritically carried their interest in governance into
regime support theory, and all essentially concede to the primacy of
policy outcomes as the metric by which citizens evaluate their
regimes.

7.2 THE PARTICIPATORY OBJECTION

Like liberalism, participatory democratic theory in its original form
provides little that could be empirically tested. Theorists inspired by
Athenian notions of direct democracy, from enlightenment thinkers
like Rousseau (2002) to more modern scholars such as Pateman (1970)
and Barber (1984), certainly argued that participatory self-governance
could have immediate positive impacts on citizens; in this respect
this body of democratic thought is somewhat more amenable to
empirical testing, and some scholars have done so (Bowler & Donovan,
2002; Donovan, Tolbert, & Smith, 2009). However, the impacts
specified by normative democratic theory are so abstract and diffuse
that any analytical work based upon them must make some truly
heroic deductive leaps. Should the educative, developmental impact

of participation make citizens happier? More responsible? More harmonious? Perhaps all or some of the above, or something else entirely? Must citizens actually participate in politics for these effects to manifest, or need they only have the opportunity to do so? And this does not even broach the subject of the demands placed upon citizens and the modern state by allowing (indeed requiring) such constant engagement by the citizenry. I have a great deal of sympathy for Barber's critique of the atomizing influence of political and economic liberalism, but I find his proposition for Athenian-style democracy in the modern world somewhat impractical. Individuals simply have far too many competing demands on their time and energies to form a Greek polity in modern states. Even in Bolivarian Venezuela, where participation is a core part of the regime's claim to legitimacy, less than a quarter of citizens regularly avail themselves of such opportunities for self-governance (Briceño, 2012). This would seem to contradict the one observable implication of participatory democratic theory: namely that citizens will jump at any opportunity to participate. In short, the hypotheses that can be deduced from participatory theory terminate in an unsupported proposition and an unresolvable (within the bounds of the theory) puzzle: how can participatory access matter, when it can only be used sporadically?

Also like liberalism, a group of scholars from outside the realm of political theory provide a solution. Psychology has long had an interest in the question of efficacy, the ability of individuals to shape their environments, and its impact on individual well-being. As described previously, the principal insight of psychology, which allows us to deduce promising hypotheses from participatory theory, is that the *act* of participation is not what increases satisfaction within a given environment, but the mere *availability* of opportunities to do so. Rather than some abstract notion of personal development, the ability to influence the course of politics can provide something that psychologists long ago accepted as critical for well-being: a sense of control over one's environment.

7.3 ORGANIZATIONAL JUSTICE AND REGIME SUPPORT: A UNIFIED FRAMEWORK FOR ANALYSIS

As stated earlier, perhaps the most significant impediment to a greater understanding of regime support is the lack of strong theoretical grounding. Assumptions about what citizens want from their regimes are often unclear, or made in ad-hoc extensions of earlier theories that had little to do with support or legitimacy (e.g. social capital theory, Huntington's theories of institutionalization), or inferred inductively from data (Booth & Seligson, 2009). The greatest contribution of this book is the development of a unified framework for analyzing questions relating to regime support. Had psychology stopped at the question of efficacy, this would not be possible. However, applied social psychology took up these questions, and theoretical work in that discipline does allow the development of such a framework: that of organizational justice. The principal advantage of the organizational justice framework on which my own theory of support is based is that it incorporates both performance and procedures into its causal narrative, although empirical testing has shown the latter to be the more decisive factor. It also provides specific guidance about how these factors interact to produce attitudes about a specific organization.

I find it surprising that this framework has not yet been applied to the issue of regime support. This literature is not unknown in the political realm; scholars have used it to analyze the justice system (Hough, Jackson, & Bradford, 2013) and voluntary compliance with laws (Levi & Sacks, 2009; Levi et al., 2009), among other things. And its applicability seems clear: it only requires that individuals be embedded in and subject to hierarchical organizations. Political regimes would certainly seem to qualify. Nevertheless, one cannot simply adopt a theoretical framework developed for one aspect of human social life and apply it to another without testing. The findings presented here are unambiguous: the organizational justice framework is an appropriate and useful way to approach the question of regime support. And given the emphasis on procedural justice and participatory access, validated in the social psychology literature and shown here to be equally crucial in the political realm, my research comes firmly down on the side of participatory democratic theory and against democratic liberalism. Put simply: procedures matter. They matter a great deal, and they dampen the extent to which performance matters. In fact, future research may well show that, if anything, the findings here actually underestimate their influence on political attitudes.

7.4   FUTURE RESEARCH

Any long work of research will have a few unanswered questions and a few findings that cannot immediately be explained, and the present work is no exception. There are three areas of this project that require further study, although none of them seems likely to undermine the previously presented findings. However, these avenues of investigation do have the potential to provide a more thorough understanding of how performance and participation interact to shape attitudes toward political regimes. They could also contribute to our understanding of how the relationships investigated here shape political behavior.

7.4.1   *Justice Cognitions and the Evaluation of Performance*

Perhaps the simplest way to introduce the first of these is with a graph, presented in Figure 7.1. This graph provides a visualization of the relationship between objective, country-level performance, and subjective, individual-level perceptions of the same. The y-axis presents average perceptions of performance.[1] The data on the x-axis are the composite governance scores used by Mainwaring et al. (2010) in their book on democratic governance, excluding the measure of

---

[1] These figures are the average predicted score on the performance latent variable specified in the 2012 reduced LAPOP model from Chapter 4.

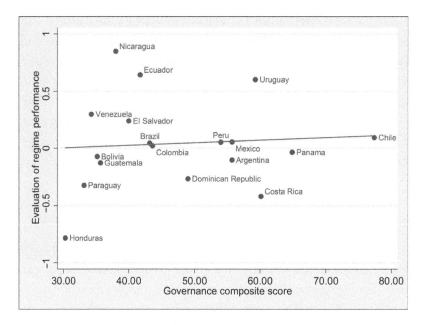

FIGURE 7.1: Average subjective evaluations of performance by objective performance

democracy, again to ensure congruence between the subjective and objective dimensions.

The weakness of the relationship shown in the graph is shocking. Ordinarily this might be attributed to poor measures, but this seems extremely unlikely for the current problem. The LAPOP questions used to form the dependent variable (evaluations of economic management, poverty reduction, and public security) are very close to the more objective country-level measures used to form the independent variable. A more promising answer lies in an aspect of attitude formation that this book has not examined in great detail. I have explored the relationship between attitudes, and how the political environment (specifically the participatory opportunities that the political regime provides) shape those attitudes. I have not, however, said much about the process by which individuals gather and process information about that environment. This process was discussed briefly in Chapter 5, when I hypothesized that *chavista* rhetoric of participatory democracy and populist struggle against the oligarchy inflated the sense of empowerment that supporters developed from participatory governance. Yet, for the most part, I have assumed that the cognitive processes by which individuals gather and process information about their regime's performance and participatory opportunities are relatively straightforward, with high levels of one or the other producing positive subjective assessments, with some random variation.

The data presented in Figure 7.1 suggest that reality is not so neat. A brief look at how countries fall on the regression line imply some interesting possibilities. Of the five overperforming countries (those above the regression line), three have populist presidents. Another, Uruguay, is well known for its extremely robust and deeply rooted democratic system. On this basis, I could engage in some inductively based speculation about why individuals in populist and participatory polities seem to be more forgiving of their regime's failures (or more exuberant about their regime's successes, in the case of Uruguay).

Fortunately, no such guesswork is necessary. The literature on organizational justice that inspires my framework has examined the cognitive element of attitude formation, and this work provides some very promising explanations for why objective and subjective performance do not match in many countries. The cognitive processes relevant to organizational justice attitudes are referred to collectively as fairness heuristics (Lind, 2001). Two factors stand out as important here: the primacy effect and substitutability.

In organizational justice theory, the primacy effect refers to the tendency to make an initial evaluation of the justice and fairness of an organization based on whatever information to which one is exposed first; those judgements then influence the evaluation of all subsequently obtained information (Lind, Kray, & Thompson, 2001). In other words, individuals do not constantly update their attitudes toward an organization as new information rolls in, with all information having roughly equal weight. Instead the first piece of information leads to a judgment that anchors evaluation of all subsequent information.

The second factor, substitutability, implies that the two dimensions (outcomes and procedures) used here are more dependent upon one another than earlier work in this area assumed. In the absence of information about one dimension, individuals will use information they possess about the other dimension to make judgments as a substitute (van den Bos et al., 2001). In other words, if a person does not have any information with which to judge the fairness or justice of an outcome, that person will use information about the justice of procedures to make judgments about outcomes.

In the political realm, new policy outputs are constantly cropping up, while the procedures that produce them remain relatively stable. By combining the primacy and substitutability effects discussed earlier, one can make some very reasonable hypotheses to account for the discrepancy apparent in Figure 7.1. Specifically, these factors imply that the interaction between performance and RBE tested in Chapter 4 may also occur even earlier in the process of attitude formation. As individuals usually have information about political procedures before they have information about specific policy outcomes, their evaluation of those outcomes are likely filtered through their procedural attitudes. High levels of RBE may not simply prevent poor performance from eroding regime support. It may in fact blind individuals to the severity of governance failures in the first place. A modified version of Figure 1.1, including this new hypothesis (labeled as H4), is presented in Figure 7.2.

Far from undermining my argument, findings that supported this hypothesis would actually provide further support. They would suggest that participatory opportunities shape attitudes in multiple ways, all of which improve support by blunting the impact of poor performance. Such findings would simply introduce another point in the process of attitude formation at which participatory opportunities could influence support, albeit indirectly through its impact on subjective evaluations of performance. Such hypotheses would be very

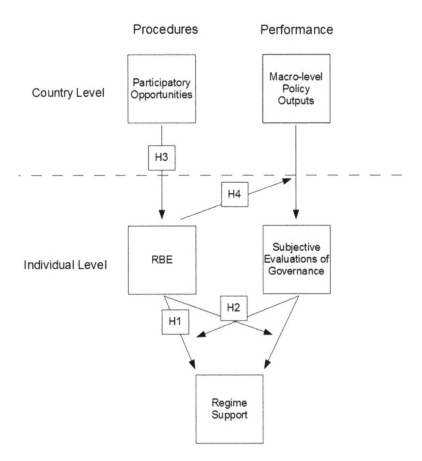

FIGURE 7.2: Theoretical framework, modified with cognitive element

difficult to test with secondary observational data. Estimating the impact of participatory opportunities (through RBE) on the cognitive process of performance evaluation would require a large number of country-year units, far larger than are available in the LAPOP dataset. This is problematic because no other large cross-national survey contains robust measures of RBE. Experimental analyses, similar to those presented in Chapter 6 of this book, could provide such tests. I plan to conduct such experiments in future research.

Without data, any discussion of the implications of this modification of the framework will be necessarily speculative. Such speculation is worthwhile, however, because the modified approach has the potential to shed considerable light on both the endurance of the Bolivarian regime under Chávez and its rapid collapse under his successor, Nicolás Maduro. Performance-centric arguments might simply point to the rapid deterioration of economic conditions in Venezuela, spurred by the collapse of worldwide oil prices, which began roughly within six to fourteen months of Maduro's ascension to the Presidency, depending upon when one marks the beginning of the cliff.[2] This decline, driven by increased production in the United States, undermined Maduro's ability to maintain the public expenditures that funded the work of the communal councils and social missions, key institutions for maintaining linkages between the Bolivarian elite and its grassroots. Yet this explanation leaves out some facts. Things were far from rosy even when Chávez won reelection in 2012; years of mismanagement and harebrained economic policies had generated a host of social problems discussed throughout this book. Inflation was rampant, crime was out of control, and the shortage problem was beginning to become serious.[3] The result of all this economic grief? A comfortable nine-point victory over the best candidate and the most united opposition effort he had ever faced.

If economic pain killed the Bolivarian movement, why did it spare Chávez? The framework used in the chapters of this book provides an answer; the modified framework discussed here could improve that answer still further. The argument of the book states that the *effect* of performance on support was mitigated by the combination of charismatic attachment, created and reinforced by

---

[2] Maduro took office in April of 2013. West Texas Intermediate, which keeps data on oil prices, shows a drop beginning in September of 2013, which briefly stabilized, then cratered after June 2014.

[3] Venezuelan coffee is notorious for its strength (and for what in the United States would be a lawsuit-inducing typical serving temperature). The reader can thus imagine my umbrage when, for the entirety of my final month in Caracas (January 2013), I was unable to find sugar for sale in any grocery store. Arepa flour, rice, and cooking oil, all key staples of Venezuelans' diets, were also becoming increasingly difficult to find by the time I left the country.

participatory opportunities. The modifications proposed in this section would go one step further: those factors not only helped maintain regime performance, but actively clouded citizens' perceptions of performance, in effect breaking the influence of "objective" regime performance on subjective perceptions of it. Chávez's death broke this attachment, and while participatory opportunities remained to make citizens feel empowered, in the absence of the populist reality began to reassert itself, especially as the crisis accelerated with the decline in oil prices. In short, this theory would not overrule that presented here, but would complement and deepen it by explaining why economic failures had so little impact on Chávez's support while obliterating that of his hand-picked successor.

7.4.2   Broader Applications of the Framework

This project focused on the role played by participatory opportunities in shaping regime support primarily because that was the most likely source of the discrepancy between performance and support in the two cases of interest. There is good reason to suppose that the kind of participatory self-governance practiced in Venezuela is unlikely to explain variation in support in other contexts. Such programs are not typical of modern democracies; participatory fora sponsored by a national regime, rather than the local governments under which they usually operate, are even more unusual.

Nevertheless, the focus on an active, meaningful role for citizen does have considerable promise for broader investigations of regime support. There are two possible analytical strategies here. The first, and by far the least promising for broader analyses, is to develop a comprehensive theory of how specific institutions (e.g. electoral systems, government structure, and legislation governing internal party democracy) shape RBE. Such an endeavor would be incredibly difficult, as institutions can interact with one another and with other elements of the political environment to produce wildly differing impacts from context to context. For example, the participatory populist framework I employed in Chapter 5 shows that participatory institutions interact with the personal charisma and populist rhetoric of Hugo Chávez to create unusually strong perceptions of RBE despite the limited scope of participatory opportunities and his authoritarian tendencies. Without the deep understanding that only single case studies can facilitate, such interactions would likely bedevil even the most carefully crafted cross-national institutional analyses.

A more promising strategy, one facilitated by recently released data, is to step back from analyses of institutions, and to focus instead on the more abstract notion of varieties of democracy. The Varieties of Democracy (V-Dem) project takes just such an approach. Its dataset provides measures of liberalism, participatory democracy, electoral democracy, egalitarianism, and deliberative democracy, among other characteristics. These measures take institutions into account, but also rely on expert assessments to account for the idiosyncrasies of individual political systems. I intend to conduct analyses based on this dataset, using both LAPOP and the World Values Survey in future research.

7.4.3   Implications for Political Behavior

Finally, this research has clear implications for theorized relationships between support and various kinds of political behavior. The most important of these is that support may not have a uniform impact on behavior; a lack of support may produce different types of behaviors, depending on whether it is based on perceptions of performance or procedures. The most obvious place where this would be relevant is in the most studied behavior impact of support: on the decision to engage in contentious politics. Many scholars have argued that low regime support tends to lead citizens to forsake institutional mechanisms of participation in favor of taking to the streets (Crow, 2007, 2010; Klosko et al., 1987; Muller & Opp, 1986; Opp et al., 1981). The framework presented here provides a more nuanced set of predictions. For example, we might expect citizens who are critical of their regime's performance but trust its institutions to have relatively weak support, but to continue to engage with the formal political system. This could, for example, help to explain why protests in Venezuela have been largely confined to the wealthy areas of major cities, while the *barrios* and the countryside have remained mostly silent. Likewise, citizens who are relatively satisfied with policy outcomes but critical of institutions may withdraw from politics into apathy. Again, this could explain why Chilean students, who have low institutional trust as well as specific and serious economic grievances, continue to protest while most Chileans, even those with little faith in the political system, merely grumble and go about their day-to-day lives. Finally, those who are critical of both dimensions will be the most likely to engage in contentious politics.

Although there are interesting implications here, the literature on support and contentious politics is already quite extensive. I find the more interesting implication for behavior to be in an area that has received less scholarly attention: how regime support shapes decisions to support or oppose populist politicians. The theory and evidence presented here (especially for the Venezuelan case) strongly suggests that support for populist leaders is driven by feelings of political impotence. If populists are able to win massive support by promising to empower citizens (as Chávez was), it stands to reason that citizens who feel that existing institutions and procedures already grant them the ability to influence the political process will be inoculated against such appeals. In other words, political systems that provide few participatory opportunities may leave themselves vulnerable to anti-system outsiders. Such a finding would have major implications for one of democracy's most intractable dilemmas: the tension between stability and participation.

7.5   STABILITY, PARTICIPATION, AND REGIME SUPPORT

A major question is strongly implied by this research, which I have thus far not addressed: is the Bolivarian populism of Venezuela really "better" than the liberal democracy of Chile? Can regime support be treated as a measure of democratic quality? Venezuela's citizens certainly were more supportive of their regime prior to the death of Chávez. One might be tempted to deduce from my argument that participatory populism is preferable to the elitist democracy practiced in Chile. This would be a mistake. The actual normative implications of my argument are more complex. As the classical liberals argued, what makes large groups of citizens happy in the short term does not necessarily imply moral superiority or contribute to long-term sustainability. And events in Venezuela, which in the absence of the unifying force of the populist has descended into chaos, suggest that the support that the Bolivarian regime enjoyed under its founder was bought on credit, the bill for which has come due at last. Meanwhile Chile lumbers along, slouching slowly yet steadily toward a more complete democratic system.

Pitting Bolivarian Venezuela's chaotic, constantly mobilized political system against Chile's elitist stability echoes long-standing debates that see participation and stability as fundamentally at odds with one another. The seminal work by Crozier et al. (1975) tied this dilemma explicitly to the decline of support in the trilateral nations throughout the 1970s. These scholars built upon Huntington's theory of institutional decay, caused by upswings in citizen engagement with democratic systems, which led to excessive demands that even highly developed states could not manage (Huntington, 1965). Overburdened states could not help but stumble, and the resulting failures of governance led to a frustrated and disenchanted citizenry. Within such a framework, the stability and integrity of political institutions should be held sacrosanct; the political role of the citizenry must be constrained (even if those citizens grumble about it), lest the entire edifice of the state be compromised. At first glance, the cases analyzed here might seem to support this argument: participatory Venezuela is in the process of collapse, while the Chilean partyarchy marches on. The actual lessons to be gleamed from the cases, in light of my findings, are not nearly so simple.

7.5.1   Participation and Stability in Bolivarian Venezuela

Although the agreement reached by Venezuelan leaders who met at *Punto Fijo* preceded Huntington by a decade, the arrangement they implemented in the wake of a devastating period of military rule was based on a similar logic. *Puntofijismo*, with its oligopolistic competition between parties that controlled their social bases through the distribution of rents, effectively prevented the kind of excessive demand making that Huntington and his followers would later come to fear. And for decades, the system worked: of the countries of South America that comprise part of Latin America, only Venezuela and Colombia[4] did not experience a period of military rule in the latter half of the twentieth century. Huntington's preference for stability over participation was seemingly vindicated.

Participation may have a heavy price, but stability does not come cheap either. The *Punto Fijo* system was ultimately shown to be a giant with feet of clay. Economic collapse impelled neoliberal reforms, and those reforms broke the system of rent distribution that kept the regime from falling to earth. It had no other basis on which to rest; in other words, the reservoir of goodwill that Easton cited as a source of strength during turbulent times was nonexistent. The people of Venezuela did not see a succession of governments making incredibly difficult decisions in good faith, but an oligarchy masquerading as a democracy, exposed for what it was. This situation was ideal for a would-be populist demagogue like Chávez to rise.

Nor does the crisis of *chavismo* provide the compelling evidence of the destructive influence of participation that Huntington's acolytes might see. In Chapter 5, I labeled the Bolivarian political strategy as "participatory populism," a system in which national hegemony is legitimized by local participation. If one seeks to identify the source of collapse, one should look to the noun, rather than the adjective. Hegemony is what allowed Chávez and his closest allies at

---

[4] And Colombia had a similarly negotiated settlement between previously antagonistic political parties.

the highest reaches of the regime to make one devastating blunder after another, to sit by as the livelihoods (not to mention the lives) of the people whose avatar he claimed to be came under increasing threat. To the extent that the various participatory fora sponsored by his regime had a role in this calamitous process, it was an indirect one. As I have argued, they lent Chávez's rhetorical paeans to "participatory protagonist democracy" a veneer of plausibility, enough so that his followers kept the faith long after his incompetence as head of state and the limits of his will to truly empower his subjects should have been clear to all.

In short, the collapse of the Bolivarian regime cannot be laid at the feet of participation's excesses. Chávez used participatory access in a tightly limited sphere to justify his evisceration of all mechanisms for holding his government accountable. It is the dearth of accountability that has allowed the Bolivarian elite to escape punishment for their foolishness. The citizenry cannot be held entirely innocent here; many Venezuelans, entranced by the illusion of "participatory protagonist democracy" that hides a system based on limited self-governance locally and hegemony nationally, have willingly allowed their citizenship to be diminished. Nor are the intellectual apologists for Chávez entirely blameless; too many were too eager to embrace what they saw as a form of radical democracy, despite the almost messianic position Chávez sought to claim. However, ultimate responsibility must lie with the man who used this obfuscation to his advantage. Had Chávez truly empowered his followers in all political spheres, national and local, perhaps they could have punished him for his failures and forced a correction of course before things became untenable. Had he truly embraced the empowerment to which he paid lip service, perhaps his legacy would not be tarnishing so quickly.

7.5.2   The Chilean Gamble

Chile seems like an ideal example of why regimes should prioritize stability and institutionalization over participation. The successes of

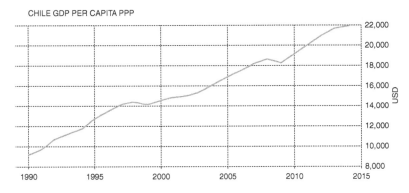

FIGURE 7.3: Chilean GDP per capita, PPP

this strategy cannot be denied: the political system survived an uncertain transition away from military rule to become a fully consolidated democracy and the economic envy of the region. However, we should be wary about drawing conclusions from these successes, as the Chilean strategy has never faced the kind of crisis that might reveal its real stability. My findings show that Chile's cautious approach to democratization had its own risks.

The Chilean political class essentially gambled the legitimacy of the political regime on its ability to steward the economy well enough to fund social improvements. This was by no means a sure bet; in an increasingly interconnected world, no one can be fully confident of their ability to dodge the slings and arrows thrown by the global economy. As it happens, the bet has largely paid off: the following graph shows Chilean GDP per capita (PPP) from 1996 to 2016.

Aside from very brief dips in 1998 and 2008 (both the result of financial crises originating in other countries), the economy's expansion has been constant and strong, although growth has slowed in recent years as the commodity boom has weakened. Given the undeniable competence of successive Chilean governments, shouldn't this be taken as evidence that stability should be preferred, whatever the cost?

The problem with such a conclusion is that it underestimates the inherent risk of such a strategy. This tactic amounts to putting it all on black: the regime bets that it can weather any storm that may come its way. This ignores a troubling question: what happens to such a regime were some economic crisis to arise that it could not manage its way out of? My research suggests that such a crisis would have a disastrous impact on regime support. First, a regime like Chile's that excludes citizens from most aspects of the political process has no reservoir of goodwill from which to draw when the good times cease to roll. Furthermore, the interactive effect described in Chapters 3 and 4 has a flipside: just as participatory opportunities can ameliorate the impact of poor performance, their absence dramatically amplifies the importance of good governance for maintaining legitimacy.

Concluding that stability and the economic performance it supposedly facilitates are more important than participation based on Chile's history ignores the fact that Chile has never had to pass through the crucible of a protracted economic crisis since the return to democracy. Even the extremely brief and minor correction in 1998 caused a drastic decline in support that effectively ended the honeymoon period of Chile's new democracy (Posner, 1999). One shudders to think what might have been if the government had been unable to correct course so quickly. Even Chile's economic prowess cannot guarantee stability, as economic management is not the only area in which regimes can fail to perform: the Chilean government's bungled response to the earthquake of 2010 (and the tsunami that followed) also led to a rapid cratering of support (Carlin, Love, & Zechmeister, 2014). Although we of course cannot observe a Chile where some greater calamity struck, we do have a historical example of such a process: this description conforms quite nicely to Venezuela during the collapse of *puntofijismo*.

7.5.3 Stability or Participation: An Intractable Dilemma?

None of this provides a direct answer to the question that initiated this discussion: is the Bolivarian system "better" than Chile's limited democracy? While each regime type has its costs and risks, taking into account each regime's historical trajectory heavily favors the Chilean approach. The Chilean regime, for all its faults, is clearly moving in the right direction (albeit at an agonizingly languid pace). As discussed in Chapter 6, the most embarrassingly authoritarian elements of the regime have been excised over time. One of the principal pillars of protective democracy, the binomial electoral system, was repealed mere weeks before this book was completed. This paves the way for pro-reform elements to finally build the kind of majorities needed to begin making major reforms, and fundamentally alters the incentives of Chilean elites vis-a-vis mobilization of the masses. Whatever its faults, the system managed to survive long enough for the dust of military rule and transition to democracy to settle, and the gradualist process seems to be on track toward a deeper democracy in the future. Chileans seem to recognize this; the same CEP survey data that shows citizens are quite critical of the system currently also shows a healthy optimism regarding the future.

One would have to search far and wide to find an optimistic Venezuelan these days, regardless of their political bent. The Bolivarian system is inarguably in a process of collapse. The founding myth of participatory protagonist democracy cannot sustain itself on a foundation of locally bounded participatory fora without the charisma of the populist to imbue those programs with greater meaning. In its death throws, *chavismo* has largely abandoned all pretense of democracy, using increasingly authoritarian and illegal tactics to maintain power. The eventual victory of the opposition provides little hope for a better tomorrow. The class antagonisms that *puntofijimo* subsumed and *chavismo* unleashed and amplified are not going away anytime soon. The opposition seems to have little insight into how to move the country forward; instead they seem permanently focused on the past, attempting to erase Chávez from memory. This inability to grapple with a new reality hardly inspires confidence in their ability to heal their country's wounds.

With these competing histories in mind, I see two major implications of this research. The first is simple: participation matters. Regimes that sacrifice it for stability, or sound economic management, or anything else, should be aware of the risks they take. I submit that no government, no matter how competent, can be sure of its ability to avoid any and all crises in the modern world. Should such a crisis arrive, the consequences for a regime whose citizens feel powerless and excluded are likely to be dire. The great irony of the Chilean system is that it was designed to prevent the rise of "populism" after nearly two decades of repression. And yet as Venezuela under *Punto Fijo* shows, that system in fact provided the ideal context for populism to develop, and only a combination of competence and luck prevented it from doing so.

The second implication is a cautionary corollary to the first: beware of elites bringing empowerment. To paraphrase *el comandante*, such elites often leave a faint whiff of brimstone in their wake. The course of *chavismo* shows the clear danger posed when an elitist system collapses: political outsiders can use promises of empowerment and political access to win support, even if the actual power they devolve is minor. A version of this process can also be seen in pre-Allende Chile, where greater political rights for ordinary citizens were usually granted not as the result of bottom-up demands, but by elites seeking to use the people as a bludgeon against their political opponents. In both cases, political leaders demonstrated far more concern for their own empowerment than for that of the people. That the people suffered as a result is hardly surprising. This research supports empowering the people, but only through processes directed by the people themselves. Such processes, which require continual challenging of elites, are likely to be slow and gradual. However, if the alternative is populist domination or a cycle of heightened expectations that the state cannot possibly meet, patience seems a small price to pay.

7.5.4 Concluding Thoughts: Regime Support and the Populist Wave

The process of writing a book is slow, and events have a way of shifting the ground beneath an author's feet. When the first words of this book were written, Hugo Chávez was still alive and actively campaigning for a third term in office. His death, and the calamity that followed forced a reckoning, as even his supporters (both in Venezuela and internationally) were confronted with the reality of his actions, unmasked by the force of his personality. As I write these concluding thoughts, another shift has taken place: populism has gone global.

Of course populism has never been confined to Latin America. The word itself was coined to describe the Farmer's Alliance movement (and its political party, the People's Party) in the United States (Kazin, 1998). Beginning in the late 60s and early 70s, nationalist parties all over Europe began adopting populist postures (Mudde, 2007). Yet recent events, particularly the secession of Great Britain from the European Union and the stunning upset victory of Donald Trump suggest that momentum may be gathering behind anti-system movements worldwide. Although a great deal of research remains to be done, the central arguments of this book suggest that the common interpretation of these movements' successes as the product of xenophobia, racism, and reactionary nationalism is at best incomplete. Perhaps liberal democracy is under threat because, as this book suggests, it is not as well-suited to meeting deep-seated needs for autonomy and collective self-governance as many believe it to be. I conclude this book by suggesting that, although prejudice and xenophobic nationalism should be condemned at every turn, perhaps devotees of liberal democracy should pause and contemplate if the systems they promote are in need of reform. Given recent events, it seems the almost commodified brand of citizenship that lies at the heart of liberal politics may not be sufficient to command the loyalty of the governed.

References

Acemoglu, D., & Robinson, J. (2006). *The economic origins of dictatorship and democracy*. Cambridge: Cambridge University Press.

Adams, J. (2000). A defense of the Constitution of the United States of America. In G. W. Carey (Ed.), *The political writings of John Adams*. Washington D.C.: Regnery Publishing, Inc.

Albert, M., & Hanhel, R. (1991). *The political economy of participatory economics*. Princeton, NJ: Princeton University Press.

Allison, P. D. (2009). *Fixed effects regression models*. Thousand Oaks, CA: Sage Publications, Inc.

Allison, P. D. (2012). Handling missing data by maximum likelihood. *SAS Global Forum 2012*. Retrieved from www.statisticalhorizons.com/wp-content/uploads/MissingDataByML.pdf.

Almond, G., & Verba, S. (1963). *The civic culture: Political attitudes and democracy in five nations*. Newbury Park, CA: Sage Publications.

Álvarez, R., & García-Guadilla, M. P. (2011). Contraloría social y clientelismo: la praxis de los consejos comunales en Venezuela. *Politeia, 34*(46), 175–207.

Anderson, C. J., & Guillory, C. A. (1997). Political institutions and satisfaction with democracy: A cross-national analysis of consensus and majoritarian systems. *American Political Science Review, 91*(1), 66–81.

Anderson, C. J., & Singer, M. M. (2008). The sensitive left and the impervious right: Multilevel models and the politics of inequality, ideology, and legitimacy in Europe. *Comparative Political Studies, 41*(4/5), 564–599.

Angell, A. (2010). Democratic governance in Chile. In S. Mainwaring & T. R. Scully (Eds.), *Democratic governance in Latin America* (pp. 269–306). Stanford, CA: Stanford University Press.

Angyal, A. (1941). *Foundations for a science of personality*. New York, NY: The Commonwealth Fund.

Araujo, K. (2012, December 19). *Telephone interview by author with Fondacomunal employee*.

Aristotle. (1959). *Politics*. Cambridge, MA: Harvard University Press.

Armstein, S. R. (1969). A ladder of participation. *Journal of the American Institute of Planners, 35*(4), 216–224.

Avritzer, L. (2002). *Democracy in the public space in Latin America*. Princeton, NJ: Princeton University Press.

Baland, J.-M., & Robinson, J. A. (2006). *Land and power: Theory and evidence from Chile*. Cambridge, MA: National Bureau of Economic Research. Retrieved from http://www.nber.org/papers/w12517.pdf.

Bandura, A. (1977). Self-efficacy: Toward a unifying theory of behavioral change. *Psychological Review, 84*(2), 191–215.

Barber, B. R. (1984). *Strong democracy: Participatory politics for a new age*. Berkeley, CA: University of California Press.

Bélanger, É. (2004). Antipartyism and third-party vote choice: A comparison of Canada, Britain, and Australia. *Comparative Political Studies, 37*(9), 1054–1078.

Bellin, E. (2000). Contingent democrats: Industrialists, labor and democratization in late-developing countries. *World Politics, 52*(2), 175–205.

Biaocchi, G. (2001). Participation, activism, and politics: The Porto Alegre experiment and deliberative democratic theory. *Politics and Society, 29*(1), 43–72.

Bica, Y. (2013, June 23). *Interview by author*.

Bitar, S. (1986). *Chile: Experiment in democracy* (Vol. 6). Philadelphia, PA: Institute for the Study of Human Issues.

Boeninger, E. (1997). *Democracia en Chile: Lecciones para la gobernabilidad*. Santiago: Editorial Andres Bello.

Boix, C. (2006). The roots of democracy: Equality, inequality and the choice of political institutions. *Policy Review, 135*, 3–21.

Bollen, K. (1989). *Structural equations with latent variables*. New York, NY: Wiley.

Booth, J. A., & Seligson, M. (2009). *The legitimacy puzzle: Political support and democracy in eight nations*. Cambridge: Cambridge University Press.

Bowler, S., & Donovan, T. (2002). Democracy, institutions and attitudes about citizen influence on government. *British Journal of Political Science, 32*(2), 371–390.

Bowman, Q. (2013). *Interview with Fondacomunal employee*.

Briceño, H. (2012, August 11). *Interview by author with UCV-CENDES Professor*.

Burbach, R., & Piñeiro, C. (2007). Venezuela's participatory socialism. *Journal of the Research Group on Socialism and Democracy Online, 21*(3).

Campbell, A., Gurin, G., & Miller, W. E. (1954). *The voter decides*. Evanston, IL: Row, Peterson.

Canache, D. (2007). *Chavismo and democracy in Venezuela*. Paper presented at the Prospects for democracy in Latin America, University of North-Texas.

Canache, D., Mondak, J., & Seligson, M. (2001). Meaning and measurement in cross-national research on satisfaction with democracy. *Public Opinion Quarterly, 65*(4), 506–528.

Cannon, B. (2004). Venezuela, April 2002: Coup or popular rebellion? The myth of a united Venezuela. *Bulletin of Latin American Research, 23*(3), 285–302.

Canovan, M. (1999). Trust the people! Populism and the two faces of democracy. *Political Studies, 47*(1), 2–16.

Cariola, C., & Miguel, L. (2005). Los bordes de la esperanza: nuevas formas de participación popular y gobiernos locales en la periferia de Caracas. *Revista Venezolana de Economía y Ciencias Sociales, 11*(1), 21–41.

Caripa, B. (2012, October 11). Constructores trabajarán con consejos comunales: proyectan hacer un centro de convenciones en La Carlota. *Últimas noticias.* Retrieved from www.ultimasnoticias.com.ve/noticias/actualidad/economia/constructores-trabajaran-con-consejos-comunales.aspx.

Carlin, R. E. (2011). Distrusting democrats and political participation in new democracies: Lessons from Chile. *Political Research Quarterly, 64*(3), 668–687.

Carlin, R. E. (2014). What's not to trust? Rubrics of political party trustworthiness in Chile and Argentina. *Party Politics, 20*(1), 63–77.

Carlin, R. E., Love, G. J., & Zechmeister, E. J. (2014). Natural disaster and democratic legitimacy: The public opinion consequences of Chile's 2010 earthquake and tsunami. *Political Research Quarterly, 67*(1), 3–15.

Carlin, R. E., & Singer, M. M. (2011). Support for polyarchy in the Americas. *Comparative Political Studies, 44*(11), 1500–1526.

Ciccariello-Maher, G. (2013). *We created Chávez.* Durham, NC: Duke University Press.

Cohen, M. R., & Nagel, E. (1934). *An introduction to logic and the scientific method.* New York, NY: Harcourt, Brace & World, Inc.

Collier, D., & Levitsky, S. (1997). Democracy with adjectives: Conceptual innovation in comparative research. *World Politics, 49*(3), 430–451.

Collier, R. B., & Collier, D. (2002). *Shaping the political arena.* South Bend, IN: Notre Dame University Press.

Constable, P., & Valenzuela, A. (1991). *A nation of enemies: Chile under Pinochet.* New York, NY: W.W. Norton & Company, Inc.

Coppedge, D. (1994). *Strong parties and lame ducks: Presidential partyarchy and factionalism in Venezuela.* Stanford, CA: Stanford University Press.

Corrales, J. (2010). The repeating revolution: Chávez's new politics and old economics. In K. Weyland, R. Madrid, & W. Hunter (Eds.), *Leftist governments in Latin America: Successes and shortcomings* (pp. 28–56). Cambridge: Cambridge University Press.

Corrales, J. (2011). Why polarize? Advantages and disadvantages of a rational-choice analysis of government-opposition relations under Hugo Chávez. In T. Ponniah & J. Eastwood (Eds.), *The revolution in Venezuela: Social and political change under Chávez* (pp. 67–98). Cambridge, MA: Harvard University Press.

Corrales, J. (2014). Venezuela's middle ground. *Foreign Policy*. Retrieved from http://foreignpolicy.com/2014/04/22/venezuelas-middle-ground.

Corrales, J., & Penfold, M. (2015). *Dragon in the tropics: Venezuela and the legacy of Hugo Chávez* (2nd ed.). New York, NY: Brookings Institution Press.

Craig, S. C., Niemi, R. G., & Silver, G. E. (1990). Political efficacy and trust: A report on the NES pilot study items. *Political Behavior, 12*(3), 289–314.

Crow, D. (2007). *Citizen disenchantment in new democracies: The case of Mexico.* (PhD Dissertation), University of Texas at Austin, Austin.

Crow, D. (2010). The party's over: Citizen conceptions of democracy and political dissatisfaction in Mexico. *Comparative Politics, 43*(1), 41–61.

Crozier, M., Huntington, S., & Watanuki, J. (1975). *The crisis of democracy.* New York, NY: New York University Press.

Dahl, R. A. (1971). *Polyarchy: Participation and opposition.* New Haven: Yale University Press.

Dahl, R. A. (1989). *Democracy and its critics.* New Haven: Yale University Press.

Davis, L. (1964). The cost of realism: Contemporary restatements of democracy. *Western Political Quarterly, 17*(1), 37–46.

De la Torre, C. (2010). *Populist seduction in Latin America* (2nd ed.). Athens: Ohio University Center for International Studies.

de Tocqueville, A. (1990). *Democracy in America* (Vol. 44). Chicago: Encyclopedia Britannica.

DeCharms, R. (1968). *Personal causation: The internal affective determinants of behavior.* New York, NY: Academic Press.

Deci, E. L. (1971). Effects of externally mediated rewards on intrinsic motivation. *Journal of Personality and Social Psychology, 18*(1), 105–115.

Deci, E. L. (1975). *Intrinsic motivation.* New York, NY: Plenum Press.

Deci, E. L., & Ryan, R. M. (1985). *Intrinsic motivation and self-determination in human behavior.* New York, NY: Plenum Press.

Deci, E. L., & Ryan, R. M. (2000). The "what" and "why" of goal pursuits: Human needs and the self-determination of behavior. *Psychological Inquiry, 11*(4), 227–268.

Deci, E. L., Ryan, R. M., & Koestner, R. (1999). A meta-analytic review of experiments examining the effects of extrinsic rewards on intrinsic motivation. *Psychological Bulletin, 125*(6), 627–668.

Dettrey, B. J. (2013). Relative losses and economic voting: Sociotropic considerations or "keeping up with the Joneses"? *Politics & Policy, 41*(5), 788–806.

Diamond, L. (1996). Is the third wave over? *Journal of Democracy, 7*(3), 20–37.

Difunden lista completa con 1500 ex agentes de la DINA que incluye a alcalde Cristián Labbé. (2012, April 13). *Biobiochile.cl.* Retrieved from www.biobiochile.cl/2012/04/13/difunden-lista-completa-con-1500-ex-agentes-de-la-dina-que-incluye-a-alcalde-cristian-labbe.shtml.

Donovan, T., Tolbert, C. J., & Smith, D. A. (2009). Political engagement, mobilization, and direct democracy. *Public Opinion Quarterly, 73*(1), 98–118.

Downs, A. (1957). *An economic theory of democracy.* New York, NY: Harper and Row.

Easton, D. (1975). A reassessment of the concept of political support. *British Journal of Political Science, 5*(4), 435–457.

Easton, D., & Dennis, J. (1967). The child's acquisition of regime norms: Political efficacy. *American Political Science Review, 61*(1), 25–38.

Easton, D., & Dennis, J. (1969). *Children in the political system: Origins of political legitimacy.* New York: McGraw Hill.

Eastwood, J. (2011). Introduction: The revolution in Venezuela. In T. Ponniah & D. Easton (Eds.), *The revolution in Venezuela: Social and political change under Chávez* (pp. 1–36). Cambridge, MA: Harvard University Press.

Ellner, S. (2003a). Introduction: A search for explanations. In S. Ellner & D. Hellinger (Eds.), *Venezuelan politics in the Chávez era: Class, polarization and conflict* (pp. 7–26). Boulder, CO: Lynne Rienner Publishers.

Ellner, S. (2003b). Organized labor and the challenge of chavismo. In S. Ellner & D. Hellinger (Eds.), *Venezuelan politics in the Chávez era: Class, polarization and conflict* (pp. 161–178). Boulder, CO: Lynne Rienner Publishers.

Ellner, S. (2011). Venezuela's social-based democratic model: innovations and limitations. *Journal of Latin American Studies, 43*(3), 421–449.

Encarnación, O. G. (2005). Do political pacts freeze democracy? Spanish and South American lessons. *West European Politics, 28*(1), 182–203.

Equipo de Planificación, C. P. (2013, October 15) *Interview by author.*

Estudiantes del liceo Lastarria se reintegran mañana a clases. (2006, October 23). *La Nación.* Retrieved from www.lanacion.cl/prontus_noticias/site/artic/20061023/pags/20061023183443.html.

Finkel, S. E. (1987). The effects of participation on political efficacy and political support: Evidence from a West German panel. *Journal of Politics, 49*(2), 441–464.

Finkel, S. E., Muller, E. N., & Seligson, M. (1989). Economic crisis, incumbent performance and regime support: A comparison of longitudinal data from West Germany and Costa Rica. *British Journal of Political Science, 19*(3), 329–351.

Folger, R., & Cropanzano, R. (2001). Fairness theory: Justice as accountability. In J. Greenberg & R. Cropanzano (Eds.), *Advances in organizational justice* (pp. 1–55). Stanford, CA: Stanford University Press.

Fontaine Aldunate, A. (1988). *Los economistas y el presidente Pinochet.* Santiago: Zig-Zag.

Foxley, A. (1983). *Latin American experiments in neoconservative economics.* Berkeley: University of California Press.

Frey, B. S., Benz, M., & Stutzer, A. (2004). Introducing procedural utility: Not only what, but also how matters. *Journal of Institutional and Theoretical Economics, 160*(3), 377–401.

Fuentes, C. (2013, 03/28/2013) *Interview by author.*

Gamson, W. A. (1968). *Power and discontent.* Homewood: The Dorsey Press.

García-Guadilla, M. P. (2003). Civil Society: Institutionalization, fragmentation, autonomy. In S. Ellner & D. Hellinger (Eds.), *Venezuelan politics in the Chávez era: Class, polarization, and conflict* (pp. 179–196). Boulder, CO: Lynne Rienner Publishers.

García-Guadilla, M. P. (2008). La praxis de los consejos comunales en Venezuela: ¿Poder popular o instancia clientelar? *Revista Venezolana de Economía y Ciencias Sociales, 14*(1), 125–151.

García-Guadilla, M. P. (2011). Urban Land Committees: Co-optation, autonomy and protagonism. In D. Smilde & D. Hellinger (Eds.), *Venezuela's Bolivarian democracy* (pp. 80–103). Durham, NC: Duke University Press.

García-Guadilla, M. P. (2013) *E-mail interview by author with Universidad de Simón Bolivar professor.*

Garretón, M. A. (1989a). *The Chilean political process* (S. Kellum & G. W. Merkx, Trans.). Boston: Unwin Hyman.

Garretón, M. A. (1989b). *La posibilidad democrática en Chile.* Santiago: Flacso.

Garretón, M. A. (2003). *Incomplete democracy.* Chapel Hill, NC: University of North Carolina Press.

Germani, G. (1978). *Authoritarianism, facism, and national populism.* New Brunswick: Transaction Books.

Gott, R. (2011). *Hugo Chávez and the Bolivarian revolution.* London: Verso.

Greene, K. F. (2009). *Why dominant parties lose: Mexico's democratization in comparative perspective.* Cambridge: Cambridge University Press.

Handlin, S. (2012). Social protection and the politicization of class cleavages during Latin America's left turn. *Comparative Political Studies, 46*(12), 1582–1609.

Hardin, R. (2000). The public trust? In S. Pharr & R. D. Putnam (Eds.), *Disaffected democracies: What's troubling the trilateral countries?* (pp. 31–51). Princeton, NJ: Princeton University Press.

Hardin, R. (2002). *Trust and trustworthiness* (Vol. 4). New York, NY: Russell Sage Foundation.

Hawkins, K. A. (2009). Is Chávez populist? Measuring populist discourse in comparative perspective. *Comparative Political Studies, 42*(8), 1040–1067.

Hawkins, K. A. (2010). *Venezuela's chavismo and populism in comparative perspective.* Cambridge: Cambridge University Press.

Hawkins, K. A., & Hansen, D. R. (2006). Dependent Civil Society: The Circulos Bolivarianos in Venezuela. *Latin American Research Review, 41*(1), 102–132.

Hawkins, K. A., Rosas, G., & Johnson, M. E. (2011). The misiones of the Chávez government. In D. Smilde & D. Hellinger (Eds.), *Venezuela's Bolivarian democracy: Participation, politics and culture under Chávez* (pp. 186–218). Durham, NC: Duke University Press.

Held, D. (2007). *Models of democracy* (3rd ed.). Stanford, CA: Stanford University Press.

Hellinger, D. (1978). Electoral change in the Chilean countryside: The Presidential elections of 1958 and 1970. *Western Political Quarterly, 31*(2), 253–273.

Hellinger, D. (2003). Political overview: The breakdown of *puntofijismo* and the rise of *chavismo*. In S. Ellner & D. Hellinger (Eds.), *Venezuelan politics in the Chávez era: Class, polarization, and conflict* (pp. 27–54). Boulder, CO: Lynne Rienner Publishers.

Hellinger, D. (2007). When "no" means "yes to revolution": Electoral politics in Bolivarian Venezuela. In S. Ellner & M. Tinker Salas (Eds.), *Venezuela: Hugo Chávez and the decline of an "exceptional democracy"* (pp. 157–184). Lanham: Rowman & Littlefield Publishers, Inc.

Hellinger, D. (2011). Defying the iron law of oligarchy I: how does "el pueblo" conceive democracy? In D. Smilde & D. Hellinger (Eds.), *Venezuela's Bolivarian democracy: participation, politics, and culture under Chávez* (pp. 28–57). Durham, NC: Duke University Press.

Hibbing, J. R., & Theiss-Morse, E. (2001). Process preferences and American politics: What the people want government to be. *American Political Science Review, 95*(1), 145–153.

Hibbing, J. R., & Theiss-Morse, E. (2002). *Stealth democracy.* Cambridge: Cambridge University Press.

Higley, J., & Burton, M. (2006). *Elite foundations of liberal democracy.* Lanham, MD: Rowman & Littlefield Publishers, Inc.

Hillman, R. S. (2006). Intellectuals: An elite divided. In J. McCoy & D. Myers (Eds.), *The unraveling of representative democracy in Venezuela* (pp. 115–129). Baltimore, MD: Johns Hopkins University Press.

Hirschman, A. O. (1970). *Exit, voice, and loyalty: Response to decline in firms, organizations and states.* Cambridge, MA: Harvard University Press.

Hobbes, T. (1985). *Leviathan.* New York, NY: Penguin Classics.

Holland, A. (2006). Venezuela's Urban Land Committees and Participatory Democracy. *Venezuelanalysis.com.* Retrieved from http://venezuelanalysis.com/analysis/1611.

Hough, M., Jackson, J., & Bradford, B. (2013). Legitimacy, trust and compliance: an empirical test of procedural justice theory using the European Social Survey In J. Tankebe & A. Liebling (Eds.), *Legitimacy and criminal justice: An international exploration.* Oxford: Oxford University Press.

Hox, J. (2010). *Multilevel analysis: Techniques and applications.* New York, NY: Routledge.

Hu, L.-t., & Bentler, P. M. (1999). Cutoff criteria for fit indexes in covariance structure analysis: Conventional criteria versus new alternatives. *Structural Equation Modeling: A Multidisciplinary Journal, 6*(1), 1–55.

Huber, E., Pribble, J., & Stephens, J. (2010). The Chilean left in power: Achievements, failures, and omissions. In K. Weyland, R. Madrid, & W. Hunter (Eds.), *Leftist governments in Latin America: Successes and shortcomings* (pp. 77–97). Cambridge: Cambridge University Press.

Hull, C. L. (1943). *Principles of behavior: An introduction to behavior theory.* New York, NY: Appleton-Century-Crofts.

Huntington, S. (1965). Political development and decay. *World Politics, 17*(3), 386–430.

Informe cabildos abril 2013, etapa 1: sueños, diagnósticos y propuestas. (2013). Retrieved from http://piensa.providencia.cl/images/documentos/03-informe-cabildos-sueos_-diagnosticos-y-propuestas.pdf.

Inglehart, R. (2003). How solid is mass support for democracy - and how can we measure it? *PS: Political Science and Politics, 36*(1), 51–57.

Inglehart, R., & Welzel, C. (2005). *Modernization, cultural change, and democracy.* Cambridge: Cambridge University Press.

James, D. (1988). *Resistance and integration.* Cambridge: Cambridge University Press.

Johnson, J. H., & Sarason, I. G. (1978). Life stress, depression and anxiety: Internal-external control as a moderator variable. *Journal of Psychosomatic Research, 22* (3), 205–208.

Jones, B. (2009). *Hugo! The Hugo Chávez story from mud hut to perpetual revolution* (Kindle ed.). Hanover, NH: Steerforth Press.

Karl, T. L. (1987). Petroleum and political pacts: The transition to democracy in Venezuela. *Latin American Research Review, 22*(1), 63–94.

Kazin, M. (1998). *The populist persuasion: An American history*. Ithaca, NY: Cornell University Press.

Kinder, D., & Kiewiet, D. R. (1981). Sociotropic politics: The American case. *British Journal of Political Science, 11*(2), 129–161.

Klein, A. G., & Moosbrugger, H. (2000). Maximum likelihood estimation of latent interaction effects with the LMS Method. *Psychometrika, 65*(4), 457–474.

Klein, A. G., & Muthén, B. O. (2007). Quasi-maximum likelihood estimation of structural equation models with multiple interaction and quadratic effects. *Multivariate Behavioral Research, 42*(4), 647–673.

Kline, R. B. (2011). *Principles and practice of structural equation modeling* (3rd ed.). New York, NY: The Guilford Press.

Klingemann, H.-D. (1999). Mapping political support in the 1990s: A global analysis. In P. Norris (Ed.), *Critical citizens: Global support for democratic governance* (pp. 31–56). Oxford: Oxford University Press.

Klosko, G., Muller, E. N., & Opp, K.-D. (1987). Rebellious collective action revisited. *American Political Science Review, 81*(2), 557–564.

Kölln, A.-K., Esaiasson, P., & Turper, S. (2013). *External efficacy and perceived responsiveness – Same, same or different?* Paper presented at the Election, Public Opinion and Parties Conference, Lancaster University, UK. Retrieved from www.lancaster.ac.uk/fass/events/epop2013/docs/External%20efficacy%20and%20responsiveness%201209.pdf.

Kurtz, M. J. (2004a). The dilemmas of democracy in the open economy: Lessons from Latin America. *World Politics, 56*(2), 262–302.

Kurtz, M. J. (2004b). *Free market democracy and the Chilean and Mexican countryside*. Cambridge: Cambridge University Press.

Laclau, E. (1977). *Politics and ideology in Marxist theory*. London: New Left Books.

Laclau, E. (2005). Populism: What's in a name? In F. Panizza (Ed.), *Populism and the mirror of democracy* (pp. 32–49). New York, NY: Verso.

Laclau, E., & Mouffe, C. (1985). *Hegemony and socialist theory*. London: Verso.

Lane, R. E. (1962). *Political ideology: Why the American common man believes what he does*. New York, NY: The Free Press.

Lapp, N. D. (2004). *Landing votes: Representation and land reform in Latin America*: Palgrave Macmillan.

Latinobarómetro. (2008). Latinobarómetro annual polls, 1995–2008. Retrieved from www.latinobarometro.org/latContents.jsp.

Levi, M., & Sacks, A. (2009). Legitimating beliefs: Sources and indicators. *Regulation & Governance, 3*, 311–333.

Levi, M., Sacks, A., & Tyler, T. (2009). Conceptualizing legitimacy, measuring legitimating beliefs. *American Behavioral Scientist, 53*, 354–375.

Lewis-Beck, M. S. (1985). Pocketbook voting in U.S. National Election Studies: Fact or artifact? *American Journal of Political Science, 29*(2), 348–356.

Ley orgánica constitucional de municipalidades, Biblioteca del Congreso Nacional de Chile, Pub. L. No. 18.695 (2006, May 9).

Ley orgánica de los consejos comunales, (2006).

Ley orgánica de los consejos comunales, (2009).

Lichbach, M. (1995). *The rebel's dilemma*. Ann Arbor, MI: University of Michigan Press.

Liendro, F. (2012a, October 22). *E-mail communication by author with comite de viviende de Francisco de Miranda member.*

Liendro, F. (2012b, October 27). *Interview by author with member of el comite de viviende de Francisco de Miranda*

Lijphart, A. (1984). *Democracies*. New Haven, CT: Yale University Press.

Lind, E. A. (2001). Fairness heuristic theory: Justice judgments as pivotal cognitions in organizational relations. In J. Greenberg & R. Cropanzano (Eds.), *Advances in organizational justice* (pp. 56–88). Stanford, CA: Stanford University Press.

Lind, E. A., Kray, L., & Thompson, L. (2001). Primacy effects in justice judgments: testing predictions from fairness heuristic theory. *Organizational Behavior and Human Decision Processes, 85*(2), 189–210.

Lind, E. A., & Tyler, T. (1988). *The social psychology of procedural justice*. New York, NY: Plenum Press.

Linde, J., & Ekman, J. (2003). Satisfaction with democracy: A note on a frequently used indicator in comparative politics. *European Journal of Political Research, 42*(3), 391–408.

Lipset, S. M. (1963). *Political man: The social bases of politics*. Garden City: Anchor Books.

Lipset, S. M., & Schneider, W. (1983). The decline of confidence in American institutions. *Political Science Quarterly, 98*(3), 379–402.

Locke, J. (2003). *Two treatises of government*. New Haven, CT: Yale University Press.

López Maya, M. (1997). The rise of Causa R in Venezuela. In D. A. Chalmers, C. M. Vilas, K. Hite, S. B. Martin, K. Piester, & M. Segarra (Eds.), *The new politics of inequality in Latin America: Rethinking participation and representation* (pp. 117–143). Oxford: Oxford University Press.

López Maya, M. (1999a). La protesta venezolana entre 1989 y 1993 (en un umbral del neolibralismo). In M. López Maya (Ed.), *Lucha popular, democracia, neoliberalismo: protesta popular en América Latina en los años de ajuste* (pp. 211–238). Caracas: Editorial Nueva Sociedad.

López Maya, M. (1999b). Venezuela: la rebelión popular del 27 de febrero de 1989: ¿Resistencia a la modernidad? *Revista Venezolana de Economía y Ciencias Sociales*, 5(2–3), 177–200.

Lòpez Maya, M. (2001). *Venezuela después del Caracazo: Formas de la protesta en un contexto desinstitucionalizado*. Kellog Institution. Retrieved from www.kellogginstitute.org/sites/www.kellogginstitute.org/files/docu ments/287.pdf.

López Maya, M. (2003). Hugo Chávez Frías: His movement and his presidency. In S. Ellner & D. Hellinger (Eds.), *Venezuelan politics in the Chávez era: Class, polarization and conflict* (pp. 73–92). Boulder, CO: Lynne Rienner Publishers.

Lòpez Maya, M. (2003). The Venezuelan Caracazo of 1989: Popular protest and institutional weakness. *Journal of Latin American Studies*, 35(1), 117–137.

López Maya, M., & Lander, L. E. (2011). Participatory democracy in Venezuela: Origins, ideas, and implementation. In D. Hellinger & D. Smilde (Eds.), *Venezuela's Bolivarian democracy: Participation, politics, and culture under Chávez* (pp. 58–79). Durham, NC: Duke University Press.

López Maya, M., & Panzarelli, A. (2013). Populism, renterism and socialism in twenty-first-century Venezuela. In C. de la Torre & C. J. Arnson (Eds.), *Latin American populism in the twenty-first century* (pp. 239–268). Washington, D.C.: Johns Hopkins University Press.

Loveman, B. (2001). *Chile: The legacy of Hispanic capitalism*. New York, NY: Oxford University Press, USA.

Lovera, A. (2008). Los consejos comunales en Venezuela: ¿Democracia participativa o delegativa? *Revista Venezolana de Economía y Ciencias Sociales*, 14(1), 107–124.

Luna, J. P. (2016). Chile's crisis of representation. *Journal of Democracy*, 27(3), 129–138.

Machado, J. E. (2008). *Estudio de los Consejos Comunales en Venezuela*. Caracas: Centro Gumilla. Retrieved from http://gumilla.org/files/documents/Estudio-Consejos-Comunales01.pdf.

Machado, J. E. (2009). *Estudio cuantitativo de opinión sobre los Consejos Comunales*. Caracas: Centro Gumilla. Retrieved from www.civilisac.org/civilis/wp-content/uploads/estudio-cualitativo-de-consejos-comunales-gumilla-2009-1.pdf.

Macpherson, C. B. (1977). *The life and times of liberal democracy*. Oxford: Oxford University Press.

Madison, J. (1952). *The Federalist Papers* (Vol. 43). Chicago, IL: Encyclopedia Britannica, Inc.

Madrid, R., Hunter, W., & Weyland, K. (2010). The policies and performance of the contestory and moderate left. In K. Weyland, R. Madrid, & W. Hunter (Eds.),

Leftist governments in Latin America: Successes and shortcomings (pp. 140–180). Cambridge: Cambridge University Press.

Madrid, R., & Rhodes-Purdy, M. (2016). Descriptive representation and regime support in Latin America. *Political Studies, 64*(4), 890–909. doi:10.1177/0032321715617772

Madsen, D. (1987). Political self-efficacy tested. *American Political Science Review, 81*(2), 571–582.

Madsen, D., & Snow, P. G. (1991). *The charismatic bond: Political behavior in a time of crisis.* Cambridge, MA: Harvard University Press.

Mainwaring, S., & Pérez-Liñán, A. (2013). *Democracies and dictatorships in Latin America: Emergence, survival and fall.* New York, NY: Cambridge University Press.

Mainwaring, S., Scully, T. R., & Vargas Cullell, J. (2010). Measuring success in democratic governance. In S. Mainwaring & T. R. Scully (Eds.), *Democratic governance in Latin America* (pp. 11–51). Stanford, CA: Stanford University Press.

McAdam, D., & Tarrow, S. (2010). Ballots and barricades: On the reciprocal relations between elections and social movements. *Perspectives on Politics, 8*(2), 529–542.

McCoy, J. (2006). From representative to participatory democracy? In J. McCoy & D. Myers (Eds.), *The unraveling of representative democracy in Venezuela* (pp. 263–296). Baltimore, MD: Johns Hopkins University Press.

McCoy, J. & Myers, D. (Eds.) (2006). *The unraveling of representative democracy in Venezuela* (pp. 263–296). Baltimore, MD: Johns Hopkins University Press.

McDonald, R. H. (1969). Apportionment and party politics in Santiago, Chile. *Midwest Journal of Political Science, 13*(3), 455–470.

McFarlin, D. B., & Sweeney, P. D. (1992). Distributive and procedural justice as predictors of satisfaction with personal and organizational outcomes. *Academy of Management Journal, 35*(3), 626–637.

McFaul, M. (2002). The fourth wave of democracy and dictatorship: Noncooperative transitions in the postcommunist world. *World Politics, 54*(2), 212–244.

Michels, R. (2001). *Political parties: A sociological study of the oligarchical tendencies of modern democracy* (E. Paul & C. Paul, Trans.). Kitchener, Ontario: Batoche Books.

Middlebrook, K. J. (1995). *The paradox of revolution.* Baltimore, MD: Johns Hopkins University Press.

Mill, J. S. (2009). *Considerations on representative government.* Auckland: The Floating Press.

Millar, R. (1981). *La elección presidencial de 1920: Tendencias y prácticas políticas en el Chile parlamentario*. Santiago: Editorial Universitaria.

Miller, A., & Listhaug, O. (1999). Political performance and institutional trust. In P. Norris (Ed.), *Critical citizens: Global support for democratic governance* (pp. 204–216). Oxford: Oxford University Press.

Moehler, D. C. (2008). *Distrusting democrats: Outcomes of participatory constitution making*. Ann Arbor, MI: University of Michigan Press.

Molina, J. E. (2006). The unraveling of Venezuela's party system: From party rule to personalistic politics and deinstitutionalization. In J. McCoy & D. Myers (Eds.), *The unraveling of representative democracy in Venezuela* (pp. 152–180). Baltimore, MD: Johns Hopkins University Press.

Mommer, B. (2003). Subversive oil. In S. Ellner & D. Hellinger (Eds.), *Venezuelan politics in the Chávez era: Class, polarization and conflict* (pp. 131–146). Boulder, CO: Lynne Rienner Publishers.

Mosca, G. (1939). *The ruling class* (H. D. Kahn, Trans.). New York, NY: McGraw-Hill Book Company, Inc.

Mudde, C. (2007). *Populist radical right parties in Europe*. Cambridge: Cambridge University Press.

Mudde, C., & Rovira Kaltwasser, C. (2013). Populism and (liberal) democracy: A framework for analysis. In C. Mudde & C. Rovira Kaltwasser (Eds.), *Populism in Europe and the Americas: Threat or corrective for democracy?* Cambridge: Cambridge University Press.

Muller, E. N. (1970). The representation of citizens by political authorities: Consequences for regime support. *American Political Science Review, 64*(4), 1149–1166.

Muller, E. N., & Opp, K.-D. (1986). Rational choice and rebellious collective action. *American Political Science Review, 80*(2), 471–488.

Muller, E. N., & Williams, C. J. (1980). Dynamics of political support-alienation. *Comparative Political Studies, 13*(1), 35–59.

Myers, D. (2006). The normalization of Punto Fijo democracy. In J. McCoy & D. Myers (Eds.), *The unraveling of representative democracy in Venezuela* (pp. 11–32). Baltimore, MD: Johns Hopkins University Press.

Navia, P. (2010). Living in actually existing democracies: Democracy to the extent possible in Chile. *Latin American Research Review, 45*, 298–328.

Newton, K., & Norris, P. (2000). Confidence in public institutions: Faith, culture or performance? In S. Pharr & R. D. Putnam (Eds.), *Disaffected democracies: What's troubling the trilateral countries?* (pp. 52–73). Princeton, NJ: Princeton University Press.

Niemi, R. G., Craig, S. C., & Mattei, F. (1991). Measuring internal political efficacy in the 1988 National Election Study. *American Political Science Review, 85*(4), 1407–1413.

Norris, P. (1999a). Institutional explanations for political support. In P. Norris (Ed.), *Critical citizens: Global support for democratic governance* (pp. 217–235). Oxford: Oxford University Press.

Norris, P. (1999b). Introduction: The growth of critical citizens. In P. Norris (Ed.), *Critical citizens: Global support for democratic governance* (pp. 1–30). Oxford: Oxford University Press.

O'Brien, R. (1994). Identification of simple measuremnt models with multiple latent variables and correlated errors. *Sociological Methodology*, (24), 137–170.

O'Donnell, G. (1994). Delegative democracy. *Journal of Democracy, 5*(1), 55–69.

O'Donnell, G. (1998). Horizontal accountability in new democracies. *Journal of Democracy, 9*(3), 112–126.

Opp, K.-D., Burow-Auffarth, K., & Heinrichs, U. (1981). Conditions for conventional and unconventional political participation: An empirical test of economic and sociological hypotheses. *European Journal of Political Research, 9* (2), 147–168.

Oppenheim, L. (2007). *Politics in Chile: Socialism, authoritarianism and market democracy*. Boulder, CO: Westview Press.

Orpen, C. (1994). The effects of self-esteem and personal control on the relationship between job insecurity and psychological well-being. *Social Behavior and Personality, 22*(1), 53–56.

Oxhorn, P. (1994). Understanding political change after authoritarian rule: The popular sectors and Chile's new democratic regime. *Journal of Latin American Studies, 26*(3), 737–759.

Oxhorn, P. (1995). *Organizing civil society: The popular sectors and the struggle for democracy in Chile*. University Park, PA: Penn State University Press.

Panizza, F. (2005). Introduction: Populism and the mirror of democracy. In F. Panizza (Ed.), *Populism and the mirror of democracy* (pp. 1–31). New York, NY: Verso.

Pateman, C. (1970). *Participation and democratic theory*. Cambridge: Cambridge University Press.

Pharr, S., Putnam, R. D., & Dalton, R. (2000). Introduction. In S. Pharr & R. D. Putnam (Eds.), *Disaffected democracies: What's troubling the trilateral countries?* (pp. 3–20). Princeton, NJ: Princeton University Press.

Pierson, P. (2000). Increasing returns, path dependence, and the study of politics. *American Political Science Review, 94*(2), 251–267.

Pinto, A. (1996). *Chile, un caso de desarrollo frustrado*. Santiago: Editorial Universidad de Santiago.

Pitkin, H. F. (1967). *The concept of representation*. Berkeley, CA: University of California Press.

Plamenatz, J. (1963). *Man and society: Political and social theory, Machiavelli through Rousseau* (Vol. 1). New York, NY: McGraw-Hill Book Company, Inc.

Plato. (2014). *The republic*. CreateSpace Independent Publishing Platform.

Plotke, D. (1997). Representation is democracy. *Constellations, 4*(1), 19–34.

Poguntke, T. (1996). Anti-party sentiment – conceptual thoughts and empirical evidence: Explorations into a minefield. *European Journal of Political Research, 29*(3), 319–344.

Polga-Hecimovich, J., & Siavelis, P. M. (2015). Here's the bias! A (re-) reassessment of the Chilean electoral system. *Electoral Studies, 40*, 268–279.

Posner, P. W. (1999). Popular representation and political dissatisfaction in Chile's new democracy. *Journal of InterAmerican Studies and World Affairs, 41*(1), 59–85.

Posner, P. W. (2004). Local democracy and the transformation of popular participation in Chile. *Latin American Politics and Society, 46*(3), 55–81.

Przeworski, A. (1988). Democracy as a contingent outcome of conflict. In J. Elster & R. Slagstad (Eds.), *Constitutionalism and democracy* (pp. 59–80). Cambridge: Cambridge University Press.

Przeworski, A. (1991). *Democracy and the market*. Cambridge: Cambridge University Press.

Putnam, R. D. (1993). *Making democracy work: Civic traditions in modern Italy*. Princeton, NJ: Princeton University Press.

Putnam, R. D. (1995). Tuning in, tuning out. *PS: Political Science and Politics, 24* (8), 664–683.

Ramírez, C. V. (2005). Venezuela's Bolivarian revolution: Who are the chavistas? *Latin American Perspectives, 32*(3), 79–97.

Rhodes-Purdy, M. (2012). *Participation paradoxes: Voting, contention and support for democracy*. Paper presented at the American Political Science Association Annual Meeting, New Orleans, LA. http://ssrn.com/abstract=2110012

Rhodes-Purdy, M. (2014). *Piensa Providencia program evaluation*. Report prepared for Providencia Municipality.

Rhodes-Purdy, M. (2015). Participatory populism: Theory and evidence from Bolivarian Venezuela. *Political Research Quarterly, 68*(3), 415–427.

Rhodes-Purdy, M. (2017). Beyond the balance sheet: Performance, participation and regime support in Latin America. *Comparative Politics, 49*(2), 252–272.

Rihoux, B., & Ragin, C. (Eds.). (2009). *Configurational comparative methods: Qualitative Comparative Analysis (QCA) and related techniques.* Thousand Oaks, CA: Sage Publications.

Riker, W. H. (1988). *Liberalism against populism: A confrontation between the theory of democracy and the theory of social choice.* San Francisco, CA: W.H. Freeman and Company.

Ripley, G. (2012, November 12) *Interview by author with vocero from El Valle (comuna Galipan).*

Roberts, K. M. (1998). *Deepening democracy? The modern left and social movements in Chile and Peru* (1st ed.). Stanford, CA: Stanford University Press.

Roberts, K. M. (2006). Populism, political conflict, and grass-roots organization in Latin America. *Comparative Politics, 38*(2), 127–148.

Rogowski, R. (1974). *Rational legitimacy: A theory of political support.* Princeton, NJ: Princeton University Press.

Rosenblatt, F. (2013). *How to party? Static and dynamic party survival in Latin American consolidated democracies.* (PhD), Pontificia Universidad Católica de Chile, Santiago.

Rotter, J. B. (1954). *Social learning and clinical psychology.* Englewood Cliff, NJ: Prentice-Hall, Inc.

Rotter, J. B. (1966). Generalized expectancies for internal versus external control of reinforcement. *Psychological Mongraphs: General and Applied, 80*(1), 1–28.

Rousseau, J.-J. (2002). The social contract. In S. Dunn (Ed.), *The social contract and the first and second discourses* (pp. 149–256). New Haven, CT: Yale University Press.

Rueschemeyer, D., Stephens, E., & Stephens, J. (1992). *Capitalist development and democracy.* Chicago, IL: University of Chicago Press.

Ryan, R. M., & Deci, E. L. (2006). Self-regulation and the problem of human autonomy: Does psychology need choice, self-determination, and will? *Journal of Personality, 74*(6), 1557–1586.

Santos, A. (2005). The Chilean dilemma: Between economic development and the deepening of democracy. *Social Forces, 84*(1), 1–21.

Sarsfield, R., & Echegaray, F. (2005). Opening the black box: How satisfaction with democracy and its perceived efficacy affect regime preference in Latin America. *International Journal of Public Opinion Research, 18*(2), 153–173.

Sartori, G. (1984). In G. Sartori (Ed.), Chapter 1. "Guidelines for concept analysis" *Social science concepts: A systematic analysis* (Vol. Guidelines for Concept Analysis, pp. 15–85). Beverly Hills, CA: Sage Publications.

Sartori, G. (1987). *The theory of democracy revisited, part one: The contemporary debate.* Chatham, NJ: Chatham House Publishers, Inc.

Schaffer, F. A. (2010). Thin descriptions: the limits of survey research on the meaning of democracy. *Polity, 46*(3), 303–330.

Schedler, A. (2002). The menu of manipulation. *Journal of Democracy, 13*(2), 36–50.

Schmitter, P. C., & O'Donnell, G. (1986). *Transitions from authoritarian rule volume 4: Tentative conclusions about uncertain democracies*. Baltimore, MD: Johns Hopkins University Press.

Schumpeter, J. A. (2008). *Capitalism, socialism, and democracy* (3rd ed.). New York, NY: Harper Perennial Modern Classics.

Scully, T. R. (1992). *Rethinking the center: Party politics in the nineteenth-and twentieth-century Chile*. Stanford, CA: Stanford University Press.

Shils, E. (1962). *Political development in the new states*. The Hague: Mouton

Siavelis, P. M. (2009). Elite-mass congruence, partidocracia and the quality of Chilean Democracy. *Journal of Politics in Latin America, 3*(1), 3–31.

Silva, P. (1991). Technocrats and politics in Chile: From the Chicago Boys to the CIEPLAN Monks. *Journal of Latin American Studies, 23*(2), 385–410.

Silva, P. (2008). *In the name of reason: Technocrats and politics in Chile*. University Park, PA: The Pennsylvania State University Press.

Singh, S. P., & Carlin, R. E. (2015). Happy medium, happy citizens: Presidential power and democratic regime support. *Political Research Quarterly, 68*(1), 3–17.

Skocpol, T. (1979). *States and social revolutions: A comparative analysis of France, Russia, and China*. Cambridge: Cambridge University Press.

Skocpol, T. (1985). Bringing the state back in: strategies of analysis in current research. In P. Evans, D. Rueschemeyer, & T. Skocpol (Eds.), *Bringing the state back in* (pp. 3–37). Cambridge: Cambridge University Press.

Spalding, H. A. J. (1977). *Organized labor in Latin America*. New York, NY: New York University Press.

Stallings, B. (1978). *Class conflict and economic development in Chile, 1958–1973*. Stanford, CA: Stanford University Press.

Tarrow, S. (1998). *Power in movement: Social movements and contentious politics*. Cambridge: Cambridge University Press.

Tarrow, S. (2000). Mad cows and social activists: Contentious politics in the trilateral democracies. In S. Pharr & R. D. Putnam (Eds.), *Disaffected democracies: What's troubling the trilateral countries?* (pp. 270–290). Princeton, NJ: Princeton University Press.

The Latin American Public Opinion Project (2012). *Americas barometer* Combined country datset (v1.5). Retrieved from http://datasets.americasbarometer.org/database-login/usersearch.php?merged=yes.

Thibaut, J., & Walker, L. (1975). *Procedural justice: A psychological analysis.* Hillsdale, N.J.: Lawrence Erlbaum Associates.

Tie breaker: a new voting system should liven up politics. (2015, February 14). *The Economist.*

Triviño Salazar, J. C. (2013). The promise of transformation through participation: An analysis of Communal Councils in Caracas, Venezuela. Retrieved from http://repub.eur.nl/pub/39829.

Urbinati, N., & Warren, M. E. (2008). The concept of representation in contemporary democratic theory. *Annual Review of Political Science, 11,* 381–412.

Valenzuela, A. (1972). The scope of the Chilean party system. *Comparative Politics, 4*(2), 179–199.

Valenzuela, A. (1978). *The breakdown of democratic regimes: Chile.* Baltimore, MD: Johns Hopkins University Press.

Valenzuela, N. (2013, July 11) *Interview by author.*

van den Bos, K., Lind, E. A., & Wilke, H. A. M. (2001). The psychology of procedural and distributive justice viewed from the perspective of fairness heuristic theory. In R. Cropanzano (Ed.), *Justice in the workplace: From theory to practice* (Vol. 2, pp. 49–66). Mahwah, NJ: Lawrence Erlbaum Associates, Inc.

Velasco, A. (2015). *Barrio rising: Urban popular politics and the making of modern Venezuela.* Oakland, CA: University of California Press.

von Mettenheim, K. (1990). The Brazilian voter in democratic transition, 1974–1982. *Comparative Politics, 23*(1), 23–44.

von Mettenheim, K. (1995). *The Brazilian voter: Mass politics in democratic transition, 1974–1986.* Pittsburgh, PA: University of Pittsburgh Press.

Walker, J. (2001). *Control and the psychology of health: Theory, measurement and applications.* Buckingham: Open University Press.

Weber, M. (1978). The types of legitimate domination. In G. Roth & C. Wittich (Eds.), *Economy & society* (pp. 212–254). Berkeley, CA: University of California Press.

Weeks, G., & Borzutzky, S. (2012). Michelle Bachelet's government: The paradoxes of a Chilean president. *Journal of Politics in Latin America, 4*(3), 97–121.

Weyland, K. (2001). Clarifying a contested concept: Populism in the study of Latin American Politics. *Comparative Politics, 34*(1), 1–22.

White, R. W. (1959). Motivation reconsidered: The concept of competence. *Psychological Review, 66*(5), 297–333.

Wiles, P. (1969). A syndrome, not a doctrine. In G. Ionescu & E. Gellner (Eds.), *Populism: Its meaning and national characteristics* (pp. 166–179). New York, NY: Macmillan Company.

Wilpert, G. (2005). Venezuela: Participatory democracy or government as usual? *Socialism and Democracy, 19*(1), 7–32. doi:10.1080/0885430042000338408

Wilpert, G. (2011). Venezuela's experiment in participatory democracy. In T. Ponniah & J. Eastwood (Eds.), *The revolution in Venezuela: Social and political change under Chávez* (pp. 99–130). Cambridge, MA: Harvard University Press.

Winn, P. (1986). *Weavers of revolution: The Yarur workers and Chile's road to socialism.* New York, NY: Oxford University Press, USA.

Yepes, J. A. (2006). Public opinion, political socialization, and regime stabilization. In J. McCoy & D. Myers (Eds.), *The unraveling of representative democracy in Venezuela* (pp. 231–262). Baltimore, MD: Johns Hopkins University Press.

Zucco, C. (2006). Where's the bias? A reassessment of the Chilean electoral system. *Electoral Studies, 26*(2), 303–314.

Index

Lightning Source UK Ltd.
Milton Keynes UK
UKHW042007170220
358890UK00001B/5